Creole Noise

Creole Noise

Early Caribbean Dialect Literature and Performance

BELINDA EDMONDSON

OXFORD
UNIVERSITY PRESS

OXFORD
UNIVERSITY PRESS

Great Clarendon Street, Oxford, OX2 6DP,
United Kingdom

Oxford University Press is a department of the University of Oxford.
It furthers the University's objective of excellence in research, scholarship,
and education by publishing worldwide. Oxford is a registered trade mark of
Oxford University Press in the UK and in certain other countries

Published in the United States of America by Oxford University Press
198 Madison Avenue, New York, NY 10016, United States of America

British Library Cataloguing in Publication Data
Data available

Library of Congress Control Number: 2021951336

ISBN 978-0-19-285683-8

DOI: 10.1093/oso/9780192856838.001.0001

Printed and bound by
CPI Group (UK) Ltd, Croydon, CR0 4YY

Links to third party websites are provided by Oxford in good faith and
for information only. Oxford disclaims any responsibility for the materials
contained in any third party website referenced in this work.

For Leila and Stanford,
Nona and Chris

Acknowledgments

This book has been a long time coming. In the years since I began this project there have been two momentous presidential elections; a global pandemic, the likes of which has never been seen; explosive social justice protests; and terrifying racist violence. Somehow this book, about a subject that some would consider abstruse, feels like a reflection of it all, the violence and the aspiration for something better, the longing to be more true to who we are as a society. The past is prologue, after all.

So many people have helped make this project a reality that I cannot name them all. A few must suffice. First, I wish to acknowledge the extraordinary work of an earlier generation of Caribbeanists, scholars like the late Errol Hill who did not have the benefit of Google, digitized libraries or scanners, yet without their painstaking archival work I could never have completed this book. Thanks to my editors at Oxford University Press for shepherding this project through to completion. I leaned on the expertise of curators and archivists, among these Maira Liriano and Tamar Evangelestia-Dougherty of the Schomburg Center for Research in Black Culture and Shani Roper at the University of the West Indies Museum. Melay Araya and Shana Russell knew where to start digging. My colleagues and students at Rutgers-Newark helped in ways large and small, particularly the late Dean Jan Lewis, who even when she was ailing herself encouraged me to finish this project when I was at a low point in my life. Lively discussions with audiences at the University of Illinois Urbana-Champaign, the North American Victorian Studies Association (NAVSA), Harvard University and Vanderbilt University opened new pathways for me to explore. I wish to acknowledge the support of the Scholars in Residence Program at the Schomburg Center for Research in Black Culture, where I was a National Endowment for the Humanities Fellow, and where I benefited from the helpful comments of other scholars, especially Yarimar Bonilla and Farah Jasmine Griffin. Brent Edwards has championed this project from its inception. It is no exaggeration to say I could not have completed this book without my fellowship at Harvard's Hutchins Center. A big thank you to Skip Gates, Krishna Lewis, and to my fellow Fellows who offered suggestions on revisions or helped me hunt down difficult sources, among these Bárbaro Ruiz, David Bindman, Bill Schwarz, and especially the fabulous Hutchins Accountability Group, Eve Dunbar, Martha Patterson, Darius Bost, Will Pruitt, and Jesse Shipley. (You made it happen, Eve!) Thanks also to my excellent—and unfazed—editorial assistant Bernie Lombardi.

Jean D'Costa has been a treasure trove of information on historical Jamaican Creole. I have benefited from the generosity of Nigel Westmaas, John Cowley, and Kenneth Bilby, who shared with me rare archival documents from the colonial Caribbean. Velma Pollard, Lise Winer, Marjorie Whylie, John Rickford, Roxana Kawall, Rupert Lewis, Salvador DeCaires, and Diana McTurk have all been helpful. My gratitude also to Michelle Stephens, Vera Kutzinski, Hortense Spillers, Pamela Gilbert, Lauren Goodlad, Leah Rosenberg, Laurie Taylor, Donette Francis, and Tim Watson. Faith Smith is, as ever, my favorite interlocutor. Darrell Moore gave me valuable feedback on Chapter 5. I have been touched by the personal generosity of many good friends, including Tahi Hunter, Fred Harris, Caroline Holder, Marion DeCaires Lake, Bonu DeCaires, Colette Foster, Mia Bay, Claire Ciliotta, Andy Milne, Charlie Hunter, Debbie Levy, Jackie Mroz, Deborah Knudsen, Suzanne Farkas, Jon Greenberg, Fran Bartkowski, Sherri-Ann Butterfield, Kim DaCosta Holton, Jamie Lew, and Mara Sidney, who gave me what I needed when I needed it, whether it was office space, a sympathetic ear, or a good laugh.

My family has been essential to everything I do. My grandparents Leila and Stanford are the inspiration for this book. My sister Nona has been with me every step of the way. My brother Chris died before it was completed. I dedicate it to them.

Portions of Chapters 1 and 2 were previously published in "Literary and Performative Culture in 1860s Jamaica," *Journal of Caribbean History*, vol. 50, issue 2 (2016): 189–99.

Contents

List of Illustrations

Introduction

Speaking Badly (In Prose)

Gal if yuh love me an yuh no write it
How me fe know?
Gal if yuh love me an yuh no write it
How me fe know?
Gal if yuh write it an me cyaan read it
How me fe know?
Talk it ah mout!
Talk it ah mout!
Talk it ah mout!

Anonymous, Jamaica

Growing up in Jamaica, I learned two forms of oral narrative. On the one hand were the stories of my grandfather Stanford, a black educator with an advanced degree who, when confronted with my cheerful "Hi, grandfather!" replied, "Hi? 'Hie' means 'to go'! You must say 'Good morning, grandfather; good afternoon, grandfather; good evening, grandfather.'" He, like other middle-class black Jamaicans of his generation, spoke only the most precise standard English. He never spoke in Creole.

He knew it, though. Well.

Stanford wanted to educate his grandchildren in Jamaica's folk tradition, and so he told us Anansi stories. He, and other Jamaican educators like him, regarded the African-derived Anansi story as a form of nation-building. But when Stanford told us Anansi stories he told them in standard English. Surely that was not how he had first heard them, growing up in early twentieth-century St. Thomas, Jamaica's poorest, blackest, most rebellious parish, site of the Morant Bay rebellion barely 50 years before. But in the heady nationalism of post-independence Jamaica that is how the patriotic Stanford transmitted our Caribbean literary heritage to us: in the Queen's English.

On the other hand, and on the other side of my family, were the mesmerizing sayings of my uneducated "Jamaica white" (that is, very light-skinned) grandmother Leila, who would have scorned to call any part of herself black. The proud daughter of a white farmer, she spoke a wonderfully inventive hybrid of Creole and English, peppering her everyday language with a heavy dose of proverbs and what Stanford would have dismissed as malapropisms. From Leila I learned that

Creole Noise: Early Caribbean Dialect Literature and Performance. Belinda Edmondson, Oxford University Press.
© Belinda Edmondson 2022. DOI: 10.1093/oso/9780192856838.003.0001

"the higher monkey climb, the more im batty show;" that "if you cyan ketch quashie ketch im shu't;" that "craven choke puppy;" and that the elaborate light fixture on the ceiling was a "shandiglare." Leila was, as one of my educated relatives put it scornfully, "one of those red St. Elizabeth women who speak so badly." If my black grandfather never spoke Creole, my "white" grandmother was hard pressed to speak anything but.

I offer these portraits of my grandparents from both sides of my family tree because they complicate two scholarly truisms: one, that Creole and its literary tradition are solely the heritage of its African-descended people, nurtured and advanced by them; and two, that the push to advance Creole traditions was fundamentally at odds with the respectability politics of the colonial black and brown middle class.[1] Stanford understood the oral tradition to be part of a nationalist project of self-determination, and imparted it as such. If the post-independence nationalism of the 1970s Caribbean tended to middle-class reproductions of a working-class referent, all the better: Creole literary traditions could thus be recuperated from the taint of blackness, poverty, illiteracy. In sanitizing Anansi for pedagogical purposes Stanford was, in his own way, following the lead of a host of middle-class black folk storytellers engaged in a similar recuperative project.[2] They were not everyday Creole speakers.

Leila, on the other hand, was. She did not tell us Anansi stories because we needed to be well-educated nationalists. Leila had no interest in the oral tradition, the nationalist project, or a university education. But as Leila opened her mouth Anansi, Bredda Rat, the batty-showing monkey and the rest of the cast just fell out. She did not impart the oral tradition; she *was* the oral tradition.

In my family the oral tradition was "white," the literary tradition was black.

To be clear, I am not arguing that Leila and her non-African origins are the real source of Creole literature and culture. To deny Creole's obvious basis in African languages is to be, if not a fool, a revisionist of a very high order. That is not my intent here. Nor is Creole, to borrow Earl Lovelace's satirical phrase, an "all o' we is one" mélange of depoliticized language, where its European antecedents hold just as much sway as its African ones.[3] Nor am I arguing that Stanford and other black middle-class non-speakers were inauthentic because they rejected Creole narratives in favor of standard English ones. In and of itself, Stanford's ability to

---

[1] For examples of the clash between Caribbean middle-class respectability and the radical black Creole tradition, see Kamau Brathwaite, *Contradictory Omens: Cultural Diversity and Integration in the Caribbean* (Kingston: Savacou Publications, 1974); Anthony Bogues, "Nationalism and Jamaican Political Thought," pp. 363–87, in *Jamaica in Slavery and Freedom: History, Heritage and Culture*, edited by Kathleen Monteith and Glen Richards (Mona, Jamaica: University of the West Indies Press, 2002); Mimi Sheller, *Citizenship from Below: Erotic Agency and Caribbean Freedom* (Durham and London: Duke University Press, 2012).

[2] Notable folklorists of the 1970s and 1980s include Louise Bennett in Jamaica, Wordsworth McAndrew in Guyana and Paul Keens-Douglas in Trinidad and Tobago.

[3] Earl Lovelace, *The Dragon Can't Dance* (1979). "All o' we is one" is a refrain that runs throughout the novel.

orally translate Anansi stories from Creole to standard English shows a level of expertise in Creole that invalidates the "inauthentic" label. Even my ironic use of the word "sanitized" to describe the de-Creolification of Creole is problematic: Stanford's Anansi story was not a sanitizing or poorly executed version of a "real," gloriously messy and dirty oral tradition: it was simply another genre altogether. It was what might be called performative literary Creole.

What I do hope to achieve here is to complicate the entrenched Caribbean belief—symptomatic of a wider colonial mythology—in the "blackness" of orality and the "whiteness" of narrative. If languages are bodied as good or bad, dirty, or clean, then English is as clean and white as Creole is dirty and black. Any commingling, recognized or no, becomes essentially a blackening project. In years past, the scholarly assessment of literary dialect was a slight variant of the same idea; any attempt to write Creole was a commingling of that which could not be commingled, writing down what was essentially an oral form. This binarized, racialized view of the spoken and the written is summed up in Nadia Nurhussein's term "literary miscegenation."[4] Yet none of it is true. It never was. As this study will show, there is no easy division between the oral and the written traditions of Creole, no easy division between "inauthentic" white literary dialect and authentic black Creole.

The anecdote of how I, an English professor who makes her living parsing narrative, came to understand the role of the oral tradition in my education is more complicated than it appears. Yes, stories are indelibly communicated when someone, as the folksong puts it, "talks it ah mout.'" Indeed, "Talk It Ah Mout'" occupies the title page of the section on the Caribbean's oral tradition in *The Penguin Book of Caribbean Verse in English*.[5] The folksong is a post-Emancipation "Bruckins" tune that accompanies a popular nineteenth-century dance. Its historical lineage makes it tempting to see it as a declaration of the "emancipation" of the oral over the written, of foundational African heritage over colonial European.

But that, too, is deceptive.

The Bruckins songs were part of an Emancipation celebration that involved "speechifying," praising Queen Victoria at a time when literacy was highly prized among a population only decades removed from slavery.[6] Let us examine the

---

[4] See Nadia Nurhussein, *Rhetorics of Literacy: The Cultivation of American Dialect Poetry* (Columbus, OH: Ohio State University Press, 2013), p. 4.

[5] See Paula Burnett, ed., *The Penguin Book of Caribbean Verse in English* (New York: Penguin, 1986), p. 1.

[6] Jean D'Costa, Marjorie Whylie, emails to author, October 16, 2020. I thank Jean D'Costa for identifying the song's emphasis on literacy, and Marjorie Whylie for providing the historical backdrop for Talk It A Mout'. Jamaican folklorist Olive Lewin notes the confluence of colonial and African tropes in the Bruckins celebrations in Jamaica in 1967, especially the endurance of the myth that Queen Victoria freed enslaved black people. See Olive Lewin, *Rock It Come Over: The Folk Music of Jamaica* (Mona, Jamaica: University of the West Indies Press, 2000), p. 116, quoted in Tim Barringer and Wayne Modest, Introduction, pp. 1–2, in Tim Barringer and Wayne Modest, eds., *Victorian Jamaica* (Durham and London: Duke University Press, 2018).

lyrics. The male narrator first questions why his female lover won't *write* her love; and then, when she does, declares her written declaration useless because "me cyaan read it." The narrator then declares that his love must "talk it ah mout.'" In other words, the song does not endorse the oral over the written; rather, it is a comic rendering of the uneasy relationship between the oral and the written. The song's gender politics are also salient. The comedy resides in the fact that a (presumably black) man makes a great show of literacy that he does not possess. The written word is, associatively, a male act, a European act. The oral is by default black and, if not female, certainly feminized. The written declaration of love is desired but, in the end, inauthentic because the illiterate narrator cannot read it, and therefore useless. Unsurprisingly, the Penguin editor interprets the song as the triumph of the oral over the written in order to establish the oral tradition as foundational to the literary. However, the very fact of the song's transcription ironizes that triumph: the real joke is that the song lives on *because* of writing. It is now the preserve of musicologists and scholarly folk choirs whose members must *read* its lyrics, along with its musical notations, in order to sing it "ah mout.'" Its satirical tone suggests a literate audience, one that laughs knowingly at male rubes who want written proof of love they can't read.

"Talk It A Mout'" and other examples of early Caribbean literary dialect are at the center of this study because they complicate the fundamental belief in the Africaneity of Creole found in creolization theory and, more broadly, scholarship on black Atlantic literary dialect. If speaking in dialect was a sign of a feminized, racialized subaltern status in the colonial era, in the twentieth century, with the rise of black aesthetics movements in the Black Atlantic—the New Negro Movement in the United States and, in the Caribbean, the Negritude, Indigenist, and Afrocubanísmo movements—writing in dialect became the preserve of literary men, race men, New Negros. The emphasis on Creole's fundamental Africaneity reflected a black nationalist pride that marked the dawn of a civil rights struggle in the realm of aesthetics. For example, in his 1987 landmark monograph *Figures in Black* Henry Louis Gates argues that African-American dialect poetry is inherently oppositional:

> The poet has in this mutation—this dialect—an accessible linguistic system that turns the literate language upon itself, exploiting the metaphor against its master. Afro-American dialects exist between two poles, one English and one lost in some mythical linguistic kingdom, now irrecoverable. Dialect is our only key to that unknown tongue, and in its obvious relation and reaction to English it contains, as does the Yoruban mask, a verbal dialectic, a dialectic between some form of an African *antithesis* all the while obviating the English *thesis*.[7]

[7] Henry Louis Gates, *Figures in Black: Words, Signs, and the "Racial" Self* (London and New York: Oxford University Press, 1987), p. 172.

Similarly, scholars of Caribbean creolization theory read its process as a confirmation of Creole's fundamental Africaneity and thus attribute to it a certain imperviousness, a certain resistance, to (neo)colonial influence. Yet, even as this version of creolization emphasizes its African core, in its determination to reject the possibility of non-African origins it seems to imply its obverse: the "melting pot" theory.[8] The fact is that Creole the language is derived from creoles, the people: creoles speak Creole. And in the cultural logic of the Caribbean, creoles can be white, black, or mixed, but never Asian. Creole, whether the site of racial struggle or multiracial harmony, is a black and white cultural form, reflective of the "indigenous" modernities of the Caribbean. Creole excludes as much as it includes: everyone can speak Creole, but not everyone is creole. Not everyone belongs.

African and European languages are the basis of Creole, yes, but there is another way to think about the interaction of these two foundational influences. Language is more than linguistics. It is also culture, currency, politics; it is a reflection of society itself. Language is more than a question of "owns" it. It is defined not simply by its ethno-national origins but by who deploys it, when and how. These users, whether habitual, occasional or strategic; whether white, black or Asian; whether cultural nationalists or colonial apologists; also shape our understanding of Creole and its literary tradition. Therefore it is another form of myth-making to ignore or downplay the non-African origins of Creole to maintain a linear, nationalist narrative of how the independent Caribbean came into being. If not exactly "all o' we is one," Creole's heritage *is* distinctly multi-ethnic: in early English accounts it is white creoles, not blacks, who are blamed for Caribbean "half-negrish" "gibberish."[9] White creoles, in turn, blamed browns (or so-called coloreds) for that same tainted "black and white Lingo"[10]; who in turn point the finger at creole blacks;[11] who, along with whites and browns, point the finger at the poor newcomers, "pagan" Indians and Portuguese, as the twentieth century dawns.[12]

---

[8]   See Kamau Brathwaite, *Contradictory Omens* (1974), which builds on his foundational work, *The Development of Creole Society, 1770–1820* (1971) to articulate the concept of creolization in the English-speaking Caribbean.

[9]   See J. B. Moreton, *West Indian Customs and Manners* (London: W. Richardson, H. Gardner, J. Walter, 1790/1793), and John Armstrong, "To Omicron *Lick-Devil, Esq.," in *Universal Almanac: Miscellanies*, vol. 2 (London: T. Cadell, 1770), pp. 175–6.

[10]   See, for example, H.G. de Lisser's critical portrait of the Creole-speaking brown middle class in *Jane's Career* (1913), whose speech is rendered in distinct contrast to that of the more dignified Creole-speaking black characters.

[11]   See Belinda Edmondson, Chapter 2 ("Brownness, Social Desire, and the Early Novel"), pp. 50–85, in *Caribbean Middlebrow: Leisure Culture and the Middle Class* (Cornell University Press, 2009). I discuss the racist stereotype of the Afro-Trinidadian character Jack Jimmy, posed in distinct contrast to the aristocratic language of the brown hero, in *Emmanuel Appadocca*, by brown Trinidadian author Michel Maxwell Philip. Jack Jimmy and other Afro-Trinidadian creoles are rendered as dialect speaking simpletons in contrast not just to brown people but to actual Africans, whose speech is rendered in standard English.

[12]   British Guiana's white newspaper the *Argosy* contains several comic renderings of Creole-speaking Portuguese in the late nineteenth century; as well as several newspaper items in both the

What is clear is that everybody spoke Creole, or some version of it. V. S. Naipaul, not known to celebrate the Caribbean's African heritage, nevertheless believed that the literary dialect found in Trinidad's popular newspaper columns was the region's true literary voice.[13] So apparently did "white"[14] pro-colonial Jamaican writer H.G. de Lisser, whose 1913 novel *Jane's Career* featured the anglophone Caribbean's first serious Creole-speaking black heroine, a portrayal critiqued—in my view, incorrectly—by Carolyn Cooper as essentially satirical of Creole's "habitual speakers."[15] So: if not African and not merely multi-ethnic; if not just oral but also written; then, what exactly *is* the Creole tradition?

That question has two main components, both of which this book attempts to thread together. The story of Creole literature is, yes, the story of a racist satirical tradition. But the story of Creole literature is also the story of how that racist tradition sowed the seeds of its own destruction and was transformed into a symbol of black uplift and progress. How the two stories became delinked is its own story, too. Early textual renderings of Caribbean Creole (that is, dialect literature, or "literary dialect"[16]) were mostly aimed at criticizing people of African descent, using their debased language as a sign of their inferiority. Yet the conflicting claims as to who can correctly render this supposedly inferior language reveals its strategic importance to Caribbean people across class and color lines. When a white creole author rebuts an English author's critical portrait of Caribbean slave society in 1793, he focuses on the Englishman's poor rendering of dialect as evidence of its inaccuracy, and his own ability to do so correctly as evidence of his truthful claims.[17] In the mid-nineteenth century, a brown Jamaican editor similarly excoriates an English author's attempt to render Jamaican dialect by arguing that "the Creole dialect is really a sealed book, to one who has not lisp'd it from his earliest years."[18] A few years later Henry Garland Murray, the first black Creole author and performer, stakes a similar claim except this time he implies that it is Africaneity, more than indigeneity, which is the central feature of authentic Caribbean identity because an authentic rendering of Creole "will always require one born of the African, to delineate [black people's speech] correctly."[19] By the time Claude McKay's brother (a well-known black schoolteacher) in 1915 defends as "true patriotism" the use of Creole in *Jane's Career* and recasts as an art the

Argosy and the black/brown-owned *The Creole* rendering the Creole speech of rural Indian indentured laborers.

[13] See V. S. Naipaul, *The Middle Passage* (Vintage, 1962), p. 69.

[14] H.G. de Lisser was actually "Jamaica white," or a light-skinned brown man.

[15] Carolyn Cooper, *Noises in the Blood* (Duke University Press, 1995), p. 6.

[16] Nadia Nurhussein, Introduction, *Rhetorics of Literacy: The Cultivation of American Dialect Poetry* (2013).

[17] See Samuel Augustus Mathews, *The Lying Hero, or An Answer to J.B. Moreton's Manners and Customs in the West Indies* (St. Eustatius: E. L. Low & Co., 1793).

[18] *Morning Journal* (November 2, 1868).

[19] See Henry G. Murray, preface, *Brown Sammy in Search of a Wife* (Kingston: R. Jordon, 1874).

exclusive Creole that is spoken "with *purity* and accomplishment," it is clear that literary dialect has become an indicator of cultural nationalism.[20] The words "purity" and "patriotism" are used to recast as a desirable, essential *educated* Caribbean cultural feature that which heretofore was considered *un*desirable: Creole's tainted, illiterate mongrel ancestry.

In our contemporary moment, when Creole narratives are justly celebrated for breaking into the global mainstream through metropolitan anthologies and awards, it is tempting to engage in revisionary history of Creole literature's origins, resetting the originary moment closer to the anti-colonial period preceding independence in the twentieth century. But what was true 250 years ago is often true today: Creole language itself is a fight. A race-based, class-based, who's-on-top-who's-not fight. One that has never exactly resolved itself. But, and this is crucial, it is not *necessarily* a weapon of the subaltern against the powerful. It can be a weapon of the powerful against the subaltern, or subaltern against subaltern. Brian Moore's observation of nineteenth-century British Guiana can be extended to the entire nglophone Caribbean: "Nineteenth century Guyana...was by no means a melting-pot. On the contrary, there was a consistently high level of suspicion, tension and violence which characterized inter-group relations. [...] there was...friction between blacks and Indians, Indians and Chinese, Chinese and whites, whites and blacks, Indians and whites, and even among different categories of Indians, and between [Caribbean migrant blacks] and [c]reole blacks."[21]

For a society burdened by the historical perception that it is at best a poor imitation of a European, African, or Asian original, Creole's cultural assertiveness as an unquestionably original Caribbean product represents a paradox of modernity. That is, Creole both stands in for that which is unassimilable, that which cannot be subsumed into (neo)colonial projects of modernity, and that mark of authentic culture which must consumed and showcased.[22] Indeed, its very inability to be assimilated is what makes it authentic, desirable. This supposed unassimilability manifests most clearly in Caribbean music, historically (if not always accurately) understood to be the voice of the people. Where political strategies failed and non-elites were denied access to simple human rights, Caribbean music could utter the unspeakable. It has always done double duty. Caribbean music was, and is, the unavoidable noise that pervades the public space in Caribbean cities and towns. This disruption of the status quo is surely what Bob Marley had in mind in

---

[20] U. Theo McKay, "The Use of Dialect" (Letter to the Editor), *Daily Gleaner* (January 28, 1915).

[21] Brian L. Moore, *Cultural Power, Resistance and Pluralism: Colonial Guyana 1838–1900* (McGill-Queen's University Press, Montreal & Kingston: The Press University of the West Indies, 1995), p. 11.

[22] For extended discussions of authenticity and the consumption of black culture see Martin Favor, *Authentic Blackness: The Folk in the New Negro Renaissance* (Durham and London: Duke University Press, 1999); and Mimi Sheller, *Consuming the Caribbean: From Arawaks to Zombies* (New York: Routledge, 2003).

1980 when he sang of his desire to "disturb my neighbor" by blasting his disco speakers in the urban anthem *Bad Card*.[23]

The politics of noise in the Caribbean are, as Carolyn Cooper has argued, also the politics of class: "Night noises that pollute middle-class neighbourhoods, disturbing a neighbour's sleep, are a threatening challenge to those uneasily awake in comfortable beds."[24] The cultures of the contemporary urban Caribbean are most associated with its working-class communities, and thus with a kind of hyperblackness. In these urban cultures Creole and Noise are indissociable elements of the Caribbean soundscape, reminders of the volatile class inequalities of the region. As the most accessible medium for non-elite Caribbean populations, Caribbean music plays a considerable part in the evolution of Creole literature and performance. Throughout this study I use Caribbean music as a form of oral Creole narrative, but it would be a mistake to conclude that therefore music, unlike the written Creole tradition, has an unmediated and transparent connection to the largely working-class, Creole-speaking majorities of the Caribbean. As this study will reveal, the transatlantic musical acts and the popular elocutionary performances of Creole from the nineteenth century to the contemporary moment were very much mediated acts, even acts of cultural ventriloquism.

Held in contempt even by its speakers for most of its existence, Creole has the strange distinction of being at once despised and desired, both liability and asset. Liability in that it has long been a marker of the region's primitive or "backward" nature; asset in that it gives the lie to the argument that the Caribbean is a cultureless backwater, a poor imitation of Europe. Creole is essential to all nationalist projects, be they politically radical, colonialist or, frankly, materialist. Now that, after centuries of censure and derision, Creole is considered the lingua franca of the Caribbean[25] and Creole literature has found an international audience, does anyone still object to the Creolification of Caribbean literature? Surely not the international audience that has made Creole authors like Claude McKay (and now, Marlon James) famous, or the British and American publishers who promote their books and encourage them to write without a Creole glossary.[26] What was true over a century ago is true today: dialect is big business.[27] Objections, if any, are mostly regional, and of a didactic nature: to wit, speaking and reading in

---

[23] Bob Marley and the Wailers, "Bad Card," *Uprising* (Jamaica: Island Records, 1980).

[24] Carolyn Cooper, *Noises in the Blood: Orality, Gender, and the "Vulgar" Body of Jamaican Popular Culture* (Durham and London: Duke University Press, 1995), p. 5.

[25] See for example, the prevailing view of regional linguists such as Hubert Devonish in *Language and Liberation: Creole Language Politics in the Caribbean* (Trenton: Red Sea Press, 1986).

[26] See Annie Paul, "Reading, Writing, Religion: Mark McWatt and Marlon James Talk with Annie Paul," *Caribbean Review of Books* (November 10, 2006), accessed February 5, 2016, http://caribbeanreviewofbooks.com/crb-archive/10-november-2006/reading-writing-religion/

[27] Nadia Nurhussein excavates the financial benefits of "tacking on" of dialect to a story during the "mania for dialect" era of the late-nineteenth century United States in *The Rhetorics of Literacy: the Cultivation of American Dialect Poetry* (2013), pp. 1–3.

Creole prevents Caribbean students from learning English and becoming global citizens.[28] It is a contemporary version of what earlier generations of black Creole writers encountered: anti-Creole crusaders who are, themselves, Caribbean, and as often as not black or non-white themselves.[29] But if the objections belong to black Caribbean people, surely so too does Creole and its ascendance. It is therefore understandable if it is regarded as an attempt to wrest Creole from people the suggestion that the Creole literary tradition is other than a direct product of its African heritage. That is not my intent either. But at this moment of Creole's arrival into the pantheon of discursive languages it is crucial to excavate the question that undergirds so much of our academic and, increasingly, popular discourse: Who owns the Creole literary tradition? Only African descendants, Creole-speaking or not? Only Creole speakers, African-descended or not? Only its literary practitioners, Creole-speaking or not? The history is strange, twisty, and winding as the region itself, full of back turns.

Black Noise? The Origins of Creole

The word itself is slippery. Today we call it Creole, Creolese, or Caribbean English. Or we nationalize it: Jamaican, Trinidadian, Barbadian. Yesterday we called it "bad" grammar. In fact, many of us *still* call it bad grammar: the very term itself is saturated with historical conflicts. Mostly we call it dialect, a subsidiary term which suggests something incorrect, inferior; a debased language always to be understood in relation to the "real" language, in this case English. But if "dialect" indicates the subaltern status of its speaker, "Creole" indicates their linguistic—and social—equality. It didn't always.

"Creole"—with a capital C—was initially the English term for the Caribbean natives, white or black, who were born and raised in the Caribbean. To be a native was, in the view of the European metropole, to be Othered. But one didn't have to be an actual native to be "nativized." Even whites who were not born in the Caribbean but lived there and were, presumably, infected with native culture, were referred to as Creoles by the English.[30] Native status was totalizing, transfiguring,

---

[28] See Karyl Walker, "Patois Bible Not a Retrograde Step," *Jamaica Observer* (November 27, 2012), accessed October 6, 2019, http://www.jamaicaobserver.com/news/Patois-Bible-not-a-retrograde-step _13096374?profile=&template=PrinterVersion; "Jamaica's patois bible: the word of God in creole" (Youtube), uploaded December 24, 2011, accessed September 29, 2019. (https://www.youtube.com/ watch?v=rRI3srdcia0.

[29] Henry Garland Murray's acknowledges his audience's sensitivities of this nature in the Preface to *Brown Sammy in Search of a Wife* (Kingston: R. Jordan, 1874); see also the editorial comments towards dialect letters in British Guiana's colored newspaper *The Creole* ("Notice to Correspondents," December 13, 1856.) Louise Bennett's "Bans O' Killing," in *Jamaica Labrish* (Jamaica: Sangster's, 1966/1972), p. 218.

[30] See Lyndon Dominique, Introduction, in Anonymous, *The Woman of Colour: A Tale*, ed. Lyndon Dominique (Peterborough: Broadview, 2008/1804), p. 22.

racializing. A Creole was marked as such by their speech. A Creole spoke Creole. The language carried the features of the people: hybrid, unassimilable, lascivious. Inferior.

In the contemporary moment, however, Creole has shifted has a place, however tenuous, in the realm of recognizable language, buttressed on the one hand by the authoritative pronouncements of linguists and, on the other, nationalist politics that claim an authentic Caribbean language not beholden to imperialist legacies. But the further back in time we go, the more Creole slips from its precarious perch in the realm of language down to its more familiar place at the bottom of the linguistic and social hierarchy: back to *That* Way of Speaking, to *Don't speak that way if you want to move up in life*. So it goes, ever devolving back in colonial time: from Creole to dialect; from dialect to "bad grammar"; from "bad grammar" to "gibberish." Falling back to the dawn of the modern Caribbean we find, again, that most elemental designation of sound that grates on human consciousness: Noise.

Noise is background sound, the disharmony that frames the Subject, the signifier of an essential incommensurability. Noise is not merely sound. A cultural and ideological concept, it is the audial representation of the enslaved, the working class, the immigrant: the Other. Amid the upheaval and violence of transatlantic slavery, noise "textualized the disorientation of African culture," as David Novak notes.[31] It is what the Europeans deemed the anarchic sounds emitted by the enslaved Africans. Noise is what these uncivilized beings, not-quite-humans made. When they attempted "speech"—meaning English or other European languages— it was a degraded version: a dialect, a pidgin, the antithesis of language itself. A real language was organized, symmetrical harmonious, *civilized*. Creole was a poor but necessary imitation, a foil for real language. Just as Europeans required colonial black, brown or Asian Others to be truly European, so did European languages require colonial dialects, pidgins, patoises to be truly legitimate.[32] (Never mind that European languages were—and are—themselves a mishmash of dialects and patoises; we are talking about the imperial ideology of language.) Shakespeare knew the difference, knew the political *value* of that difference: in *The Tempest* Caliban retorts to Prospero, "You taught me language; and my profit on't/Is, I know how to curse."[33] It is a line that has come to symbolize anti-colonial discourse. Yet Caliban also delights in the *noises* of his native island home:

---

[31] David Novak, "Noise," in *Key Words for Sound Studies*(Durham and London: Duke University Press, 2015), pp. 126, 130. My thanks to Darius Bost for alerting me to this article.

[32] See Faith Smith's discussion of English national anxieties to render "Englishness" distinct from "Jamaicanness" from the Victorian era to the present in Faith Smith, "'A Mysterious Murder': Considering Jamaican Victorianism," in *Victorian Jamaica*, edited by Tim Barringer and Wayne Modest (Durham and London: Duke University Press, 2018), p. 658.

[33] William Shakespeare, *The Tempest*, Act 1, Scene 2.

Be not afeard; the isle is full of noises,
Sounds and sweet airs, that give delight and hurt not.
Sometimes a thousand twangling instruments
Will hum about mine ears, and sometime voices
That, if I then had waked after long sleep,
Will make me sleep again: and then, in dreaming,
The clouds methought would open and show riches
Ready to drop upon me that, when I waked,
I cried to dream again.[34]

An earlier generation of Caribbean intellectuals claimed Caliban's distortion of Prospero's language as a metonymy of Creole. They argued that Caliban's language is Caribbean language incarnate, its very nature satire or protest, a dialectical form of dialect, a way of speaking Truth to Power.[35] Colonial mimicry is weaponized as Noise. "You taught me language, and my profit on't/Is I know how to curse," Caliban tells his slave master. Caribbean discourse is, in this reading, oppositional at its core. Yet the "sounds and sweet airs" that are native to Caliban's island might also be read not as dialectical at all but rather as original Creole languages; languages that are not necessarily discordant, but simply native, in harmony with the speaker and the landscape.

The Europeans who visited the Caribbean felt differently.

A biting satire of Caliban's plaintive speech was printed in the Kingston magazine *The Columbian* in Jamaica, 1799:

Sayings, ça iras, drums, flags, twanging instruments,
A thousand different cries, sometimes riots,
Do stun my ears by day; unruly horses,
And scoffing negroes, break my rest at night:
Or, if I sleep, in dreaming I awake
With shrieks of fire; methinks I see the street
In horrid blaze around me, that I long
To quit this isle for Britain once again.[36]

Drums. Twanging instruments. Cries. Riots. An interval of two hundred years vanishes. The black noise of 1799 may as well be Public Enemy's "Fight the Power,"

---

[34] *The Tempest*, Act 3, Scene 2.

[35] See, for example, Bill Ashcroft, *Caliban's Language: The Transformation of English in Post-Colonial Literatures* (London and New York: Routledge, 2009), p. 2; for a poetic rendering of the same, see Edward Kamau Brathwaite, "Caliban," *The Arrivants* (1973). For earlier, non-anglophone uses of Caliban-as-anticolonial symbol, see Roberto Fernández Retamar, *Caliban and Other Essays* (1989).

[36] "Parody of Shakespeare," *Columbian Magazine: or The Monthly Miscellany* (Kingston, Jamaica, 1799), p. 251, quoted in Dillon, p. 209, footnote 117.

circa 1989.[37] Black music and black rebellion are, again, made synonymous. What to Caliban are "sweet sounds" to the anonymous British author are the ominous rumblings of violent revolution. The first line makes a reference to "ça ira" ("it will be fine"), a refrain of a popular song during the French Revolution, the full verse of which is "it will be fine, it will be fine, let's hang the aristocrats to the lamp-post."[38] If England's order and harmony was reflected in its language then, the thinking went, the anarchy and *dis*order of Caribbean society was reflected in *its* language. The Caribbean functioned both as tabula rasa and mini-Africa of the New World, a place of terrifying formlessness—but inviting financial possibility—in the European imagination. For the English, the language and the wider soundscape of the Caribbean were intimately aligned, as the narrator implies when he bemoans the "thousand different cries" of the "scoffing negroes." Caliban's music is, for him, alien island noise that "stun[s]" his ears and makes him want to "quit this isle for Britain once again." It was surely the Jamaican soundscape that so oppressed Lady Nugent, the English governor's wife in 1804, when she wrote, "Noise all night; and, if possible, today worse than ever."[39]

Taken as mere noisemaking Creole proves that, as nineteenth-century British historian James Anthony Froude infamously put it, "there are no people [in the Caribbean] in the true sense of the word, with a character and purpose of their own."[40] In this formulation the noise that tormented Lady Nugent is a signifier of nothing more than Otherness, racial in character but beyond race. It doesn't matter that there are a multitude of Creoles in the region: they signify the same liminality.

This study thus claims the vocabulary of Noise, and all of the attendant pejorative language of erasure, imperialism, and marginalization, as part of its restorative historical project. Noise, Dialect, Pidgen, Vernacular, Creole. These words carry their own particular history. The history of Creole literature is, therefore, the history of these senseless utterances, these ominous noises, these fighting words. They are the sounds of a mongrel society, white, brown, and black, on a journey from senselessness to sense-making, from the disorder of formlessness to the symmetry of definition. Such were the views of Froude and other early English and European travelers, who reported that the natives spoke a *kind* of language, an inchoate, protean form of communication. The question of who, exactly, it belonged to, was up for debate. Some believed that it was the result of the Africans'

---

[37] Public Enemy, "Fight the Power," Def/Jam CBS Records, from *Do the Right Thing* (soundtrack; Spike Lee, dir.: Forty Acres and a Mule Productions, 1989).

[38] Ça Ira," Oxford Reference, accessed January 26, 2021. In the original French: "a ira, a ira, les aristocrates la lanterne," "Definitions for ça ira," accessed October 4, 2020, https://www.definitions.net/definition/ca±ira.

[39] Lady Maria Nugent, *Lady Nugent's Journal* 1839, entry, December 27, 1804 (Cambridge: Cambridge University Press, 2010), p. 279.

[40] See James Anthony Froude, *The English in the West Indies, or the Bow of Ulysses* (London: Longmans, Green, and Co., 1888), p. 94.

inability to speak English correctly (whichever of the many forms of English that might be). Others like white creole historian (and slave owner) Edward Long believed that his fellow white creoles were "infected" by a form of negrofication that resulted in a "disgusting" form of broken English, a view affirmed by Lady Nugent yet again, who famously notes that "the Creole language is not confined to the negroes" and describes white creole women as speaking "a sort of broken English, with an indolent drawing out of their words, that is very tiresome if not disgusting."[41]

A third view was articulated by John Atkins, an eighteenth-century English traveler to Jamaica, who early on identified Creole as the authentic language of, not the blacks, but the white creoles. In a region whose original inhabitants and histories were eviscerated so that the Europeans could proceed with their tabula rasa fantasy of conquest, the question of who was truly native had considerable currency. For Atkins, it was the white creoles who were the region's true natives: "The Creoles...which are properly the Natives of the Island, are a spurious Race.... They are half Negrish in their Manners, proceeding from the promiscuous and confined Conversation with their Relations, the Servants at the Plantations, and have a Language especially Pleasant, a kind of Gypsy Gibberish, that runs smoothest in swearing."[42] Atkins' observation is insistently affirmed in other eighteenth-century English texts such as that by the Scottish satirist John Armstrong, who mocks "that beautiful pybald, black and white Lingo, pallaber'd in its greatest *purity* by the Creolians [white creoles] of Jamaica."[43] [emphasis mine]

I underscore this early belief that Creole was essentially a "negrofied" white creole invention because ever after, right up to our contemporary moment, Creole is associated with the inferiority—or, more recently, the creativity—of the working-class, African-descended, or black, populations of the Caribbean.[44]

---

[41] Edward Long writes that Creole "infects many of the White Creoles, who learn it from their (black or colored) nurses in infancy," in his *The History of Jamaica*, vol. 2 (London: T. Lowndes, 1774), p. 427. Lady Nugent, *Lady Nugent's Journal of her residence in Jamaica from 1801 to 1805*(Kingston: Institute of Jamaica, 1966), p. 98.

[42] John Atkins, *A Voyage to Guinea, Brasil, and the West Indies* (London: Cesar Ward and Richard Chandler, 1736: 244–5, cited in D'Costa and Lalla, *Language in Exile: Three Hundred Years of Jamaican Creole* (Tuscaloosa: University of Alabama, 1990), pp. 23–4. Ironically, white Americans appeared to entertain the opposite view; that only "pure" blacks could speak "pure" dialect. See African American writer Charles Chesnutt's complaint that white authors of dialect fiction inevitably used "full-blooded blacks" with "dog-like fidelity" to whites for dialect speech: Charles Chesnutt to George Washington Cable, June 1890, cited in Richard Broadhead, ed., Introduction, *The Conjure Woman and Other Tales* (Duke University Press, 1993), p. 14.

[43] John Armstrong, "Omicron *Lick-Devil, Esq.," *Universal Almanac: Miscellanies*, vol. 2 (1770), pp. 175–6. Armstrong is alluding to what he considers the pretensions of publishers to use non-English speech to sell books, perhaps an oblique reference to the popularity of dialect during the period.

[44] It should be noted that some contemporary linguists also link black and white speech during this period: Jerome Handler and John Rickford note that seventeenth-century Barbadian blacks and indentured whites were understood to speak a similar language. See Jerome Handler and John Rickford, "Textual Evidence on the Nature of Early Barbadian Speech, 1676–1835," *Journal of Pidgin and Creole Languages* 9 (2) (1994), p. 221.

Whether embodiments of cultural inferiority or creativity, what joins these otherwise opposing views is the underlying presumption that Creole is, at its core, an essentially black cultural product. What this view of Creole's fundamental blackness obscures is that, to Europeans, white creoles were, themselves, the embodiment of a suspect cultural hybridity; white in ancestry but black in manners and habits, especially sexual ones. They were also of uncertain political inclinations: vociferous defenders of British rule in one moment, ardent Caribbean nationalists in another.

If the perversions of white creoles originated in this taint of blackness then that perversion was reflected in their speech. English bookkeeper J. B. Moreton describes two elegant white creole women, "all lovely, all divine," who are sexually forward and speak in a vulgar dialect (" 'Sir, Ise don't love turkey rump—Ise love turkey bubby [breasts].")[45] For just such racial ambiguity is white creole Antoinette Cosway regarded with fascinated repulsion by her English husband in Jean Rhys' *Wide Sargasso Sea* ("Long, sad, dark alien eyes. Creole of pure English descent she may be, but they are not English or European either."[46])

By contrast, for both black and white creoles Africans embodied both a racial and cultural purity, albeit a purity that could signify black savagery or nobility depending on the political context, but purity nevertheless.[47] Even pioneering scholars of Caribbean Creole in the late-nineteenth and early-twentieth centuries refer to it as "Negro English," as if it were only spoken by blacks.[48] The belief that "pybald" Creole is essentially an African holdover is one that remains remarkably current. "The fact that all races have adopted [Creole] speech does not make it any less African," argues one contemporary writer of a Jamaican grammar book, summarizing a popular perspective.[49] Creole's explicit national appeal is reflected in much of twentieth-century Caribbean literary criticism; it is the basis of what in 1980 Kamau Brathwaite famously termed the region's "nation language." Nation language is what Brathwaite sees as the region's unassimilable Africaneity, encoded

[45]   See J. B. Moreton's descriptions of both male and female white creoles in *West India Customs and Manners* (1790), pp. 108–27, quoted in Anonymous, *The Woman of Colour: A Tale*, edited by Lyndon J. Dominique (Peterborough: Broadview, 2008), p. 247.

[46]   Jean Rhys, *Wide Sargasso Sea* (New York: Norton1966/1982), p. 67.

[47]   For example, the pro-Eyre, anti-rebel accounts of the Maroons during the Morant Bay uprising praise the Maroons as embodying a kind of savage African nobility deployed in the service of whites, which creole blacks have violated. See account of Jamaican Maroons in Anonymous, "The Jamaican Maroons," a *New York Tribune* article reproduced in *The Sacramento Daily Union* 96 (101) (November 30, 1898), p. 7; see also Henry Garland's portrayals of Africans in his *Brown Sammy* stories as well as others. In the earliest known novel by an African-descended author in the Caribbean, the titular character is rendered noble by his mixture of English and African/Maroon heritage.

[48]   See Frank Cundall, founder of the Institute of Jamaica, in "The West Indies Today, 1908," National Library of Jamaica MST, 934, 102; and Walter Jekyll, *Jamaican Song and Story: Annancy Stories, Digging Songs, Ring Tues, and Dancing Tunes* (Jamaica, 1906), p. 3; both cited in *They Do as They Please: The Jamaican Struggle for Freedom after Morant Bay*, Brian L. Moore and Michele A. Johnson (Mona: University of the West Indies Press, 2011), p. 84.

[49]   L. Emilie Adams, *Understanding Jamaican Patois: An Introduction to Afro-Jamaican Grammar* (Kingston: Kingston Publishers Ltd, 1991), p. 5.

in an Africanesque language that is not simply African but also politically radical precisely because of its unassimilability, its resistance to imperial influence.[50] In other words nation language, like Gates' formulation of black literary dialect, is opposed to standard English in both form and content; its very existence is radical. Notably, for Brathwaite, noise is indispensable to nation language: "Noise is that decorative energy that invests the nation performance. Unnecessary but without which not enough."[51]

Although in our postcolonial moment the Creole tradition is now mostly associated with African oral traditions it clearly has roots in the British dialect tradition as well—and in the dialectical traditions of both Africa and Europe. Early twentieth century calypso in colonial Trinidad was often articulated as a war between the "good," standard English grammar of educated, urban—and native-born Trinidadian—calypsonians and the "bad" grammar of so-called small island immigrants, to the point where contemporary calypso has been described as reflective of, not essential Afro-creole culture, but rather "*re*-Afro-creolization."[52] Dialect is call and response: but dialect is also the contact zone between point and counterpoint, hegemon versus subaltern, "proper" grammar versus "bad" grammar: language versus noise. In particular, its lineage appears to be directly related to the explosively popular Scottish dialect poetry and music featuring dialect lyrics that saturated the anglophone Caribbean from the late eighteenth century well into the twentieth via the Scottish sailors, doctors, book-keepers, and plantation workers who made up a significant number of white immigrants to the region. Scottish dialect poetry and humorous stories featuring dialect-speaking Scots could be found in almost every anglophone Caribbean newspaper well into the twentieth century. Chaucer was not available to everybody in the eighteenth-century Caribbean; but Robert Burns was.

Violence and Blackface

Perhaps the most singularly fascinating phenomenon that I have uncovered in my research is the "missing link" in the story of Creole literature, the primary means by which physical performance was transformed into books and stories. That link is the astonishing ubiquity of blackface minstrelsy in the Caribbean, throughout most of the nineteenth century right until about 50 or 60 years ago. I am certainly not the first scholar to discover this—Louis Chude-Sokei's groundbreaking

---

[50] Kamau Brathwaite, "The History of the Voice," pp. 265–6, reprinted in *Roots* (Ann Arbor: University of Michigan Press, 1993/1986).

[51] See Edward Kamau Brathwaite, *History of the Voice: The Development of Nation Language in Anglophone Caribbean Poetry* (London: New Beacon Books, 1984), pp. 301–2, footnote 49.

[52] See Lise Winer, quoting Don Hill, in "Socio-cultural Change and the Language of Calypso," *New West Indian Guide* 60 (¾) (1986), p. 119.

research in *The Last Darky* (2006) comes to mind—but what is striking to me, as someone who grew up in the Caribbean, is how that history has been obscured or elided in contemporary discourses about our cultural heritage, whether popular, political, or personal. As I read archival accounts of the popular blackface comedy duos who performed across the region in the 1920s and 1930s I asked my mother if she had any knowledge or experience of blackface performances growing up in Jamaica. She was dismissive. Blackface minstrelsy was an American problem, a by-product of that country's violent racist history, not ours. Great Britain, not the United States, was the major cultural influence. She then recounted for me the fun folk songs and dances that she had learned in school, among them "Jump Jim Crow," a blackface song-and-dance number popularized by white American Thomas Rice in the early nineteenth century. My mother reminisced fondly about Bim and Bam, the hilarious comedy duo performed regularly at Kingston's venerable Ward Theatre for the annual Christmas pantomime. But Bim and Bam performed in blackface, I reminded her. So they did, she said with dawning horror, but we never thought anything of it. They were *funny*.

Literature is not an art form that we associate typically with the physical world. But the physical and the literary have always been intertwined, never more so than with literary dialect. And that physicality was intimately connected to violence as a visceral, lived expression of hostility. The passion of nineteenth-century blacks and non-whites for Caribbean Creole literature and performance was born of a complex matrix of emerging literacy, imported periodicals, blackface minstrelsy, and lit by the powder keg of violence, actual or threatened. The rise of the subaltern class was a threat to elite interests; Creole, literary or performative, was a weapon. But it was also a tool of advancement. In Jamaica, an epicenter of literary dialect, the violent suppression of the Morant Bay Rebellion in 1865 also occasioned an explosion of performative and literary dialect, and gave rise to the first black author of Creole literature. In British Guiana, the importation of the Portuguese, Indians, and others to replace the black workers on the plantations occasioned often violent civil unrest. It also prompted one of the earliest pub-lished books of Creole poetry, by a local white, in 1877.[53]

As my mother's experience illustrates, the influence of nearby U.S. culture is consistently underestimated. Dialect-laden comic sketches from United States media were reproduced in Caribbean newspapers as early as the 1830s.[54]

---

[53] Brian Moore's work in both the Jamaican and Guyanese contexts is particularly noteworthy here. For an in-depth discussion of the cultural context of the Morant Bay Rebellion see Brian L. Moore and Michele A. Johnson, *"They Do As They Please:" The Jamaican Struggle for Cultural Freedom after Morant Bay* (University of the West Indies Press, 2011); and *Cultural Power, Resistance and Pluralism: Colonial Guyana 1838–1900* (McGill-Queen's University Press (Montreal & Kingston: The Press University of the West Indies, 1995).

[54] See Lise Winer, "Six Vernacular Texts from Trinidad, 1838–1851," in *Englishes Around the World: Studies in Honour of Manfred Gorlach*, edited by Edgar W. Schneider and Manfred Gorlach (Amsterdam: John Benjamins, 1997).

American theatrical and performing companies visited the Caribbean with regularity from as early as the late eighteenth century, among these the hugely popular blackface minstrel companies of the mid-to-late-nineteenth century, whose depiction of blacks and use of "negro dialect" were the very heart of their performances.[55] Difficult for twenty-first century readers to understand is the reality that, for nineteenth century Caribbean audiences, these visiting blackface troupes did not just represent a nostalgia for slavery, they also represented a kind of vernacular cosmopolitanism, a way to be both black and modern in the emerging post-slavery world. Their dialect-laden "plantation" songs were recast as "Negro spirituals" for a later generation, songs which became the main attraction of the classically trained African-American choir the Jubilee Singers, who wowed black audiences around the world when they toured in the late nineteenth century. The influence of the Jubilee Singers was made manifest in the formally trained black choirs from Africa to the Caribbean, such as South Africa's African Choir and, as early as 1882, Jamaica's Kingston Choral Union (later renamed the Native Jamaica Choir). Both would tour Great Britain as "native" choirs in the succeeding decades.[56] There was a reason, after all, why blackface was popular with black audiences.

Early Creole Grammar Books

The noise of what Brathwaite calls nation performance is, as I have noted elsewhere, not just a raced concept but also a classed and gendered one.[57] The stereotype of the black virago is incomplete without the sonic accompaniment of dialect. Even in contemporary narratives, the vaunted verbal dexterity of Caribbean women usually involves "tracing" or cursing in Creole. Colonial archives are full of allusions to working class blacks, particularly women, who refuse to behave respectably; or, more importantly, refuse to work within the wage labor system of the plantations.[58] As Mimi Sheller notes, "Many examples of 'violent language' in the British records were spoken by women...when violence occurred, working-class women were often at the forefront, brandishing not only insults and provocation but also,

[55] See Errol Hill, Chapter 10 ("Performance Modes after Slavery"), pp. 247–71, in *The Jamaican Stage 1655–1900* (Amherst: University of Massachusetts Press, 1992); also Jill Lane, *Blackface Cuba, 1840–1895* (Philadelphia: University of Pennsylvania Press, 2020).

[56] See Jane Collins, "'Umuntu, Ngumuntu, Ngabantu': The Story of the African Choir," *Studies in Theatre and Performance* 27 (2) (2007), pp. 95–114.

[57] For an extended discussion of dialect, nationalism and gentrification see Edmondson, Chapter 3 ("Gentrifying Dialect, or The Taming of Miss Lou"), pp. 86–109, in *Caribbean Middlebrow* (2009).

[58] See Faith Smith, *Creole Recitations* (Charlottesville: University of Virginia Press, 2002), p. 18; and Mimi Sheller, *Citizenship from Below: Erotic Agency and Caribbean Freedom* (Durham and London: Duke University Press, 2012), pp. 70–5.

quite often, weapons."[59] In one telling example from 1847 Jamaica, a Kingston minister complains that a recent Christian fellowship meeting at his church devolved into "a noisy indecent discussion" because, in his estimation, two-thirds of the leaders of the meetings were black illiterate women "of active and restless disposition" who were "beyond the control of the ministers...."[60]

But if Creole's early cultural form was made visible by the public performances of black working-class women, it was also the case that Creole literature was uniformly a private masculine endeavor. In fact, it was a gentleman's practice. As early as 1822 white creole Samuel Augustus Mathews, author of the combative, Creole-laced polemic *The Lying Hero*, published *The Willshire Squeeze*, an alternately comedic and serious compendium of what he called "Negro proverbs," thus inaugurating a series of publications by local and foreign whites throughout the next century to transcribe and make sense of "the Negro language."[61] By casting himself as merely a semi-literate entertainer with an amusing hobby, Mathews underplays his own genuine intellectual interest in, and respect for, black creole language and culture. In the section on "negro familiar dialect" he methodically transcribes a number of black creole proverbs with thoughtful translations and explanations attached.[62] It was an ethnic balancing act with repercussions for generations of non-white authors. Towards the end of the century the authors of publications on and in Creole became distinctly non-white.

In 1868, after a politically tumultuous decade in Jamaica, an avowed gentleman by the name of Thomas Russell wrote a landmark text with the not-exactly-tongue in cheek title, *Etymology of Jamaican Grammar by a Young Gentleman*.[63] This slim grammar book—twenty-two pages—has been overlooked by scholars, perhaps, because it is an awkward narrative hybrid. On the one hand it reads like a weighty, learned tome; on the other it effects a breezy, brief social commentary. *Etymology* attempts to straddle the didactic aims of linguistic scholarship with the wink-wink condescension of Caribbean elites towards "bad" grammar. We have no evidence of the author's race, but it has been speculated that Russell was a member of the white or near-white elite.[64] The volume's tone is alternately

[59] See Mimi Sheller, *Citizenship from Below* (2012), p. 75.

[60] See Mimi Sheller, *Citizenship from Below* (2012), pp. 70–1.

[61] Samuel Augustus Mathews, *The Willshire Squeeze: A Ballad Founded Upon Facts to Which Are Added Specimens of the Negro Familiar Dialect and Proverbial Sayings, with Songs* (Demerara: Printed for the Author at the Guiana Chronicle Office, Georgetown, 1822.)

[62] Samuel Augustus Mathews, *The Willshire Squeeze* (1822), pp. 77–81.

[63] See Thomas Russell, *Etymology of Jamaican Grammar by a Young Gentleman* (Kingston, Jamaica: M. DeCordova Printers, 1868), accessed November 19, 2020. https://archive.org/details/etymologyjamaic00russgoog.

[64] "The tone and structure of his work, written in a particularly tumultuous moment for Jamaican politics, suggests that he came from a good education, which in turn leads us to suppose that he was white or mostly white and belonged to the middling to upper classes." See Phillip Hatfield, "Our 'Young Gentleman' Thomas Russell and the emerging 'Problem' of the Caribbean Language," American Collections Blog post, British Library, accessed June 22, 2016, http://britishlibrary.typepad.co.uk/.m/americas/2015/07/our-young-gentleman-thomas-russell-and-the-emerging-problem-of-the-caribbean-language.html.

ponderous and self-consciously witty, striving to project both scholarly erudition and amused condescension. Similar to *The Willshire Squeeze* in its almost schizophrenic tonal shifts, Russell's *Etymology* illustrates how the contradictions of literary dialect reflect the difficult social positioning of its practitioners.

White creoles were indeed awkwardly placed as Caribbean subjects. Their heritage was English, but not their culture—or their language. Education was used by the colonial state as a whitening, or at least Englishifying, project. But for whom? As V. S. Naipaul once noted dryly of the Caribbean's white elite, "Education was strictly for the poor; and the poor were invariably black."[65] To appear to strive for learnedness was to be too aspirational, too not-the-thing-itself: too black. For nineteenth-century black scholars, as Faith Smith has pointed out, erudition as a form of labor was associated with black striving, a condition of trying but not necessarily succeeding.[66] Further, as I have shown elsewhere, in the nineteenth-century Caribbean the "gentleman of letters" was a masculine prototype for men of color to aspire to, not at all incompatible with anti-colonial or proto-black nationalist leanings.[67] Nurhussein and Smith further elaborate on the labor of Creole literature by distinguishing between Creole speakers and Creole writers, the former associated with ease and authenticity, the latter with labor and *in*authenticity.[68]

If inauthenticity is a hallmark of Creole literature then in this sense Russell's slim volume is the first truly Creole grammar book, both in form and content. It highlights its own distance from native Creole speakers while making the case for Creole as a legitimate language form. On the one hand *Etymology* is the work of a serious grammarian. It consists of chapters dedicated to scholarly subjects such as "Articles," "Case and Gender," "Interjectional Phrases," and "Possessive Pronouns, Distributive and Demonstrative." The author earnestly reminds us that inasmuch as Creole is "[a] form of *language* which has now been spoken for nearly two centuries," it deserves more rigorous study than the "occasional pilfering of its rich and expressive construction...to wring out a laugh...when 'dry' English fails."[69] Russell identifies Jamaican Creole as a blend of cultures, from the "Spanish" words and phrases to those of "purely African" origin.[70] Yet he also demurs from the obvious point of the book—to make a serious argument in favor of Creole as a language—by retreating to the excuse that "This little work was never intended originally to meet the eye of the Public." He declares that he

[65] V. S. Naipaul, *The Middle Passage* (New York: Vintage, 1981/1962), p. 57.

[66] See Faith Smith, Chapter 1 (" 'Writing Was Easy to Him:' Education, Labor, Distinction"), in Faith Smith, *Creole Recitations* (2002).

[67] Belinda Edmondson, Chapter 2 ("Literary Men and the English Canonical Tradition"), in *Making Men: Gender, Literary Authority, and Women's Writing in Caribbean Narrative* (Duke University Press, 1999).

[68] Faith Smith, *Creole Recitations* (2002), pp. 23–66; and Nadia Nurhussein, *Rhetorics of Literacy* (2012), p. 121.

[69] Thomas Russell, *Etymology of Jamaican Grammar* (1868), p. 13.

[70] Thomas Russell, *Etymology of Jamaican Grammar* (1868), pp. 6–7.

"merely prepared it as a source of social amusement" to his friends. Further, he insists—contradictorily—on calling Creole a "corruption" of English, and mockingly suggests that the country's elite should become "pupils" of Creole so that they can better deal with the lower orders of society. "The writer is most willing to give letters of introduction to any anxious to enjoy the benefit of a living teacher," he snidely concludes, distancing himself from the very idea that the working class can have anything to teach the elite.[71]

Not so the better-known, and emphatically black, middle-class teacher John Jacob Thomas. A year after *Etymology* was published, the Afro-Trinidadian author published *The Theory and Practice of Creole Grammar* (1870), the watershed volume on the French Creole spoken by blacks in Trinidad. The anti-racist politics of Thomas' Creole grammar book is best understood in relation to his more famous *Froudacity: West Indian Fables Explained* (1889), a polemical counterpunch to J. A. Froude's anti-black *The English in the West Indies* (1888). *Froudacity*, declares Thomas, aims to "exorcise this negrophobic political hobgoblin" from the historical record.[72] Read as the start of a dialectical continuum of anti-racist scholarship, then, *Creole Grammar* becomes not just an exercise in gentleman-making but even more so an assertion of Afro-Trinidadian value.

The difference in approach of the two Caribbean grammarians may be explained by the difference in what it meant to be a white (or near-white) gentleman author and what it meant to be a black author. For the most likely white or near-white Thomas Russell, a gentleman author was one for whom—if one aimed for true whiteness—education must be treated as merely an accessory to whiteness. (Indeed, noting the elasticity of race and class in the use of "backra," or white man, in Creole terminology, Russell observes that if a black man "by his education and position, or money, move much in the upper class society, then he is said to turn 'pure pure backra.'"[73]) For a black author like John Jacob Thomas, however, education was a core attribute, an indispensable passport into a higher class. Unlike Russell, therefore, Thomas makes a point of emphasizing, not minimizing, his book's didactic aims. In his preface he explains that his motives for writing the book are essentially in the cause of nationalism and racial uplift: he wishes to help "Creole-speaking natives who may desire to study other languages etymologically" and to aid "[i]n the administration of Justice in this Colony," since "it is notorious [that] our best interpreters... commonly fail in their renderings, especially from Creole into English."[74] Thomas' volume was credited in a later vol-

---

[71] Thomas Russell, *Etymology of Jamaican Grammar* (1868), p. xi.

[72] See John Jacob Thomas, Preface, in John Jacob Thomas, *Froudacity: West Indian Fables by James Anthony Froude Explained by J.J. Thomas* (London: T. Fisher Unwin, 1889).

[73] Thomas Russell, *Etymology of Jamaican Grammar* (1868), p. 15.

[74] John Jacob Thomas, *The Theory and Practice of Creole Grammar* (Port of Spain: Chronicle Publishing Company,1869), pp. xxx–iv. For a more extensive discussion of the social and political context in which this volume was produced, see Faith Smith, *Creole Recitations* (2002).

ume by Irish scholar Lafcadio Hearn when he published a dictionary on Creole proverbs of the blacks of Louisiana, reminding us that even then Caribbean Creoles were always part of a transnational circuitry.[75] Even Russell's locally-published *Etymology* found its way into the library of the anti-racist Harvard professor Alpheus Crosby, suggesting that despite his demurral Russell was laboring in the same vineyards of racial/national uplift as Thomas.[76]

Taken together, both texts underscore the dueling imperialist and nationalist compulsions of early Caribbean scholarship on Creole. On the one hand both illustrate the imperial urge to catalogue. By similarly showcasing their authors' erudition in the decoding of "primitive" languages, these texts are the medium by which the authors fashion themselves into that most desirable entity, a gentleman of letters. On the other hand, these texts assert that Caribbean culture *is* Culture, with rules, history, meaning. At the moment when black and brown populations were making gains in education and economic progress, the cataloging of Creole, the display of it, the dismissal of it, becomes freighted with all of the contradictory impulses of this colonial/decolonial moment. The status of Creole as both a reviled and treasured measure of Caribbeanness bears the full weight of this paradoxical inheritance.

The Modern Politics of Creole

The declaration of Creole's fundamental Africaneity in the postcolonial present, therefore, should be understood in the context of the centuries-long fight over Creole. As I have indicated, the tussle over language ownership precedes the era of independence. In 1916, even as his peers spoke of the "negro language" of the Caribbean and the New World, white Guyanese philologist J. Graham Cruickshank argued that "the talk of the black people in America (meaning the Americas) *is not African* except in shreds."[77] He asserted that Guyanese blacks got their English not from the English but from black Barbadian immigrants, who in turn got their dialect from white indentured servants from Devonshire.[78] If not exactly exemplary of the melting pot thesis, Cruikshank's understanding of the origins of "black" dialect is distinctly multi-ethnic. This, pro-multiracial, anti-African view is amplified by iconic twentieth century Jamaican poet Louise Bennett in her famously skeptical 1947 Creole poem "Back to Africa?," in which

---

[75] Lafcadio Hearn, *Gombo Zhebes: Little Dictionary of Creole Proverbs* (1885).

[76] See Philip Hatfield, "Our 'Young Gentleman' Thomas Russell," American Collections Blog post, British Library, accessed June 22, 2016. http://britishlibrary.typepad.co.uk/.m/americas/2015/07/our-young-gentleman-thomas-russell-and-the-emerging-problem-of-the-caribbean-language.html. Also, John Jacob Thomas, *Froudacity* (London: T. Fisher Unwin, 1889).

[77] J. Graham Cruickshank, *"Black Talk," Being Notes on Negro Dialect in British Guiana, with (inevitably) a Chapter on the Vernacular of Barbados* (Georgetown: The Argosy, 1916), p. ii.

[78] J. Graham Cruickshank, *"Black Talk"* (1916), pp. iii–iv.

she questions a Garveyite's desire to "return" to Africa and asserts that "Yuh haffe come from some weh fus, / Before yuh go back deh."[79] Her use of Creole as the voice of authentic Caribbean culture emphasizes Creole's twentieth century status as a non-African mainstay. Bennett's poem highlights the modern political stakes in invoking the non-Africaneity of Creole, a stance that has more to do with the contemporary political question of who owns Caribbean culture and less to do with the actual historical record. In the independence era of the mid-twentieth century, with the emergence of a voting black majority, the issue of who is a true native of the region assumed a new urgency. The light-skinned and non-black elites could not be left out of the nation-building initiatives. Centuries later, a Creole heritage, an association which was anathema to early white creoles could in the twentieth century be reclaimed as a sign of authentic Caribbean identity.

It is hard not to get trapped in the circularity of these arguments:

Creole is—shamefully? gloriously?—multiracial. Or "tainted."
No, it's black and pure.
It's degraded.
No, it's elevated.
It's a symptom of cultural backwardness.
No, it means that we have arrived at Culture.

On it goes. Yet it is this very circularity, ironically, that indicates the vital and continuing relevance of Creole literatures. Even as the genre of "dialect poetry" or indeed dialect prose has become an anachronism in the United States, it lives on, indeed thrives, in the anglophone Caribbean, where an enduring discomfort with Creole is commingled with a fierce love of the language, and thus provides the rationale for its ascension. Despite the entreaties for "good" grammar, any move to eradicate "bad" grammar risks destroying a foundational regional attribute. What we have here is the collision of two apparently mutual exclusive ideas: one, that speaking solely in Creole signifies cultural inferiority but also cultural authenticity; two, that speaking mainly in standard English signifies cultural superiority but also cultural *in*authenticity. So we are back to the uneasy distinction between the oral and the literary, the two always tied to each other: to *speak* Creole—at least as one's principal language—is a sign of inferiority, but to *transcribe* Creole is a sign of erudition. Better yet, to invent a written language, to codify its rules and govern its meanings, is to make oneself visible, to become a subject in the semiotics of the printscape. In a bid for just such visibility the Rastafarians of Jamaica famously created their own vernacular, complete with

---

[79] Louise Bennett, *Jamaica Labrish* (Kingston: Sangster's Bookstores, 1966/1973), p. 214.

grammar rules, that has expanded through music and poetry into a transnational language of social protest.[80]

From Samuel Augustus Mathews' efforts to transcribe Creole in the 1790s, to the first Creole grammar books in the anglophone Caribbean in the 1860s and 1870s, to the "fun" Creole dictionaries of today, transcription is essential to the equality movements in the Caribbean. So it is that the early efforts of nineteenth-century Caribbean grammarians to designate Creole a bona fide language inter-sects with the aims of the current crop of popular grammar books.[81] In the tourist-oriented airports of the Caribbean one can pick up quick reads on "How to Speak [Whatever Creole is Spoken]," which provide helpful dictionaries of local words and phrases, or a comic introduction to the country's culture.[82] The continuous production of dictionaries, grammar books or other lexical explana-tions of Creole for the last 150 years reveals the dual role of the language. The fascination with Creole spans both academic and popular discourse. One largely academic school of thought deems it a homegrown, pan-Caribbean language with multiple branches, one on par with other accepted languages that therefore requires respect, institutionalization and rigorous study. Another school also sees it as a homegrown language, but an inferior one, local rather than regional, best used at home, "on the street" or for comic flourishes. Caribbean theatrical come-dies are inevitably conducted in Creole—or, better yet, with an insufferable English-speaking character who gets her comeuppance by a Creole-speaking one, a performative tradition stretching all the way back to 1781.[83]

So on the one hand we have respected linguist Richard Allsopp's comprehen-sive *Dictionary of Caribbean English Usage*, which diligently catalogues the French, Indian, African Scottish, or other origins of Creole words from Curacao to Guyana; on the other we have Ken Maxwell's comic *How to Speak Jamaican*, whose tongue-in-cheek mission is "educating visitors and would-be Jamaicans all over the world as to how the *real* English should be spoken."[84]

Alongside these developments is the emerging view that Creole is neither a regional language nor a merely local idiom, but a national language with a trans-national reach, similar to English, Spanish or French. The Creole nationalists are responsible for the shift from terms like "dialect" or even "Creole" to "Jamaican"

---

[80] See Velma Pollard, *Dread Talk: The Language of Rastafari* (Barbados: Canoe Press, 2000).

[81] See John Jacob Thomas, *Theory and Practice of Creole Grammar* (1869); and Thomas Russell, *The Etymology of Jamaican Grammar by a Young Gentleman* (1868).

[82] Two examples of tourist-oriented grammar books are *How to Speak Jamaican*, Ken Maxwell (1987), and *Barbados Pocket Guide* (Thomas Cook Publishing, 2011).

[83] The Jamaica-based American actress Margaret Cheer's 1781 play, *West Indian Lady's Arrival in London* features a Creole-speaking Jamaican creole who foils her scheming English suitors with her canny use of dialect. See Richard Wright, *Revels in Jamaica* (Kingston: Bolivar Press, 1986/Dodd, Mead & Co. Inc., 1937), pp. 154–5.

[84] Richard Allsopp, *Dictionary of Caribbean English Usage* (Oxford, 1996); Ken Maxwell, *How to Speak Jamaican* (1987), italics mine.

(as Maxwell refers to it above) or "Bajan."[85] What was once seen as local is now an assertive national culture with an overtly nationalist cultural agenda. In Jamaica, for example, a 2005 survey of national attitudes towards Jamaican Creole found significant support from the population to make Jamaican Creole an official language on par with English. In another example, a Jamaican pastor promotes the new Jamaican Creole New Testament bible, which he emphasizes has been translated, like the canonical King James version, from the original Greek.[86] The argument in favor of Creole-language school books, public documents and canonical texts rests on the assumption that the spoken and the written word are the same. Therefore, to access to the written Creole text will yield more social acceptance and do the work of national uplift, both at home and on the world stage. However what is clear in the promotion of both the humorous tourist-oriented Creole dictionaries and the scholarly Creole bibles is the authors' assumption, similar to their intellectual peers of the nineteenth century, that the ability *to translate* Creole is, itself, a sign of cultural authenticity.

As my grandfather's rendering of Anansi stories into English illustrates, being able to strategically articulate language along the Creole–English continuum[87] has become a hallmark of modern Caribbean elites, an all-but-indispensable mark in any Caribbean country where Creole is, inevitably, the common language. To *speak* Creole is not necessarily to *use* Creole as a form of knowledge production, as a form of counter-knowledge. The act of creolizing language requires the obverse, that one can *de*-creolize. As Homi Bhabha notes, "To vernacularize is to 'dialectize' as a process, it is not simply to be in a dialogic relation with the native or domestic, but it is to be on the border, in between, introducing the global-cosmopolitan 'action at a distance' into the very grounds—now displaced—of the domestic."[88] So it is then that the ability to both speak *and* write in English and its vernaculars; to be both the real thing and the fake: to mimic that which is oneself; is, finally, to become a true Caribbean citizen of the world.

---

[85] See Karyl Walker, "Patois Bible Not a Retrograde Step," *Jamaica Observer* (November 27, 2012), accessed October 6, 2019, http://www.jamaicaobserver.com/news/Patois-Bible-not-a-retrograde-step_13096374?profile=&template=PrinterVersion; also Courtney Stewart, "Jamaica's patois Bible: The word of God in creole," accessed October 2, 2019, https://www.youtube.com/watch?v=rRI3srdcia0; and Xavier Murphy, "Interview: Professor Hubert Devonish, Advocate for Jamaican Patois as a Language," Jamaicans.com (2009), accessed September 27, 2019, Professor Hubert Devonish, Advocate for Jamaican Patois as a Language (jamaicans.com).

[86] See Xavier Murphy, "Interview with Hubert Devonish" (2009); and Courtney Stewart, "Jamaica's patois Bible: The word of God in creole" (December 25, 2011), accessed October 2, 2019, https://www.youtube.com/watch?v=rRI3srdcia0.

[87] Linguists in the 1960s first coined the term "Creole Continuum" to characterize the varieties of Caribbean language to be found between creole and standard English. See John Rickford, *Dimensions of a Creole Continuum: History, Texts, and Linguistic Analysis of Guyanese Creole* (Stanford: Stanford University Press, 1987), p. 15.

[88] Homi K. Bhabha, "Unsatisfied: Notes on Vernacular Cosmopolitanism," in *Text and Nation: Cross-Disciplinary Essays on Cultural and National Identities*, edited by Laura García-Moreno and Peter C. Pfeiffer (Columbia, SC: Camden House, 1996), p. 196.

Note on Use

I am using the admittedly loaded term "dialect" throughout mostly to describe what is now understood to be Caribbean Creole, to indicate how the language was—and still is—perceived, and how it was described at these key historical moments. Elsewhere I use Creole to denote its status as an authentic language. I also use "vernacular," both to distinguish Caribbean Creole from other forms of non-standard English and to link it to the African-American vernacular form. "Creole" can refer both to a person of "pure" European or African descent and to language used by these groups. I distinguish between these two uses by lower-casing creole when referring to people and upper-casing when referring to the language. It is my view that creole is a descriptor for many different ethnicities of Caribbean people, not a noun. Some authors do the opposite. Different countries designated—and continue to designate—creoles differently. In Jamaica and Barbados a creole was understood to be a white person of British heritage, whereas in Trinidad a creole was black or French. In British Guiana a creole was always black. What in other Caribbean countries was called dialect in British Guiana was called Creolese. Finally, although Black is increasingly upper-cased to denote a transnational or multi-ethnic African-descended cultural identity, I have continued to lowercase black when referring to African-descended Caribbean people in the belief that, just as the difference between adjectives and nouns are blurred in creole and Creole, a black is not always Black: a Trinidadian might be black in the Caribbean and Black in the United States, for example. Which makes them both black and Black. Language is difficult.

1

White Creoles, "Bad" Grammar, and the Birth of Dialect Literature

> I know no more of grammar, than a bastard calf does of his grandfather.
>
> Samuel Augustus Mathews, *The Lying Hero*

In 1790, after a few years' sojourn in Jamaica, English book-keeper J. B. Moreton wrote a withering critique of West Indian society.[1] Titled *Manners and Customs in the West India Islands*, the text was intended as a prospectus for potential emigrants to the region. Long on detail, its thesis was simple: slavery was bad. Slavery had turned the entire Caribbean into an extended province of "Whoredom." The blacks were immoral, the "mongrels" far worse. The Jews were thieving sharpers. But the vilest of all were the "negroefied" white creoles. These whites, of English stock, should have known better. Yet they stole, debauched, and behaved with extraordinary cruelty to those over whom they ruled. Worse yet, in habits, speech, and inclinations they were all but indistinguishable from the blacks:

> [T]he men in general, . . are . . . lazy, dull, and indolent, in all industrious matters; and volatile as air where drinking, whoring, gaming, or any kind of dissipation invites; so that their hearts and fortunes seldom agree; for they are extremely extravagant; and know not the value of money or effects till they want them. They are amazingly fond of costly, tinsel frippery; abroad they appear ridiculously gay, and at home slovenly and dirty; and when deprived of the advantage of an European education, are assuming and presuming, negroefied, awkward, ignorant guegaws; their darling amusements are confined to negroe huts and mulatto balls; though a Creole was languishing on his death-bed, I believe the sound of the gumbay[2] or violin would induce him to get up and dance till he killed himself.[3]

---

[1] The first edition was written in 1790. A second edition with a slightly different title—*West India Customs and Manners*—was issued in 1793, suggesting that the book was popular. All references will be from the 1793 edition.

[2] An African instrument.

[3] J. B. Moreton, *West India Customs and Manners* (London: Richardson, Gardner and Walter, 1790/1793), pp. 104–6.

Creole Noise: Early Caribbean Dialect Literature and Performance. Belinda Edmondson, Oxford University Press.
© Belinda Edmondson 2022. DOI: 10.1093/oso/9780192856838.003.0002

The engraving "A Surinam Planter in his Morning Dress," by abolitionist William Blake, captures the English view of white creoles: violent hedonists who inspect the flogging of their human property while drinking and "whoring" with the naked mixed-race women who serve them (Figure 1.1). Even so, Moreton is merely amused, rather than repulsed, by the creoles' "negroefied" speech, a condescension that is usually reserved for blacks: "I often laughed heartily at hearing a Creole master or miss say, 'Do, momma, get me some mauby,[4] mine head no 'tand good.'"[5]

This was no sentimental, pious abolitionist tale of the Victorian era. There were no chaste victims of slavery, in Moreton's telling. His view of Jamaica society—for it was only Jamaica to which he had traveled, in spite of his capacious title—came at a time when the British Parliament was debating ending the slave trade. Moreton and other English observers saw the degeneracy of creoles not just as the

Figure 1.1 *A Surinam Planter in his Morning Dress*, plate 10 from *Narrative of a Five Year's Expedition against the Revolted Negroes of Surinam, in Guiana...from the year 1772 to 1777*, Captain J.G. Stedman, engraving by William Blake, 1793. Courtesy of Princeton University Art Museum.

[4] Mauby is a drink of fermented tree bark, indigenous to the Caribbean.
[5] J. B. Moreton, *West India Customs and Manners* (1790/1793), p. 106.

result of slavery, but as the inevitable result of their creoleness, the fact that they were whites in the tropics, removed from European society.[6] Despite its elaborate detailing of other facets of West Indian life, the white creoles took Moreton's account for what it undeniably was: not just an attack on their livelihood, but an attack on their very cultural identity. And they returned the favor.

In 1793 white Kittitian[7] creole Samuel Augustus Mathews published *The Lying Hero, or An Answer to J.B. Moreton's Manners and Customs in the West Indies* through a regional publisher and fellow white creole, Edward L. Low (who had already published a similar response to another popular anti-slavery tract.[8]) Mathews' narrative retort to Moreton is mostly unremarkable. It reads like most pro-slavery fare: the English who migrate to the West Indies are a second-rate lot who couldn't hack it back home, you can't trust what they say; blacks are happy (if lazy) servants, devoted to their masters and overseers, who would rather be slaves in the Caribbean than miserable back in Africa; white creoles are the kindest of masters who only punish those who commit crimes; and so forth. What sets Mathews' narrative apart is the same feature which distinguishes Moreton's.

In its methodical transcription of popular "negro" dialect work songs and ballads, Moreton's account of West Indian life in the late eighteenth century differs from so many other travel narratives.[9] Whereas most pro-slavery representations of the slaves reveal merely one-dimensional simpletons, these transcribed songs illustrate the emotional range and expressiveness of their black creators. As Moreton observes, "When working, though at the hardest labour, they are commonly singing, and though their songs have neither rhime nor measure, yet many I have often laughed heartily, and have been as often struck with deep melancholy at their songs."[10] These extraordinary ballads of black lament, social satire and pointed critique provide evidence for Moreton's observations of West Indian life and the barbaric treatment of the slaves. Mathews' book also features "negro" songs, which provide counter-evidence for *his* claim that slaves are happy workers

[6] See, for example, Trevor Burnard, "'Rioting in Goatish Embraces': Marriage and Improvement in Early British Jamaica," *History of the Family*, vol. 11 (2006), pp. 185–97.

[7] "Kittitian" is the term for a native of the island of St. Kitts, originally called St. Christopher.

[8] After living for 18 years in St. Kitts, Reverend James Ramsay published *An Essay on the Treatment and Conversion of African Slaves in the British Sugar Colonies* (London: James Phillips, 1784), an influential essay on the poor treatment and conversion of African slaves. The Kittitian planters responded with their own essay, published by local printer Edward Low. See Some Gentlemen of St. Christopher, *An Answer to the Reverend James Ramsay's Essay on the Treatment and Conversion of Slaves* (Basseterre, St. Christopher: Edward Low, 1784), cited in Victoria Borg O'Flaherty, "Samuel Augustus Mathews: His Life and Times," p. 58, in *St. Kitts and the Atlantic Creoles: The Texts of Samuel Augustus Mathews in Perspective*, edited by Philip Baker and Adrienne Bruyn (London: University of Westminster Press, 1998).

[9] Jamaica plantation and slave owner Matthew Gregory "Monk" Lewis continued this tradition of using the song lyrics of the enslaved to illustrate his views of their condition, in his *Journal of a West India Proprietor* (1834). While Lewis was pro-slavery, he also details instances of cruelty by other slave owners to their slaves. See Paula Burnett, ed., *The Penguin Book of Caribbean Verse in English* (London: Penguin, 1986), p. 371.

[10] J. B. Moreton, *West India Customs and Manners* (1790/1793), p. 152.

intent only on their own affairs. The difference is that whereas Moreton positions himself merely as a faithful transcriber of black voices, Mathews establishes himself as much more than a medium. He declares that he, Samuel Augustus Mathews, is actually the *composer* of his text's "negro songs." In other words, he suggests that, through music, he possesses the unique ability to, in essence, become black.

Unsurprisingly, Mathews is dismissive of Moreton's "negro" songs; he claims that as voices of the enslaved they are suspect. Moreton's transcriptions don't reproduce the authentic speech of black people: "[T]he Lying Hero then gives you what he calls a negro song; if the reader understands anything of their lingo, he will find there appears nothing of the negro language in this song....This is as much like a negro song as I am like a poor man...."[11] The implication is that Moreton's transcriptions are actually the inventions of an Englishman with an abolitionist axe to grind. He, Mathews, should know. He is a Kittitian. In fact, he knows the blacks of almost *all* the islands due to his extensive travel in the region, unlike Moreton and his Jamaica-centric narrative. The blacks *are* all the same—in their general contentment. And so are the whites, who are not "negroefied" as Moreton charges, but more like Europeans in their lack of knowledge of black creole speech and ways. None of the whites, whether creoles or Europeans, possess Mathews' ability to "discourse in the negro language."[12] Indeed, he loves nothing better than to go out among the field slaves disguised as one of them. Moreover, his command of the "negro language" is so good that the slaves do not believe that he is really a "bocra" [white] man. Unlike Moreton's *his* negro songs are authentic:

> I have, upon my first arrival at Antigua, Dominica, and Barbadoes, disguised myself like a field negro, my *bonglow* in one hand, my *bonger* in tother, a *junkey pipe* in my mouth, and thus equipped, I have sallied out after dark, gone to the market place and drawn all the negroes around me, and I have entertained them by singing the most favorite negro songs, accompanied with the instrument, for hours together, and they have been ignorant that a white man was present; nay, I once opened their hearts and purses so much, that a gathering of half a dollar was made and tendered to me, and upon my refusing to accept the donation, a quarrel ensued, and I was compelled to make myself known, to prevent the consequences....
>
> I was so well known by the negroes in the different Islands, that I have been riding by a plantation where one hundred, or more, were at work and as soon as I was seen by one, they have hollo'd and shouted, and would not lift a hoe until I

---

[11] Samuel Augustus Mathews, *The Lying Hero: Or an Answer to J.B. Moreton's Manners and Customs in the West Indies* (St. Eustatius: Edward Low & Company, 1793), pp. 136, 139.

[12] Samuel Augustus Mathews, *The Lying Hero* (1793), p. 141.

was out of sight, so much were they pleased with seeing me; but when I stopped to speak, or sing a song to them, they were happy indeed.

I have known numbers come from the farthest part of the Island, for no other purpose but to see, and try to speak to me, and I have often observed them peeping and pointing at me, and enquiring of those that brought them, where I came from, and if I was "von bocra foo true [really a white man]." . . . [13]

Mathews' improbable story is breath-taking in its self-serving hubris: gullible enslaved blacks who refuse to work because they are so smitten with his presence; who travel great distances just to hear him sing; and are so stirred by his songs that they *force* him to take their money. But its almost comic unreliability as evidence is not the text's most salient feature.[14] What is significant is Mathews' assertion of his unique ability as a white creole to penetrate black life by performance; in other words, he could "become black" through his ability to sing, compose, and converse in the "negro language." Mathews' claim actually confirms Moreton's charge that the white creoles are indeed "negroefied." This is apparent even as Mathews attempts to distinguish himself from other whites by declaring that his singular ability to "discourse in the negro language" is the result not so much of his West Indianness as of his assiduously cultivated talent. This ability to "talk black" is what gives him the authority to challenge the likes of educated Englishmen like Moreton. What is clear to us as contemporary readers is that Mathews' supposed singularity is not singular at all. It is merely a reflection of the fact that white creoles in the Caribbean were part of a creolizing society in which the "negro language" would become the most popular medium of expression for the entire racial spectrum of society, a medium which would continue to be both despised and cherished in the generations to come.

In the interstices of the Moreton–Mathews dialectic we have a singular example of how black creole speech, the British dialectical literary tradition, racial ventriloquism,[15] and white creole "negroefication" all combined to initiate what eventually became the "dialect," or Creole, literary tradition of the anglophone

---

[13]   Samuel Augustus Mathews, *The Lying Hero* (1793), pp. 143–4.

[14]   Not all scholars of the Mathews text have interpreted his passing and racial ventriloquism in the critical manner that I have here. For example, Peter A. Roberts asserts that "Mathews' imitation [of black music], at that time, would have to be regarded as the best form of compliment paid to the slaves for the quality of their songs and music. At the same time, it can be thought of as a reverse of the festivities in which the slaves imitated their masters and mistresses." See Peter A. Roberts, *From Oral to Literate Culture: Colonial Experience in the English West Indies* (Mona, Jamaica: University of the West Indies Press, 1997), p. 52. I disagree with this assessment. There is no evidence that Mathews was inverting a slave tradition of satirical imitation; there is certainly no satire implied in his description of his "passing." And while Mathews may indeed think highly of black music and lyricism, in this example he is boasting about his own abilities to reproduce it, which is not the same thing.

[15]   Michael North first coined the term "racial ventriloquism" to describe the use of black-associated dialect or vernacular by whites, a use that was subsequently picked up by other scholars. See Michael North, *The Dialect of Modernism: Race, Language, and Twentieth-Century Literature* (London and New York: Oxford University Press, 1994).

Caribbean. The split identity of white creoles, caught between their vision of Britain as their native "home" and their increasing self-identification as culturally Caribbean, is a central component in what is otherwise deemed to be a black narrative tradition. Some were creole by birth, others by adoption. Some were racially progressive, sympathetic to black desires for empowerment. Some were unabashedly racist, hoping for a return to the plantation hierarchy. All of them were invested in Creole as the medium through which they made their views known. It is a tangled story.

White Creoles and Racial Ventriloquism

White creoles were not the first racial ventriloquists in Caribbean literature. Nor were anglophone creoles the only ones who utilized the voices of the Other. In the early nineteenth century the white criollos of Puerto Rico, protesting control of their land and rights by the Spanish colonial authorities, penned deliberately ungrammatical, dialect-filled letters to the newspapers as *jíbaros*, or peasants. These expressions of *jíbarismo* were meant to affirm, via the supposedly unvarnished voice of the common man, the elites' nationalist stance.[16] In the anglophone Caribbean the aim of this racial masquerade was somewhat different. While often similarly political to the jíbaro masquerade in nature, white creoles of the anglophone Caribbean wanted to be recognized as intimately familiar with black speech, culture, and thought. If the goal was to "sound" the most like the people they used to further their own ideological beliefs then white creoles were undoubtedly the most effective ventriloquists. This was because, as the Mathews example illustrates, white creoles essentially ventriloquized themselves.

As Thomas Krise notes, English anti-slavery advocates frequently used fictional black characters, usually Africans, to voice the anti-slavery position, or at least to urge slave-owners to be kinder and gentler to their human property.[17] However, these ventriloquizers did not attempt to reproduce even a simulacrum of Caribbean speech. The "sound" of the black Caribbean voice was inevitably the florid prose of its English author. There was no prestige in vocal verisimilitude, no attempt at representing the subjectivity of the enslaved. Most critically, the ventriloquizers knew their audience, and their audience knew them: there was no

---

[16] See Francisco A. Scarano, "The Jíbaro Masquerade and the Subaltern Politics of Creole Identity Formation in Puerto Rico, 1745–1823," *American Historical Review* 101 (5) (December 1996), pp. 1398–431.

[17] Thomas Krise, *Caribbeana: An Anthology of English Literature of the West Indies, 1657–1777* (Chicago: University of Chicago Press, 1999), p. 4. Krise lists several important ventriloquist precursors to Moreton's, among these Thomas Tryon's "A Discourse in the way of Dialogue between an *Ethiopian* or *Negro-Slave*, and a *Christian* that was his Master in *America*" (1684), based on Tryon's stay in Barbados; and Anonymous, "The Speech of Moses Bon Sàam" (1735) supposedly made by a Maroon leader.

confusion as to who was "speaking," and why—at least until the wave of dialect mania that seized late-eighteenth-century Britain found its way to the Caribbean colonies. It was here that the question of authorship, of who was "speaking" and why, laid the foundation for literary dialect in generations to come.

As early as 1700 whites in the Caribbean had started to identify as West Indian. According to Orlando Patterson, in eighteenth-century Jamaica "local patriotism was so pronounced among the early settlers, and their children who became known as the 'creole party,' that on several occasions they attempted to exclude English-born persons from filling posts in the island and even went as far as declaring that they 'will not allow themselves to be called Englishmen.'" In the 1828 novel *Marly: or, A Planter's Life in Jamaica*, the white Jamaican Singleton family is riven by members who either fiercely identify with the island or those who identify with England and are ashamed of the family's creole speech and manners.[18]

This tension between white Englishness and white creoleness was only underscored by the slavery debate. The political sparring contest between English critics and white creoles over the morality of the slave trade was, unsurprisingly, fought without any actual input from the victims themselves. Though both pro- and anti-slavery factions denied non-whites a direct voice in the political debate, both sides nevertheless sought to authenticate their views through the affirmations of the enslaved people themselves. The enslaved population, however, spoke in a hybrid language considered by Europeans to be the very essence of irrational discourse. As one English traveler to the region put it, "So excitable are these people, that a quarter of an hour never elapses without a 'scene'. Such gesticulation, such pantomime, such a roll out of unintelligible phrases, making it difficult to recognize one's own language!... [their] capacity to talk is in an inverse proportion to their capability of reason."[19]

This disorganized "bad" grammar was supposedly reflective of the emotive and illogical nature of its black and brown speakers, a grammar antithetical to all of the qualities associated with the supposedly white speakers of the "good" kind. How could whites effectively utilize "bad" grammar for evidence in a debate that required the vigorous martialing of logic, reason, and moral virtue—all qualities not associated with this new "negro language?" How could such a contradiction be maintained? The contradiction is registered in Moreton's own ambivalent response to negro dialect. On the one hand he sneers at the white creoles whose

[18] See Orlando Patterson, *The Sociology of Slavery: An Analysis of the Origins, Development, and Structure of Negro Slave Society in Jamaica* (Madison, NJ: Fairleigh Dickinson University Press, 1967), p. 34. Both Patterson and *Marly* are quoted in Jean D'Costa and Barbara Lalla, *Language in Exile* (1990), p. 23.

[19] Charles Day, *Five Years in the West Indies* (1852), pp. 111–13, quoted in Christine Corcoran and Salikoko Mufwene, "Sam Mathews' Kittitian: What Is It Evidence Of?," in *St. Kitts and the Atlantic Creoles: The Texts of Samuel Augustus Mathews in Perspective*, edited by Philip Baker and Adrienne Bruyn (1998), p. 83.

speech, indistinguishable from that of their black slaves, shows them to be a degraded (if hospitable)[20] race. On the other hand he invokes, via music, this same "negro language" to express a certain admiration for black sentience and creativity. For his part, the white Kittitian Mathews proudly declares in his preface, "I know no more of grammar than a bastard calf does of his grandfather." Unlike Moreton, Mathews wants the reader know that, his authorship of a scrupulously grammatical publication notwithstanding, he is a natural speaker—*and* writer—of "bad grammar." Otherwise a sign of a degraded humanity, bad grammar is here utilized by Mathews as a badge of authenticity, to illustrate how completely he, as a white creole, embodies the black speech he is mediating.

It is impossible to imagine a non-white author making such a pronouncement of his or her own semi-literacy either then or in the next 150 years. Black and brown West Indians had to prove the opposite: that they possessed "good" grammar, as evidence of their reliability as authors, witnesses, good citizens. In the eighteenth century Caribbean, as elsewhere, non-whites had no personhood as far as the law was concerned.[21] Yet their views, expressed obliquely or directly through their music, were still vital as "evidence" for one side or another of the slavery debate. The eye-witness accounts of the whites, whether English or creole, were not apparently considered sufficient by either to prove or disprove either argument. When blacks wrote autobiographical slave narratives it was a publishing convention for the preface to be written by other whites. The preface was used to verify the character of the author and the truth of his or her account. These white authority figures were vital to the white readership because they provided the stamp of authenticity on the narratives of the formerly enslaved, without which black testimony was not to be trusted.[22]

Taken together, however, the complementary anti-slavery and pro-slavery texts of Moreton and Mathews illustrate a peculiar twist of the slave narrative

---

[20] Despite his relentless criticism of the white creoles, Moreton seems to have enjoyed their company. He calls them a naturally hospitable and generous people See J. B. Moreton, *West India Customs and Manners* (1790/1793), p. 107. Other English and European travelers to the region observed the same qualities, regardless of their political views on slavery.

[21] Moreton, clearly an abolitionist sympathizer, disagreed with the legal non-personhood status of blacks. He writes, "...blacks in the British colonies are British subjects: therefore British subjects should no more be slaves in her colonies than in Britain; for I contend, nor can any man confute [sic] me, that every man under the sun, whom God formed after his own image, 'has a natural and inalienable *right* to liberty.'" See J .B. Moreton, *Manners and Customs in the West India Islands* (1790/1793), p. 164. Moreton deliberately uses the revolutionary rhetoric of the American Declaration of Independence in making his case for black equality under the law. In Massachusetts and other New England states a few years earlier slavery had been ended following several petitions by enslaved blacks for freedom, similarly using the rhetoric of the Declaration of Independence. (See "'Natural and Inalienable Right to Freedom': Slaves' Petition for Freedom to the Massachusetts Legislature, 1777," in *Collections of the Massachusetts Historical Society*, 5th Series, III (Boston, 1877), pp. 436–7. Moreton seems to be personally familiar with the Americas, and elsewhere makes reference to time spent in Quebec.

[22] Some of the famous examples include Mary Prince, *The History of Mary Prince: A West Indian Slave Narrative* (1831); and in the U.S. context, Frederick Douglas, *Narrative of the Life of Frederick Douglass* (1845); and Linda Brent (Harriet Jacobs), *Incidents in the Life of a Slave Girl* (1861).

convention in the Caribbean. In these white-authored Caribbean narratives, testimonials from black non-persons who could not even give testimony in a court of
law were actually considered vital evidence of the authors' veracity. These "testimonials" come in the form of black music, the purest form of evidence from a
people who were frequently described by whites as habitual liars or of a child-like
disposition. Because black music was perceived as somehow organic and
unmediated, not as synthetic, artistic, calculating, or self-interested, whatever
social commentary it provided could reveal the "truth" of black happiness or
unhappiness, guile or guilelessness. It was a very potent signifier for whites. In the
Moreton–Mathews clash, then, the ventriloquizing of black music and speech
forms by white interlocutors serves as verification in a tense war of ideology.

This begs the question: for whom was this "proof" necessary? One obvious
answer is the English reading public, which was weighing the rewards of
Empire—the luxuries of sugar and tobacco, the astounding fortunes that flowed
from the West Indies into idyllic English country houses[23]—against its increasing
discomfort with the price of those luxuries. That price was not just the human toll
of torture, murder, and degradation of Africans, but it was the very idea of English
virtue itself, which was given the lie in the face of slavery's abominations, increasingly made plain to the British public in such printed exposés.[24] While Moreton
certainly wrote for an English reading public, it is not apparent that Mathews did
so. Moreton published in London: Mathews locally, in St. Kitts. Publishing with a
regional Caribbean publisher was not the best way to reach an English public
(unless the author planned to republish the piece in England).[25] Leaving aside the
issue of whether Mathews even had access to English publishing houses, it
appears that Mathews wrote his stinging defense of slavery to mend fences with
local white authorities, of whom he had run afoul.[26] There were, of course, also
pro-slavery advocates in Britain for whom arguments such as this would be welcome. Mathews makes much of the fact that he performed his two songs, "Buddy
Quow" and "Sabina," in front of Prince William Henry in 1787, when the prince
was stationed in the Caribbean with the English navy.[27] Mathews inserts this fact
into his narrative both to show off his prowess as an entertainer and to convince

---

[23] For an incisive portrait of the "darker history" of Britain's country houses, see Sam Knight,
"Home Truth," *The New Yorker* (August 23, 2021): pp. 30–41.

[24] I distinguish between "English" and "British" here to mark the virtues of colonial ideology as
specifically English.

[25] For a more extended discussion of republication of Caribbean texts in England prior to the
twentieth century, see Belinda Edmondson, Chapter 1, "Early Literary Culture," in Edmondson,
Caribbean Middlebrow (Cornell University Press, 2009).

[26] See Victoria Borg O'Flaherty, "Samuel Augustus Mathews, His Life and Times," in *St. Kitts and
the Atlantic Creoles: The Texts of Samuel Augustus Mathews in Perspective*, edited by Philip Baker and
Adrienne Bruyn (1998).

[27] See Samuel Augustus Mathews, *The Lying Hero* (1793), p. 139.

the reader that his songs are authentic renderings of Afro-Caribbean speech and life. After all, who would tell falsehoods before the Prince of England?

In Prince William Henry, Mathews would have had an entirely sympathetic audience for his light-hearted negro songs. The prince was known to be a defender of slavery, and therefore would have been more than ordinarily welcome among the white creoles. (He also had a reputation for frequenting West Indian brothels and, in one famous incident, wrecked the establishment of Barbados' legendary brown brothel owner, Rachael Pringle.[28]) As historian Bridget Brereton notes, Mathews' dialect performance for the prince undoubtedly took place before an all-white, all-male audience, whose members would have smirked at the salacious lyrics of "Buddy Quow," with its theme of supposedly consensual interracial sex.[29]

More than a defense of slavery, though, Mathews was also looking for customers. Self-promotion of his work as a composer, singer, and general authority on "negro ballads" was critical to the fulfillment of his ambitions. "I have made [the treatment of slaves] a study, and it has been the principal amusement of my life for five and twenty years," Mathews declares, neatly eliding the difference between the serious research characteristic of someone who works for a living, and the superficial "amusements" of the leisured class, the landed gentry.[30]

Mathews' rhetorical balancing act is noteworthy for what it tells us about how he wishes to be seen. Contrary to his lofty implication that he was wealthy (he declares that Moreton's rendering of the black vernacular is "as much like a negro song *as I am like a poor man*"), Mathews was actually a struggling carpenter from a modest white creole family. His father was a mason with few slaves. Mathews did not simply live among blacks, as did all white creoles; he also worked alongside them in his trade. Skilled black and brown men had by then gained a fragile foothold in the rigid hierarchy of Caribbean slave societies as carpenters and furniture makers. Lower class whites in the eighteenth century anglophone Caribbean were not in a stable economic position. The sugar trade had suffered a recession decades earlier, which had sent many of them to America for work. Now they were further threatened by the rise of skilled non-white tradespeople and had to be appeased by the passage of a bill restricting the economic activities of the free coloreds.[31] Mathews struggled with debt to the point where he had to

---

[28]   Rachael Pringle makes an appearance in white creole J. W. Orderson's 1842 novel, *Creoleana*. See also Marisa J. Fuentes, "Power and Historical Figuring: Rachael Pringle Polgreen's Troubled Archive," *Gender and History* 22 (3) (November 10, 2010), pp. 564–84.

[29]   See Bridget Brereton, "The Historical Context of Moreton's (1790) Attack on Slavery and Mathews' (1793) Response," in *St. Kitts and the Atlantic Creoles*, edited by Philip Baker and Adrienne Bruyn (1998), p. 61.

[30]   Samuel Augustus Mathews, *The Lying Hero* (1793), p. 139.

[31]   See Edward L. Cox, *Free Coloreds in the Slave Societies of St. Kitts and Grenada* (Knoxville: Univ. of Tennessee Press, 1984) pp. 65–6, quoted in Victoria Borg O'Flaherty, "Samuel Augustus Mathews: His Life and Times," in *St. Kitts and the Atlantic Creoles*, edited by Philip Baker and Adrienne Bruyn (1998), p. 51.

flee the island several times to avoid being imprisoned for it. His proximity to blacks and browns was therefore not at all romantic or deliberate, as he claims. It was a sign of his low social status. Re-purposing his proximity as a form of upper-class slumming allowed Mathews to re-position himself as an elite whose amusing excursions among the lowly positioned him as an authority on blacks and thus as a useful interlocutor for other whites. He would no longer be the lower-to-middling class white in the rigid colonial hierarchy.[32] This would raise his social standing at a time when he sorely needed it. For Mathews was broke. His life as a singer of "negro songs" was, after all, a business for him, not merely an idle pleasure. And there was a growing appetite for his product.

White Creole Leisure Culture

Like Mathews, white creoles were famously passionate about their leisure pursuits. This was particularly true of dance and music, two cultural forms completely dependent on black artistry in the Caribbean. White creole enthusiasm for the music of the black slaves was part of a wider enthusiasm for folk music and prose during the Romantic era during the long eighteenth century that revolutionized the British arts. This enthusiasm crossed the Atlantic to the anglophone Caribbean, where black creole songs were so popular among whites that they recorded them in various ways in the ensuing decades. The lyrics to the popular Jamaican dialect song, "Quaco Sam," for instance, were painted on a series of ornamental dishes in the early nineteenth century.[33] A white man who could compose and perform such music would have a stable income, if he could get past the stigma. Dialect performances of one kind or another might have provided a convenient source of income for lower- to middle-class whites such Mathews, coming at a time when dialect poetry and ballads were all the rage in late-eighteenth-century Britain.

The speech, music, and dance of the British working class that had aroused such enthusiasm in the home countries were transmitted directly to the Caribbean by the working-class Scottish, Welsh, Irish and English sailors, soldiers and book-keepers, who comprised a significant portion (perhaps a majority) of the region's

---

[32] Christine Corcoran and Salikoko Mufwene, "Sam Mathews' Kittitian. What Is It Evidence Of?," in *St. Kitts and the Atlantic Creoles*, edited by Philip Baker and Adrienne Bruyn (1998), p. 81. Corcoran and Mufwene suggest that Mathews' negro performances are a form of racial minstrelsy performed for reasons similar to those of white immigrants who performed blackface minstrelsy in the United States in the nineteenth century; to reassure themselves that they are not on the lowest rung of the social order.

[33] Mrs. Rebecca Brandon of Kingston, Jamaica, commissioned a series of ornamental dishes with the lyrics to "Quaco Sam" printed on them in 1838. A dish from the series is on exhibit at the Institute of Jamaica in Kingston. The song still survives in rural parts of Jamaica. See Jean D'Costa and Barbara Lalla, *Language in Exile* (1990), p. 143.

white population. Scottish and Irish musical and artistic forms were more influential, arguably, than English ones in the anglophone Caribbean. For example, Scottish and African musical and dance forms merged in a number of Jamaican songs and dances. The popular early nineteenth-century Jamaican song, "Quaco Sam," sung to the tune of the Scottish military song "White Cockade,"[34] reveals such a merging:

> Oh Lard! How me wi dance when me *yerry* fiddle an drum! [hear]
> Me no tink pon *backra wuk*, me no care fe *fum-fum*! [white man's work] [beatings]
> Me wi dance de *shay-shay*, me wi dance de *'cotch reel*, [A dance of African origin] [Scotch Reel]
> Me wi dance till ebry *craps* a me foot-battam peel. [scrap][35]

Here Creole speech, through music, captures the contradictory nature of the black experience. The powerful pull of merged African and British linguistic and artistic traditions is revealed in the way "Quaco Sam" couples the casual brutality of everyday slave experience ("Me no tink pon backra wuk, me no care fe fum-fum") with the enjoyment by the enslaved of both African and British musical and dance forms.[36]

Further, as already noted, this enjoyment was not confined to the black population. Lady Nugent, the wife of Jamaica's Governor General from 1801 to 1806, reports that she "forgot all her dignity" when she heard a Scotch Reel, and joined in the dancing with the slaves, one of whom sang the lyrics to "Quaco Sam." This was not unusual: whites and blacks frequently danced together on the estates.[37] Scottish music may even have been deliberately used to foster worker

---

[34] See Barbara Lalla, "Quaco Sam—A Relic of Archaic Jamaican Speech," *Jamaica Journal*, vol. 45 (May 1981), pp. 20–9. I thank David Bindman and Judy Rudoe for alerting me to this source.

[35] See Paula Burnett, ed., *The Penguin Book of Caribbean Verse in English* (1986), p. 8. I am indebted to Velma Pollard's essay, "'Slash Me Off a Penny's Worth:' The Scots in Jamaica," in Giovanna Covi, Carla Sassi, Velma Pollard, and Joan Anim-Addo, *Caribbean-Scottish Relations—Colonial and Contemporary Inscriptions in History, Language and Literature* (London: Mango Publishing, 2007), for pointing out the connection between Scottish and African musical traditions in Jamaica.

[36] The final stanza of "Quaco Sam" comes back to the commingled themes of brutality and joy in the slave experience: "Me tek me road da cane-piece, weh de people-dem da run, / An all come behin' me, get de fum-fum. / Wid de centung da me back, chacolata da me pan, / Me da wuk, me da laugh, me da tink pan Quaco Sam." [I took the road thrugh the cane, where the people ran, / And all who came after me got a beating. / With the hoe at my back, the snack in my pan, / I continue to work, I laugh, and I think on Quaco Sam.] See Paula Burnett, ed., *The Penguin Book of Caribbean Verse in English* (1986), p. 9.

[37] In *Marly; or, a Planter's Life in Jamaica*, the young Marly observes that occasions like Crop Over were marked by a festive dance in which the overseers and book-keepers, danced with black and brown women. See Anonymous, *Marly; or, a Planter's Life in Jamaica* (Glasgow: Richard Griffin & Col, 1828), pp. 42–3.

productivity in colonial Jamaica.[38] The musical ballads and poetry of the working class Scottish dialect poet Robert Burns were sang, read, and quoted all over the Caribbean. (Indeed, Burns himself had planned to migrate to Jamaica to work as a book-keeper at one point, and even wrote the semi-autobiographical "On a Scotch Bard, Gone to the West Indies," about men like himself who left to seek their fortunes in the Caribbean.) Like "Quaco Sam," other "Negro ballads" were actually popular British songs with radically different lyrics that revealed the casual brutality that defined the lives of enslaved blacks. In particular, the lyrics to Moreton's transcription of a "Negro ballad" that I will refer to as "Altho' A Slave," reflect this dialectical inversion of a British referent. "Altho' A Slave" is a devastating indictment of slavery sung by an enslaved black woman, set to the tune of the then-popular Scottish song, "Lord! What care I for mam or dad?" The Scottish song was, itself, an ironic derivation of the Robert Burns romantic ballad, "Corn Rigs Are Bonie," about a young man's night of erotic passion in a corn field with his lover.[39] Inversions of popular British songs—or "versions" in Jamaican reggae parlance—were popular modes of indigenous music in the colonial Caribbean.

Transcribers, Ventriloquists, or Both?
The Moreton–Mathews Clash

Although Moreton's other "negro" songs are anthologized as authentic representations of early Afro-Caribbean poetry, "Altho' a Slave" is mostly interpreted as his own creation. This may be because elsewhere in his book Moreton intersperses his own standard grammar poetry.[40] However, "a vulgar Port Royal ditty" version

---

[38] See Velma Pollard, "'Slash Me Off a Penny's Worth:' The Scots in Jamaica," in Giovanna Covi, Carla Sassi, Velma Pollard, and Joan Anim-Addo, *Caribbean-Scottish Relations—Colonial and Contemporary Inscriptions in History, Language and Literature* (2007), p. 127. In early twentieth century Jamaica a Scotsman was brought into a soap factory to teach the black workers Scottish songs, the rationale being that their "African songs" were too slow and made them work slowly, whereas the Scottish songs were happier, quicker, and would improve factory production. I thank Velma Pollard for alerting me to this connection.

[39] Lyrics and sheet music for "Lord! What care I for mam or dad?" in *Calliope: or, the Musical Miscellany. A Select Collection of the Most Approved English, Scots and Irish Songs, set to music* (London: C. Elliot and T. Kay; C. Elliot, Edinburgh, 1788), p. 440. The full text of "Lord! What care I for mam or dad?" is sung from the point of a rebellious young woman who is seduced by her lover "on yonder green." Despite her parents' disapproval, she would be willing to "die so sweet a death / With such a charming fellow" again. Moreton's "negro" ballad is therefore an ironic inversion of an ironic inversion.

[40] See J. B. Moreton, *West India Customs and Manners* (1790/1793), pp. 154–5. Paula Burnett anthologizes Moreton's work songs as composed by anonymous authors, but she reproduces this one as his own composition, albeit without explanation for her choice ("…this European-style ballad is interesting as the earliest-known use of the vernacular by a white writer…"). See Paula Burnett, ed., *The Penguin Book of Caribbean Verse in English* (1986), p. 396. Earlier in Moreton's narrative, he "submits an extract from a poem" that he asserts he wrote on his first voyage to the Caribbean. However, in *Noises of the Blood* Carolyn Cooper interprets "Altho' A Slave" as an authentic Afro-Caribbean woman's text. (She titles it "Me Know No Law, Me Know No Sin," from another line in the song.) See Carolyn Cooper, Chapter 1, *Noises in the Blood: Orality, Gender, and the "Vulgar" Body of Jamaican Popular Culture* (Durham: Duke University Press, 1995), pp. 17–36.

of this black woman's lament appears several decades later in the popular English novel *Tom Cringle's Log*. The novel is authored by Michael Scott who, although English, lived in Jamaica for many years as a young man, perhaps overlapping with Moreton. Clearly Moreton was not lying, as Mathews charges, when he claims that the song was sung by an enslaved black woman. His transcription was based on an authentic popular song of the period, although perhaps interspersed with his own additions:[41]

Altho' a slave me is born and bred,
My skin is black, not yellow:
I often sold my maidenhead
To many a handsome fellow.

My massa keep me once, for true,
And gave me clothes, wid *busses*   [kisses]
Fine muslin coats, wid *bitty* too,   [small amount of money]
To gain my sweet embraces.

When *pickinniny* him come black,   [child]
My massa starve and *fum* me;   [beat]
He tear the coat from off my back,
And naked him did strip me.

Him turn me out into the field,
Wid hoe, the ground to clear-o;
Me take pickinniny on my back,
And work him te-me weary.

---

[41] Michael Scott, *Tom Cringle's Log* (Edinburgh: Blackwood, 1834), p. 275:…I was turning to go to sleep again, when a female, in a small suppressed voice, sung the following snatch of a vulgar Port Royal ditty, which I scarcely forgive myself for introducing here to polite society.

> "Young hofficer come home at night,
> Him give me ring and kisses;
> Nine months, one picaniny white,
> Him white almost like missis.
> But missis fum my back wid switch,
> Him say de child for massa;
> But massa say him"

The singer broke off suddenly, as if disturbed by the approach of some one….

I thank Jean D'Costa for alerting me to this later transcription of "Altho' A Slave" as well as availing me of her extraordinary store of knowledge on Jamaican linguistics of the eighteenth and nineteenth centuries. Author email correspondence with Jean D'Costa (November 24, 2013). See also Jean D'Costa, Chapter 1, in Jean D'Costa, Barbara Lalla, and Velma Pollard, *Caribbean Literary Discourse: Voice and Cultural Identity in the Anglophone Caribbean* (Tuscaloosa: University of Alabama Press, 2013). D'Costa explains how the songs of the enslaved create a counter-narrative to white narratives of the plantation. In particular she comments on the continuing popularity of Moreton's transcribed song: "It makes one pause to realize that *this song* stayed well-known and popular from the 1770s until the 1830s. One wonders how much of its bitter critique of the speaker's social world crept into the minds of those who wrote it down. Did they even sniff the odor of protest and resistance layered in these verses?"

Him, *Obissha*, him de come one night,   [Overseer]
And give me gown and busses;
Him get one pickinniny, white!
Almost as white as *missess*.   [mistress]

Then missess fum me wid long switch,
And say him da for massa;
My massa curse her, "lying bitch!"
And tell her, *"buss my rassa!"*   ["kiss my ass!']

Me fum'd when me no condescend
Me fum'd too if me do it;
Me no have no one for *'tand* my friend,   [stand]
So me am forc'd to do it.

Me know no law,
Me know no sin,
Me is just what ebba them make me;
This is the way dem bring me in;
So God nor devil take me!

This black woman's lament, formally disguised as a lilting romantic "air," suggests that white creoles are culpable for enslaved women's deviant sexual behavior. Elsewhere Moreton speculates that if virtuous English women were subjected to the same conditions they would be equally immoral.[44] In this remarkable song an enslaved black woman finally gets to challenge those who condemn her virtue by "speaking" of the precariousness of her position. That the singer is "black, not yellow," is relevant because of the supposedly innate promiscuous sexual qualities already associated with brown, or mixed-race, women, who make up a disproportionate share of the "housekeepers," or mistresses, of white men by this time. Moreton is more sympathetic towards blacks than coloreds, and often makes positive, even admiring, remarks about aspects of black creole culture. This song reflects the view that black women are entrapped by a brutal system of concubinage that leaves them with little or no agency: beaten if they refuse to have sex, beaten if they surrender. On full display is the cruelty of the white creole planter, who beats, humiliates, and rapes his black concubine, then turns her out into the fields to work, her baby on her back.[43] In this song white creole culture itself is

---

[42]   J. B. Moreton, *West India Customs and Manners* (1790/1793), p. 120.
[43]   The line, "And naked him did strip me," could be interpreted as a prelude to rape as well as a humiliating putdown in its own right. Putting black women out to work after sex was a commonplace event, as Moreton observes: "It is quite usual for a Creole gentleman after dinner to send to the field for one of his favourite wenches, who is instantly hurried home and conveyed to his chamber, (or if he has a wife, to some other apartment), piping hot and drowned with perspiration, in which condition he enjoys the savoury object; after which he takes a nap for an hour or so, and she returns to labour till night…." See J. B. Moreton, *West India Customs and Manners* (1790/1793), pp. 105–6.

under fire, embodied by the abusive master's curse to his equally abusive wife, "lying bitch, buss my rassa! [kiss my ass!]" The rustic lovers' tryst in the corn fields of Burns' Scottish ballad becomes a sick joke in its Caribbean version, where white men of all kinds (and black men, too) have sex with hapless enslaved black women, who are beaten and then returned to hoe the fields, the master's "pickney" on their backs, until they're "weary." The unknown black female singer's inversion of it is all the more a profound rebuttal to the original when one considers the possibility that, particularly in comparison with African songs, Scottish songs were considered happy by definition. Utilizing the same inversion technique as the unknown black composer(s), through the strategic use of this "negroe dialect" narrative Moreton inverts the happy white narrative, that romantic pro-slavery discourse of black contentment on the picturesque tropical plantations of the Caribbean.

In his other transcriptions of enslaved music Moreton similarly portrays the larger enslaved population as trapped in the suffocating confines of the plantation, brutalized by godless overseers.[44] Mathews and other white creoles clearly understood only too well the condemnation of their own behavior and the refutation of their pro-slavery arguments reflected in these negro songs. Mathews therefore mimes Moreton's transcriptions almost exactly—right down to the titles, Song 1 and Song 2—but with different content. The work songs that Mathews transcribes are for the most part forgettable ditties, not damning to white mythologies in the ways that Moreton's are.[45] Similarly, when Mathews casually drops that blacks actually stop work, or travel from the farthest reaches of the island just to hear him perform, we are meant to read this as an implicit rebuttal, not of Moreton's explicit arguments, but of what Moreton's transcribed slave songs imply about black confinement and overwork. Yet these are not merely Moreton's accusations; because they are transcribed, they are actually the slaves' themselves. Mathews' own "negro" song, "Buddy Quow," challenges not Moreton's anti-slavery argument so much as the anonymous black woman's lament.

Mathews' song "Buddy Quow" takes on Moreton's characterization of black women's sexuality:[46]

---

[44] See Moreton's transcriptions of "If me want for go in a *Ebo* / Me can't go there!" and "Tink dere is a God in a top / No use me ill, Obissha!," in J. B. Moreton, *West India Customs and Manners* (1790/1793), p. 153.

[45] Moreton's transcriptions of Song 1 ("If me want for go in a *Ebo* / Me can't go there!) and Song 2 ("Tink dere is a God in a top / No use me ill, Obissha!") are indictments of white creole brutality. Mathews reproduces versions of both songs, also titled Song 1st and Song 2nd, which he verifies as transcriptions of authentic negro songs. Song 1st is reproduced in a later document, *The Report of Saint Bartholomew* (May 18, 1805), where it is given the title "Hey Jigrejig: Ebo Song with Drum," and is ascribed to Mathews. Song 1st contains the only line in either song that can be construed as a criticism of white brutality: "Bockra work O, bruk ee haunt, O, O, lo. [White man's work broke his spirit / heart, O, O, lo." See Samuel Augustus Mathews, *The Lying Hero* (1793), pp. 138–9. Translation from Philip Baker, Adrienne Bruyn, Neville Shrimpton, and Lise Winer, "The Texts of Samuel Augustus Mathews," in *St. Kitts and the Atlantic Creoles*, edited by Philip Baker and Adrienne Bruyn (1998), p. 44.

[46] Although I have changed a few lines based on my own interpretation of Creole, I have mostly used the translation of "Buddy Quow" by Neville Shrimpton and Philip Baker. See Samuel Augustus

Vos motter Buddy Quow?	What's the matter Brother Quow?
Aw bree Obeshay bong you	I believe overseer's banged [beaten] you
You tan no sauby how	You don't seem to know how
Daw bocra mon go wrong you,	That white man is going to wrong you,
buddy Quow.	Brother Quow.
Chaw, tan way, lem me lone	Cho, stand back, let me alone
No so trouble begin now	That's how trouble begins now
Aw goo mine tik von tone	I've a good mind to take a stone
So knock you rotten shin now,	To knock your rotten shin now,
bruk you bone.	break your bone.
No haut bun morrogoo	No heart burn, country man,
Es granny ungry do you	It's a great hunger that's got you
Aw hab sum bobrocoo	I have some dumplings
Aw bring dem, aw kumfoo you, morrogoo	I'll bring them, I'll get them for you, countryman
No ungry no so dry	Not hunger nor thirst [that bothers me]
Foot true now no mo yerry	For true, now, listen to me
Mek wataw foo me yie	[what I have to say] makes water fill my eyes
Aw cry so tay aw weary vipe me yie	I cry so til I wearily wipe my eyes.
Dat time Quasheba tell,	That time Quasheba told me
Ee go bring von pickney fimme	she was going to have my baby
Aw nawngaw so, aw sell	I was so proud, I sold
Daw hog me momy gim me, berry well.	That hog my mother gave me, for a good price.
Von kote aw buy um new,	I bought her a new coat
Von rapper aw bin bring kum,	I bought her a wrapper
Von new honkisser too	one new handkerchief too
Aw neber bin go tink um newsy, true.	I never thought she'd be nasty, true.
Ven unco Quaco say	when Uncle Quaco say
De pickney he bin kum mon,	the child has been born, man,
Aaw nawngaw morer tay	I felt so proud til
Me haut bin nock pum, pum, [mon], My heart	
was knocking pum, pum, man,	
true Gran Jay. really loud.	
Gor Mighty day law bup,	God almighty there above
See how Quasheba do me,	See how Quasheba did me
Daw bocra mon ee lub	The white man she loves
Ee bring mulatto foo me, Gor na bub.	She bore a mulatto for me, God in heaven above.
Ee yie, ee nose, ee mouth,	His eye, his nose, his mouth,
Me bin goo mine foo hitum	I've a good mind to hit him,
Tan ebry mossel bout,	Every muscle standing out,
Like Obeshay bin pit him and he mout.	Like overseer spat him out his mouth.

Mathews, "The Texts of Samuel Augustus Mathews," arranged and annotated by Philip Baker, Adrienne Bruyn, Neville Shrimpton, and Lise Winer, with commentary by Alain Kihm, in *St. Kitts and the Atlantic Creoles*, edited by Philip Baker and Adrienne Bruyn (1998), pp. 8–11.

Reading the lyrics of the Moreton song and "Buddy Quow" side by side, the central focus of both comes clear. It is on black women's supposed promiscuity, a popular musical topic of extending well into the twentieth century.[47] Whereas Moreton's transcribed song is meant to be taken as a lament posing as a romantic ballad, Mathews' is a comic song posing as a lament. (Interestingly, Michael Scott, the author of *Tom Cringle's Log*, renders "Altho' A Slave" not as a lament but as a "vulgar ditty," more similar in intent to "Buddy Quow" than to Moreton's version.) "Buddy Quow," however, is a rebuttal on two fronts. While clearly challenging Moreton's black woman's lament, it also calls into question Moreton's own creative interpretations of Caribbean life by rendering a more "authentic" salacious ballad on the same topic. For *Manners and Customs in the West India Islands* also features Moreton's own risqué poem on black women's infidelity, a comic ballad written from the viewpoint of the black man and with a heroine similarly named "Quashiba:" "For Quashiba's gone to town, / To see smarter beaumen than me; / Tho' I often compell'd her to own / How false and how fickle they be."[48] Moreton bills his poem as "the complaint of a negroe man, whose helpmate had deserted him." It is written in typically florid eighteenth century prose, not in dialect, a distinction upon which Mathews gleefully seizes to highlight the text's inauthentic nature. If Moreton and Mathews are similar in their own poetic attempts to ventriloquize black men, Moreton provides a counter-discourse by black women themselves in their own "language." More critically, although Mathews is clearly rewriting Moreton's "Quashiba" poem, it is the more compelling counterweight of the black woman's text "Altho' A Slave" with which Mathews, ultimately, is concerned.

"Buddy Quow" makes a point of referencing multiple black characters with explicitly African names: "Quasheba," the faithless lover whose name was a commonly used stand-in for a black woman, as was "Quow" for a black man; the "morrogoo" friend; and "Uncle Quaco." This suggests the singer's privileged position from within an entirely black world where the listeners can glimpse authentic black voices. The blacks themselves have plenty of agency over their own lives, unlike in Moreton's black woman's version, where blacks are so thoroughly without real choices in a white-dominated society that their morality is a completely relative proposition.

---

[47] "Man Smart (Woman Smarter)," by the Trinidadian calypsonian King Radio in 1936 and popularized by Harry Belafonte in the 1950s, is an example of the theme of the duplicitous black or non-white woman. The theme goes hand-in-hand with the theme of women's rampant materialism, illustrated in calypsos such as Growling Tiger's "Money is King" and Mighty Sparrow's "No Money No Love" and "Jack Palance." For more on themes of women, sex, and materialism in calypso see Patricia Mohammed, "A Blueprint for Gender in Creole Trinidad: Exploring Gender Mythology through Calypsos of the 1920s and 1930s," pp. 129–69, in *The Culture of Gender and Sexuality in the Caribbean*, edited by Linden Lewis (Gainesville: University of Florida Press, 2003).

[48] See J. B. Moreton, *West India Customs and Manners* (1790/1793), p. 150.

Both "Altho' A Slave" and "Buddy Quow" highlight material goods as a central motif in the sexual behavior of black women. In the former the black female protagonist tells the listener that although she has sold herself to "many a handsome fellow," and although both the master and the overseer give her money and clothes to gain her consent, in the end she is "forc'd to do it." Feminine finery and material goods also feature in "Buddy Quow" (and in "Quaco Sam," for that matter).[49] However, here its purpose is very different. Material goods are illustrative of black female superficiality, not of the black woman's further objectification through—ironically—the use of objects. In Mathews' version of the black experience it is the black men who buy things, the point being that they possess the power to do so: they own animals and can even purchase luxury clothing for their "Quashebas." Even with this munificence, the greedy "Quashebas" deceive them with white overseers, whom they actually love. Although in the first verse of "Buddy Quow" his friend assumes that Buddy Quow is upset because the overseer has beaten him, it turns out that this is not the case: Quow is in despair because his Quasheba has cheated on him with the overseer and produced a brown baby. This set-up directly refutes the view held by the abolitionists and their sympathizers that the white overseers were cruel abusers of the enslaved. Contrary to the friend's—and the listener's—expectations, it is the black woman who is responsible for the black man's despair, not the white man.

Who Is "Speaking?" Ventriloquizing Black Women's Voices

The theme of the promiscuous black woman remained a constant in pro-slavery Caribbean narrative through the nineteenth century until Emancipation. "Quaco and Mimba," a pre-Emancipation dialect poem published by a Trinidadian slave-owner published in the planter-oriented *Trinidad Guardian* in 1827, details a lovers' quarrel between his two enslaved blacks. It is similar in intent and execution to Mathews' "Buddy Quow:" the author, Matthew Muscovado, claims that he overheard his two slaves arguing and was "seized with one of those rhyming fits, which, in common with all men—Poets or not—I am subject to, and resolved to try how *Quashie's* story would look in verse, using his own dialect." Mimba has been unfaithful to Quaco, but attempts to deceive him by claiming that her lover is her brother. The author asserts to the editor that such faithless behavior occurs "every day among your favorite Blackies, in spite of your high opinion of their *moral* capabilities."[50] This sneering putdown is not to convince the white planter

---

[49] "Mi hab mi Regan gown, mi hab mi gin'am cloak, / Swalla-henkychi tie me head, Massa-tenky tie mi troat." See Barbara Lalla, "Quaco Sam," *Jamaica Journal* (1981), p. 21.

[50] Matthew Muscovado, "Quaco and Mimba (A Negro Ballad)," A Planter's Port Folio, No. 2, *Trinidad Guardian* (October 2, 1827) pp. 77–8, reprinted in Lise Winer, *Trinidad and Tobago* (Amsterdam: John Benjamins, 1993), pp. 77–81.

readership that blacks are immoral, but rather to provide eye-witness evidence which affirms the white planters' pro-slavery views. Like "Buddy Quow," this was to rebut a swelling abolitionist counter-narrative that was already entrenched in public discourse. For Muscovado and other white creoles, dialect, the language of blackness, affirms their view the black women are knowing manipulators who can choose white or black lovers, experience "love" for white overseers, and cheat on everyone, black or white. In this version there are no victims of slavery, only victims of black women's perfidy.

White creole women are mostly invisible in these men's versions of plantation life, but in Moreton's they are equally complicit in their brutality towards the slaves (indeed, elsewhere Moreton notes that as a purely financial transaction white creole mistresses hire out their "negro wenches for white men.").[51] Moreton seems particularly interested in black women's experiences, moreso than black men's. He describes most of the work songs as sung by black women as they till the fields.[52] Black women are the most common vector around which racial ventriloquism, dialect narrative, and political discourse merge during this period. Despite the fact that black women as literary authors were not recognized until the twentieth century, their voices were pivotal to any representation of Caribbean society. Black women were particularly potent symbols for both abolitionists and slavery advocates.

The abolitionists sought to portray black women as hapless and brutalized sexual victims of a "natural" male proclivity to licentiousness, represented by the "quadroon" woman featured in Blake's "Surinam Planter in his Morning Dress." The pro-slavery faction countered with images of black women as the anti-thesis of the European feminine ideal: physically strapping, garrulous, cynical, amoral hucksters who themselves exploited whites (or even their own people) for gain and weren't afraid to "talk back"—in dialect, of course—to powerful whites, or anyone else. In the 1830 engraving "Offended Dignity" by popular English caricaturist William Heath a feisty black Caribbean woman, smartly dressed and hands akimbo, is personally offended by the infamous anti-slavery image of a black woman being whipped: "Dem Buckra [white men] tell big lie," she tells the well-dressed black man holding the picture, "...you an Buckra be one great fool" (Figure 1.2).

---

[51] Moreton, *West India Customs and Manners*, p. 126. Moreton further claims that white men who wish to have sex with a brown woman slave must first pay five pounds to her black mother or "solicit the favour of her mistress." He provides evidence for this by transcribing a popular negro song:

> Come carry me in a room
> Come carry me in a room
> And give them five pound apiece.
> Come carry me in a room
> Come carry me in a room
> And lay me on the bed.

[52] See J. B. Moreton, *Manners and Customs in the West India Islands* (1790/1793), p. 152.

Figure 1.2 *Offended Dignity*, colored engraving, William Heath, England, 1830.
Courtesy of the Lewis Walpole Library, Yale University.

Similarly, in 1823 the pro-slavery "English traveler" Cynric R. Williams[53]—more
likely the white creole absentee planter Charles White Williams—records a satirical
dialect song of white male sexual hypocrisy supposedly sung by Magdalene, an
enslaved and, notably, Christian black woman he encounters while in Jamaica:[54]

Hi! de Buckra, hi!
You sabby wha for he da cross de sea,
Wid him long white face and him
twinkling yeye;
He lub, make lub, as he preach to we,
He fall on his knees, but he pray for me,
Hi! de Buckra, hi!

Look! The white man, look!
You know why he crossed the sea
With his long face and his
his twinkling eye;
He loves, makes love, as he preaches to us,
He falls on his knees, but he prays for me,
Look! The white man, look!

Hi! de Buckra, hi!
Massa W---f---e da come ober de sea,

Look! The white man, look!
Mister [Wilberforce] comes over the sea

---

[53] Likely not his real name. Tim Watson persuasively argues that Cynric Williams may well have
been the Jamaican-English planter Charles White Williams, a member of a pro-planter advocacy
group in England who owned the Duckworth Plantation in Jamaica in the early nineteenth century. As
Watson notes are no records of anyone called Cynric R. Williams in Great Britain during this period.
See Tim Watson, *Caribbean Culture and British Fiction in the Atlantic World 1780–1870* (Cambridge:
Cambridge University Press, 2008), pp. 66–74. Also, see Candace Ward and Tim Watson, Introduction,
in Cynric R. Williams, *Hamel the Obeah Man*, edited by Candace Ward and Tim Watson (Peterborough:
Broadview, 2010), p. 19.

[54] Cynric R. Williams, *A Tour through the Island of Jamaica, From the Western to the Eastern End, in
the Year 1823* (London: Hunt and Clarke, 1826), p. 297. The translation of "Hi! de Buckra, hi!" is mine.

Wid him roguish heart and him tender look;	With his roguish heart and his tender look;
And while he palaver and preach him book,	And while he palavers and preaches his book [bible]
At the negro girl he'll winkie him yeye.	At the negro girl he'll wink his eye.
Hi! de Buckra, hi!	Look! The white man, look!

The Christian black singer's sly reference to the famously moral abolitionist William Wilberforce implies that these pious English abolitionists, like the immoral white creoles they criticize, also desire sex with black women. Black women's verbal dexterity and wit in "outing" English male hypocrisy, therefore, is essential to making the point that white readers must not feel sorry for these amazons, who can clearly take care of themselves. The back story to Magdalene's "Buckra" song is related in tongue-in-cheek fashion. Williams notes that Magdalene was one of several black Christian girls he met who were bathing and washing clothes in the river, all of whom were, as he puts it, "sleek as moles" with "not a scratch" on their bodies. This detail rebuts the abolitionist image of enslaved women as the ultimate victims of slavery's brutality. (Elsewhere Williams' black valet preaches an impromptu sermon to brown women imploring them to marry black men rather than commit sin with white ones, a piece of advice in "no ways to their taste."[55] They were, apparently, beyond Christian redemption.) Whether or not this is a factual account, its intention is the same: to illustrate that the abolitionist missionaries who came to the Caribbean must really want to indulge in sexual indiscretions with black women under the guise of converting them to a life of chastity.[56] By ventriloquizing the black Magdalene, however, he gets the supposed victim of slavery to skewer her supposed savior. The song functions similarly to the ways that black music is used by Moreton and Mathews as the hard evidence for their ideological arguments.

But we contemporary readers must nevertheless ask, just how authentic is this pro-slavery advocate's rendition of the voices of actual black Jamaican women? Again we are faced with the question of archival authenticity on the issue of white transcription of black voices. Early Caribbean prose of the enslaved is circumscribed by the supposedly factual nature of travel writing, political propaganda, and the creative license of fiction, all of which constantly weave in and out of both

[55] See Cynric R. Williams, *A Tour Through the Island of Jamaica: From the Western to the Eastern End in the Year 1823* (1826), p. 56.

[56] See Samuel Augustus Mathews, *The Willshire Squeeze, a ballad founded upon facts, to which are added, specimens of the Negro familiar dialect and proverbial sayings, with songs* (Demerara: Guiana Chronicle Office, 1822). Mathews lists the Methodists as first among the curses in his life (p. 5). As Victoria Borg O'Flaherty notes, "Mathews must have felt that by catering too much to the slaves, the Methodists were undermining social stability of the society." She further documents that the Methodist minister in St. Kitts in the 1790s was welcomed by free coloreds and often relied on brown and black preachers. See Victoria Borg O'Flaherty, "Samuel Augustus Mathews: his life and times," in *St. Kitts and the Atlantic Creoles*, edited by Philip Baker and Adrienne Bruyn (1998), p. 58.

fiction and non-fiction such that the lines of fact, fiction, and authorship blur. Linguist Barbara Lalla describes the difficulty of assessing transcribed narratives of non-white Caribbean people by white foreigners in eighteenth- and nineteenth-century texts:

In various senses, then, a curious continuum exists between fiction and non-fiction. The polemic, the book of domestic manners, the travelogue, and the novel of adventure shade imperceptibly into each other. In these genres occur representations of speech that I would describe as *ventriloquist dialogue*, speech (by the British author) on behalf of the silenced Caribbean voice. This rendering of Caribbean speech is in many instances invented (and in this sense fictional) rather than objectively transcribed. It is characteristically brief because it does not function as an opportunity for local expression.[57]

Although Lalla is right that the purpose of these transcriptions is not "local expression," nevertheless they are ideologically useless without that identifiable localness. Transcribed narratives function as creative texts of black and brown populations *despite*, not because of, the means by which they are recorded. Striving for the most authentic evidence possible, the transcribers appear painstaking in their effort at verisimilitude. Transcription was a two-edged sword: in suppressing the voice of the enslaved, it gave voice to the enslaved.

Given that Cynric Williams was likely a planter himself, arguably it is he, not Magdalena, who is the author of "Hi! de Buckra." Like Mathews before him, Williams' ability to toggle easily between racial ventriloquism and transcription illustrates that both strategies were clearly convenient covers for white creoles, whose own relationship to Creole was uneasy and contentious. Transcription and ventriloquism allowed them to be English—"real" whites—and black, or "real" natives. Transcription allowed them to be English when the argument called for Englishness; ventriloquism allowed them to be black when blackness was required. Williams seems to have taken advantage of both. He authored a well-regarded novel, *Hamel the Obeah Man*,[58] in the same period, so he was not merely a recorder of Jamaican life, he was also a creative interpreter of it. Indeed, the extraordinary attempt at verisimilitude suggests that, if he was not a speaker of Creole, then he lived in close proximity to those who did. There are all of the earmarks of, at the very least, creative license in Williams' supposedly non-fiction account.

On the other hand, as Jean D'Costa argues, it is likely that "Hi! de Buckra" is founded on an authentic "negro song," albeit one which Williams, like Mathews, utilizes for his own political views. As a specialist in eighteenth- and

---

[57]   See Barbara Lalla, Chapter 2 ("Black Wholes") in Jean D'Costa, Barbara Lalla, and Velma Pollard, *Caribbean Literary Discourse: Voice and Cultural Identity in the Anglophone Caribbean* (Tuscaloosa: University of Alabama Press, 2013), p. 45.

[58]   Cynric R. Williams, *Hamel the Obeah Man*, edited by Candace Ward and Tim Watson (2010).

nineteenth-century anglophone Caribbean linguistics, D'Costa's opinion here is especially relevant. She suspects that Williams took a popular black creole song called "Hi! de Buckra, hi" and improved on the text: "roguish heart," "tender look," "twinkling yeye" are, she notes, intrusions from a standard English culture. She also notes that Williams' transcriptions show a high degree of accuracy in their transcription of archaic Jamaican Creole.[59]

"Hi! de Buckra" is typical of the mocking dialectal counterpoint song s of the period.[60] The difference between the Buckra's official Word and his unofficial actions is similar to the dissonance between the romantic Burns ballad and the black woman's ironic version of it in "Altho' a slave." Black music—for it is music when it favors white interests, but "noise" when it opposes—can puncture the "truth" of abolitionist eyewitness accounts by pointing out that the white Word and white actions are not one and the same. Magdalene's song would likely have been sung as a disarming "air" with a bouncing, happy melody, rendering it impervious to serious critique. It is no accident that white creoles exploited black creole musical traditions for their pro-slavery views. Creole music was a most potent force for the oppositional views of enslaved black and non-white people, regardless of how it was utilized or manipulated by white intermediaries. If white men were keepers of the written Word, and freed black and brown men the heirs apparent in the Emancipation era, then black women had only song with which to broadcast their views. One late-eighteenth century traveler to the region noted that, on their arrival, white emigrants on board the ships were greeted at the dock by black women singing ominous songs of their impending death. In Jean Rhys' classic 1962 Caribbean novel *Wide Sargasso Sea*, the daughter of a slave-owner is driven to despair by the taunting songs of black women.[61] These different kinds of examples tell us that, regardless of their enslaved status and the fact that their words were used and manipulated by whites, black women brandished their vaunted verbal dexterity as a form of narrative resistance to their subaltern condition.

[59] Jean D'Costa, email correspondence with author, November 24, 2013.

[60] Paula Burnett lists some of these dialectical work songs such as the Moreton-transcribed "Tink Dere is a God on Top" and others in *The Penguin Book of Caribbean Verse in English* (1986).

[61] British traveler Robert Renny tells of the arrival of his ship in Port Royal Jamaica, to be greeted by black Jamaican market women singing "New come buckra / He get sick / He tek fever / He be die / He be die." Renny also hears similar songs on the streets of Kingston, "One, two tree, / All de same, / Black, white, brown, / All de same; All de same." See Robert Renny Esq., *An History of Jamaica* (London: J. Cawthorn, 1807), p. 241. These songs are also reproduced by the British missionary J. M. Phillippo in *Jamaica: Its Past and Present State* (London, 1843) quoted in Paula Burnett, ed., *Penguin Book of Caribbean Verse in English*, pp. 4–5, 373; also quoted in Vincent Brown, *The Reaper's Garden: Death, Power, and New World Slavery* (Harvard University Press, 2008), pp. 1, 3. See also Jean Rhys, *Wide Sargasso Sea* (New York: W. W. Norton, 1992), p. 101, where the taunting songs of the former slave Amelie in front of her newly-married mistress drive the former to despair: "The white cockroach she marry, / The white cockroach she buy young man / The white cockroach she marry."

"Overheard" Narratives after Slavery

Although musical lyrics were a central medium for racial ventriloquism by whites of black speech in the anglophone Caribbean, just as many examples are to be found in poetry or prose narrative. Usually these involve a standard grammar narration with dialect speech uttered by black or brown characters. Unlike Mathews, many of the authors chose to remain anonymous. The narrative convention most often deployed was that of the disinterested white observer, someone outside the circle of black life who was merely listening in, trying to understand a conversation that he only partly comprehended. In Trinidad, for example, anonymous authors penned letters to the editor of the *Spectator* purporting to have "overheard" conversations among black people that they are simply reporting and requesting the editor to comment on the subject. The writing generally described city, not rural, life. Its purpose was inevitably social or political commentary, more freely given since the author's views were disguised as black peoples' conversation and therefore immune from personal or political repercussions. There was a distinctly creative component to these letters: with anonymous monikers like "Spectator" and "Eavesdropper," these "overheard" conversations invariably were written as theatrical dialogue, with characters speaking directly to each other with little or no omniscient narration for the duration. The anonymous letters-to-the-editor tradition was, in its way, a fledgling version of today's robust picong[62] tradition of Trinidad and Tobago. The writers poked fun at the linguistic idiosyncracies of the black working class, particularly at those who were ignorant but affecting to sound educated or knowledgeable. The stories contained in these letters seem intended for more than just the white planter elite. They formed part of a wider culture of printed discourse, or printscape. As print publications proliferated in every country of the anglophone Caribbean a wider, multiracial audience for these dialect narratives was an inevitable consequence.

In "The Sorrows of Kitty," published in Trinidad a year after slavery ended in 1839, the anonymous writer (who calls himself "Spectator") relates the argument between his hard-working black washerwoman Kitty and her lazy, good-for-nothing black lover Pompey. Pompey is a formerly enslaved groom from an Estate who now, "free as Buckra," is living in the city, sponging off of his lover's earnings, drinking and eating it all up while refusing to work. Kitty curses Pompey, telling him, "You free—me work hard! Me slave to you!" whereupon Pompey tells her

---

[62] The satirical tradition of dualing banter that characterizes Trinidadian music, literature, and performance. "A spontaneous, verbal battle in rhymed song between two or more contending CALYPSONIANS, in which the wit and humorous impact of a contender's improvisation determines his supremacy…," according to Richard Allsopp, ed., *Dictionary of Caribbean English Usage* (London: Oxford University Press, 1996), p. 439. The traditional carnival characters of the English-speaking Pierrot and the dialect-speaking Pierrot Grenade in Trinidad are a similarly dueling couple.

"Me man—you woman! Your tongue too free!" "Spectator" concludes that there are far too many "idle vagabonds," lately freed from the Estates, roaming the city. Here again we see black sexual relationships the subject of white satire, with the familiarly intertwined themes of money and sex. In this post-Emancipation narrative the emphasis is on the inversion of gender roles: the black man is shiftless, emasculated and dependent on a woman, all the while insisting on his manly prerogative; the woman is "industrious and hardworking."[63] While the tone is lighthearted and comic, its conclusion that black men are a dangerous surplus to the freed population is less so. This example parallels a later example in Jamaica where black women's voices are used, in ventriloquist fashion, to comment on the post-Emancipation "problem" of black male freedom. That "problem" would set the stage for the violence of the succeeding decades.

The ventriloquist phase of Caribbean dialect literature initiated by the Moreton–Mathews conflict in the 1790s was the primary means by which dialect became a written form in the nineteenth century. The white ventriloquists were, ironically, the originators and disseminators of dialect as a narrative and literary form. The ventriloquist phase of dialect narrative was not only essential to its development, arguably it is still with us: ventriloquism of one kind or another is still an endemic feature of Caribbean Creole narrative. Early agents like Moreton, Mathews, Williams, McTurk, Cordle, and the host of anonymous writers whose work filled the pages of the early Caribbean newspapers laid a foundation for how the "common man" majority—whether the voice of the slave, the rural peasant, or the working class urban population—was to be represented. Ventriloquizing what was deemed the black working class voice proved useful for a range of objectives: it provided direct testimonials to the evils of slavery; it witnessed to slavery's innocuous nature; it served as a political critique of emancipation; it ameliorated racial tensions between white elites and the black/brown majority.

Although the entire cross-section of Caribbean society spoke dialect, it was inevitably black and African-descended people who were the focus of these ventriloquizing efforts for obvious political reasons—it was their silenced voice that, ironically, spoke loudest to those who sought to portray the basis for an original Caribbean political and cultural identity. That many of the white authors of this tradition were pro-slavery, racist, or looked down on Afro-Caribbean culture does not mean that they were not instrumental in its development as an authentically Caribbean form. That some were foreigners does not mean that they were marginal to the same. Although the ventriloquist narratives cannot be taken as conclusive "evidence" of black innocence, collusion or culpability in whatever political debate in which they were deployed, collectively these early dialect renderings are invaluable, both for the complex portrait we glimpse of enslaved and subjugated

---

[63] Spectator, "The Sorrows of Kitty," *Trinidad Standard* (February 1, 1839), p. 3.

black people themselves, but also for what they reveal about white creole strivings for a creative and authentic Caribbean voice. Ventriloquist dialect writers aimed to amplify, distort, or silence entirely the voices of the emerging black majorities of the Caribbean as black and brown people continued to rise from absolute sub-jugation to within reach of political power. An acknowledgement of this often antagonistic role ensures that we can never attribute a superficial melting pot the-sis to the role of white dialect innovators. Yet it is also true that the emergence of the Afro-Caribbean voice, and the articulation of the Afro-Caribbean experience, owes as much to these "fake," or mediated, black voices as to the more recognized forms of historical evidence, as well as to the actual voices of black people, them-selves. In the end these ventriloquists, and those that they ventriloquized, yielded a lasting template for an original Caribbean narrative form.

2

Violent Ventriloquism

The Golden Age

If racial ventriloquism was a hallmark feature of early Caribbean dialect literature, so too was violence. As Deborah Thomas notes, it is difficult *not* to write
about the violence that suffuses contemporary Caribbean societies and preoccu-
pies its governments. What is true for any account of contemporary Caribbean
society is true, or should be, for any study attempting to plot the region's early literary history.[1] In fact, the story of the evolution of Creole literature is incomplete
without a recognition of the essential feature of violence, rhetorical, metaphorical,
and actual, that accompanied its rise.

The Caribbean was always a violent place, especially for blacks, Asians, and
others who fueled its plantation economies. The Moreton–Mathews clash that
"birthed" the Creole genre took place in the context of the vicious brutality of
Caribbean, where unspeakable violence towards the enslaved justified the spectacular wealth creation that laid the foundation for much of modern Britain and
its elite family dynasties. It is therefore useful to follow Marisa Fuentes' lead in
conceptualizing the Caribbean archive itself as a space of violence because of its
role in the erasure of the brutal origins of what is now a hallowed national trait.[2]
Here I seek to restore a sense of physicality, of placedness, to the creation of the
Creole literary tradition through an exploration of the role of violence, figurative
and literal. Thus far I have emphasized the *loudness* of Creole's literary tradition:
the black noise defining the Caribbean soundscape; the entertaining literary
fights on the pages of pamphlets and newspapers; the sonic disturbances that give
rise to the pen-to-paper quality of the conflict. But the Caribbean is also a space
marked by silence. Its literary archive conceals more than it reveals about the
bodies, conflicts, and acts of suppression that created it. The poet M. NourbeSe
Philip describes the embedded role of blackness in the New World literary archive
as "Body becoming text...Not on the margins. But within the very body of the
text where the silence exists."[3]

---

[1] Deborah Thomas, *Exceptional Violence: Embodied Citizenship in Transnational Jamaica* (Durham
and London: Duke University Press, 2011), pp. 1–2.
[2] Marisa Fuentes, *Dispossessed Lives: Enslaved Women, Violence, and the Archive* (Philadelphia:
University of Pennsylvania Press, 2018).
[3] M. NourbeSe Philip, *A Geneaology of Resistance and Other Essays* (Mercury Press, 1997), p. 95.

Creole Noise: Early Caribbean Dialect Literature and Performance. Belinda Edmondson, Oxford University Press.
© Belinda Edmondson 2022. DOI: 10.1093/oso/9780192856838.003.0003

Creole, the foundational language of the modern Caribbean, is embedded within that matrix of noise, silence, and violence. Just as the story of the rise of American "dialect mania" is incomplete without its context in the aftermath of slavery, so too did literary dialect burst into furious flower in the post-Emancipation anglophone Caribbean. The latter half of the nineteenth century the Caribbean was a place of turmoil. British capital had fled, but suppressive colonial governance remained. White elites, whose identities were tied to the wealth engendered by slavery, were confronting a stark diminution of wealth and the specter of racial equality even as blacks and non-whites were aspiring to all that had been denied them: land, money, status. It was a recipe for violence.

However, even as Caribbean societies were marked by acts of physical and rhetorical violence in the latter half of the nineteenth century, the rise of literary dialect coincided with more than the effects of the flight of metropolitan capital, repressive colonial governance, or white elite hostility to blacks and non-whites. The anglophone Caribbean was increasingly urbanized, now home to a surging population of immigrants: indentured Indians, Chinese, and Portuguese in Trinidad, Jamaica, and, most of all, British Guiana. The proliferation of dialect literature was indissociable from this fertile breeding ground of violence, commerce, and social ambition. Ironically, the most violent era in the history of Creole literature was also its Golden Age. I offer two case studies from Jamaica and British Guiana, two epicenters of Caribbean literary dialect, as examples of the role of violent social upheaval in the making of the Creole literary tradition.

Literary Dialect and the Morant Bay Rebellion

A watershed moment in Jamaican history occurred on October 11, 1865. The eastern-most parish of St. Thomas erupted in violence. Black farmers rose up against the colonial authorities who denied them land, the source of all wealth. The protestors were met with extraordinary brutality by Governor Eyre. At least 500 people died, overwhelmingly black, children among them. More were executed in the trials that followed the Rebellion. In the aftermath of Morant Bay Jamaica became a Crown Colony of Great Britain, which meant direct rule from the metropole. The hard-fought political participation of blacks, browns, and Jews in the governance of the country was effectively erased.

Morant Bay was the latest in a string of violent occurrences involving the newly emancipated blacks and colonial authorities since Emancipation in 1834. Alongside this cauldron of constant violence was the increasing centrality of African-derived celebrations and traditions in the public sphere. Historian Jonathan Dalby notes that many of the violent incidences leading up to Morant revolved around the twin poles of traditional black forms of celebration and popular hostility to the newly formed police force.[4] Black Jamaicans, wary of colonial desires to return them to servitude, asserted their personhood through cultural forms, especially music. Indeed, music continued to be the most common medium of popular black protest narratives from the eighteenth century into the nineteenth. Rhonda Cobham-Sander points out that as late as 1907 at least two folk songs that protested the brutality of the authorities during the Morant Bay Rebellion were still extant, with lines such as "Oh General Jackson! You kill all the black man them!"[5]

Just as black music and cultural entertainments were sites of violent clashes with colonial authority, the performance of the amateur theatre troupe of the British military in Morant Bay in November 1866 offers a visceral example of the role of culture as a proxy for resistance and pacification. In November 1866, almost exactly one year after the Morant Bay Rebellion, black Jamaican men were still on trial for acts of treason, British provost-marshal Gordon Ramsay was court-martialed for murder and British gunboats still lay anchored off the Jamaican coast. The soldiers from the gunboats gave theatrical performances in the town, supposedly to benefit reformatories in Kingston but in all likelihood were used to ameliorate tensions with the black population, many of whom would have known the victims killed or experienced brutality themselves at the hands of those same British soldiers. It was in this atmosphere of racial tension and fear that the British soldiers performed a soldier-produced play called *Nigger Delineators*.

The "fashionable company present" for the play's inaugural performance included prosecutors and attorneys for the various Morant Bay trials taking place, including Ramsay's defense solicitors, as well as the Inspector General of Police. There was also a genuine "darkie"—meaning, apparently, a black Jamaican performer—onstage, who danced "in correct style a pleasing Virginia breakdown, which was greeted with thunders of applause."[6] (The use of the American term "darkie" to describe a black Jamaican is instructive for what it tells us about the influence of American language on the Caribbean, even in 1866.) One of the gunboat commanders had the brilliant idea of insisting that "persons of whatever class who should desire to see the performance" should be given free admission, such that "the back part of the room became crowded to suffocation with numbers of the unwashed, whose genuine expressions of

---

[4] Jonathan Dalby, "Precursors to Morant Bay: The Patterns of Popular Protest in Post-Emancipation Jamaica (1834–1865," pp. 99–129, in *Journal of Caribbean History* 50 (2) (2016), p. 100.

[5] See Rhonda Cobham-Sander, "Fictions of Gender, Fictions of Race: Retelling the Morant Bay Rebellion in Jamaican Literature," *Small Axe* 4 (September 2000), pp. 3–5. Cobham-Sander is quoting Walter Jekyll, *Jamaica Song and Story* (1907). General Jackson was one of the British military leaders instrumental in suppressing the Rebellion.

[6] Errol Hill, *The Jamaican Stage* (1992), p. 105.

wonder and pleasure at what was going on made up to the remainder of the audience for the inconvenience and discomfort otherwise occasioned by the invasion."[7]

That a supposedly innocuous blackface minstrel show could provide the vehicle for political "pacification" reveals the extent of the elite's anxiety about the majority black population. White authorities feared black culture. Or rather, they feared black *expression* of black culture. The question of who controlled it, when it was allowed and when not, was paramount. Black religion was particularly suspect. A blackface minstrel show, featuring "black" dialect and written and performed by whites, was a tool of pacification, but it also provided a link between forms of black Atlantic expression, Afro-Caribbean and African-American, mediated by whites. Paramount was the issue of which group actually controlled the performance. The *Colonial Standard*, which published the review of the gunboat amateurs' performance, was understood to be the mouthpiece of the plantocracy and white elite. Calling the rebels "bloodthirsty," "traitors," and "savages," it supported the suppression of the Morant Bay Rebellion by Ramsay and his officers. It also recognized the need to ameliorate tensions among its various constituents.[8] The newspaper was effusive in its praise of *Nigger Delineators*:

> The inhabitants of Morant Bay are warm in the gratitude to...the officers of the Garrison...for the liberal and zealous efforts they have been making to intro-duce the "innocent gaieties of life" among the society of the place, so dispirited lately by the melancholy occurrences that have taken place; whilst the lower orders of people are enthusiastic in their applause and approbation of the good "buckras." We will be bound that the sojourn of these gentlemen in Morant Bay will do more to humanize the lower orders and to bring about that peace, refine-ment, and contentedness which is so much desired, than all the Courts Martial, Special Commissions, patronising missions, addresses from the Anti-Slavery society, and pattings from *Chamerovzow and Co.*,[9] that have lately been lavished on them.

---

[7] See "Morant Bay (Theatricals)," *Colonial Standard and Despatch* (November 5, 1866).

[8] In his op-ed for the *Daily Gleaner* on the anniversary of the Morant Bay Rebellion, the Reverend Devon Dick notes the contradictory reports in the *Colonial Standard* which support the view that the newspaper reflected both the plantocracy and an emerging middle class: even as it denounced the "bloodthirsty" rebels in the aftermath during the trials one writer praised the rebel ringleader, the Reverend Paul Bogle as a good man, well-respected in the community. See Devon Dick, "Paul Bogle: A Man of Peace," *Daily Gleaner* (October 14, 2003), accessed February 4, 2014, http://jamaica-gleaner.com/gleaner/20031014/cleisure/cleisure3.html.

[9] Louis Chamerovzow was an English anti-slavery campaigner to whom George William Gordon wrote his last letter before his execution, asking that the proceedings against him be publicized. See "Chamerovzow, Louis," in The Oxford Dictionary of National Biography, accessed May 23, 2014, http://www.oxforddnb.com/view/printable/101107.

By the use of euphemisms—the "dispirited" population, the "melancholy occurrences"—the reviewer clearly indicated his understanding of the pacification mission of *Nigger Delineators*: to reconcile angry blacks to the white elite (the "good 'buckras,'") and suppress more protests. It was the carrot in the carrot-and-stick approach. This otherwise self-serving reflection of a planter mouthpiece like the *Colonial Standard* reveals that the white population understood the efficacy of blackface performance in showcasing "the benefits of life under the British flag," as Krista Thompson aptly puts it, at a moment for *both* elites and non-elites, when the country was dealt the blow of Crown Colony rule.[10] Indeed, dialect performance is represented here as a kind of healing force. The white elites could feel reassured that the blacks were being pacified, even as they maintained control of racial representation onstage. They could be reassured that the dialect-speaking blacks represented onstage were "our negroes," even if that dialect—an imitation of African-American vernacular—hardly resembled Jamaican or Caribbean Creole.

Meanwhile, the blacks and browns could view both performance and the gesture of free admission as an acknowledgement of their cultural importance, even as they were denied political rights and cultural expression of their own. In this way dialect performances, particularly ones that featured African-American dialect and cultural "types," could help to smooth over racial and class tensions by displacing them through a comic performance with a similar-yet-different racial context. In other words, from the viewpoint of black and brown Jamaicans, *those* "darkies" are emphatically *not* us; yet, they are familiar enough that we can laugh knowingly at that which is us-yet-not-us. For white Jamaicans, those "darkies" *are*, not us, but ours, and so we too laugh knowingly at what is ours-but-not-us.

In the same month that *Nigger Delineators* took place on the Jamaican stage, both the *Colonial Standard* and the other prominent newspaper, the *Daily Gleaner*, published two Creole texts, supposedly by black women. One a letter, the other a poem, both responded to the reported public comments of the Reverend Samuel Holt, a black minister and farmer who had recently given a public lecture at a Kingston Baptist church. Reverent Holt had visited England to raise money for a Jamaican marketing association, and while there had apparently been asked by the English audience whether or not black men in Jamaica had white wives. The newspaper reported that the Reverend scolded his church audience that "he had the mortification to answer 'No'" and then asked the men, "'Why have you not white wives?'"[11] Errol Hill tells us that Reverend Holt "recommended his people

[10] See Krista Thompson, *An Eye for the Tropics: Tourism, Photography, and Framing the Caribbean Picturesque Picturesque* (Durham and London: Duke University Press, 2006), p. 86.

[11] A BLACK WOMAN, "Mr. Holt at at the 'New Particular' Baptist Chapel," *Colonial Standard and Despatch* (November 19, 1866). The editorial note that precedes "Mr. Holt" describes Mr. Holt and the details of his journey to England. Decades later, a black sugar planter named Felix Holt wrote two articles in the black-owned newspaper the *Jamaica Advocate* which criticized elite planters as preying on black workers: see "Confessions of a Sugar Planter: The Black Man's Burden," *Jamaica Advocate* (September 6, 1902 and October 4, 1902). I thank Patrick Bryan for supplying this reference.

to dress in such a manner as to make them acceptable husbands to the white ladies of Jamaica."[12]

In response the venerable *Daily Gleaner* published a Creole-language letter from QUASHEBA to "Massa Edita," ironically titled "Colour fe Colour," the black rebels' slogan of racial solidarity during the Morant Bay Rebellion. Not to be outdone, three days later the stridently anti-black and pro-planter[13] *Colonial Standard* published a dialect poem titled "Mr. Holt at the 'New Particular' Baptist Chapel" by A BLACK WOMAN."[14] Both letter and poem show remarkable similarity in their mutual desire to enact physical vengeance on black men. Both allude to white figures of terror during the Morant Bay massacres. The rebel slogan "Colour fe Colour" is here inverted to suggest a comedy of black-on-black violence. Its author fulminates that "Parson Holt—him disarve to be tripped to him black black kin [stripped to his black skin,] and all de St. Elezebet black woman ought to flog him tell him dead. Him is worser dan de Marshal Law Ramsy (Provost Marshal Gordon Ramsay, a notorious English officer convicted then acquitted of murder.[15])"

The poet of "Mr. Holt" is, if possible, even more direct:

. . . . . .	. . . .
Him tun him back pon we—him no wanty Black wife—	He's turned his back on us—he doesn't want a Black wife—
tick yah him no hab fe hide from Maroon and Colonel FYFE!	Take care he doesn't have to hide from the Maroons and Colonel FYFE[16]!
But we wi' wait till him cum back na Black Ribba, yerry,	But we will wait for him to come back to Black River, listen,
Den tick yah dem no teck him from bilbo room Go bury!	Then take care they don't take him from the *bilbo room*[17] to bury!

[12] Errol Hill, *The Jamaican Stage* (1992), p. 213.

[13] See Audi Alteram Partem, *Colonial Standard* (November 19, 1866), on the "creed of the negrophilists."

[14] QUASHEBA, "Colour fe Colour," *Daily Gleaner* (November 16, 1866); and A BLACK WOMAN, "Mr. Holt at the 'New Particular' Baptist Church," *Colonial Standard and Despatch* (November 19, 1866).

[15] See *Morning Journal* (November 10, 1866), quoted in "1866: Gordon Ramsay Uses Indecent Language," *Alpha History*, accessed March 15, 2018, http://alphahistory.com/pastpeculiar/1866-gordon-ramsay-indecent-language/.

[16] The Jamaican Maroons were notorious for rounding up and killing blacks who had rebelled in the recent Morant Bay Rebellion, as well as many who had not; they were led by the Scotsman Colonel Alexander Fyfe.

[17] "Bilbo" is derived from sixteenth-century English; a "bilbo" is a long iron bar, a leg-shackle commonly used in prisons, ships, and plantation slavery through the nineteenth century, according to the Oxford English Dictionary. Here it used to mean punishment cell. My thanks to Jean D'Costa for this explanation.

Him may go back na Englant—him may teck All dat trouble, But if him no mine himself him wi' dead like	He may go back to England—he may take all that trouble, But if he doesn't mind himself he will die
Paul Bogle;	like Paul Bogle;
Him may plant as him like, an sell all de day all the Ob him life, But nebba, nebba in dis worl, wi' him get one Buckra wife!	He may plant as he likes, and sell the days of his life, But never, never in this world, will he get a White wife![18]

The anonymous authors of "Colour fe Colour" and "Mr. Holt" were almost certainly white Jamaican men ventriloquizing the voices of black Jamaican women. There are no records of black Jamaican women producing locally published writing during this period. Unlike "Altho' A Slave" and other examples that ventriloquized black women, these ventriloquist dialect narratives have no stake in pretending that the real author is a black woman. Quite the opposite.

White perceptions of black women's pathologically violent nature was instrumental to the authors' intent in these dialect narratives. Black women, poor, peasant black women in particular, were considered by both blacks and whites to be at odds with the Victorian ideal of quiet, subservient, maternal womanhood.[19] White authorities noted with disapprobation the participation of black women in the Rebellion and other disturbances preceding it. "You appear to be a very violent woman," scolded one judge to a black female defendant, while others distastefully observed "the females with their coats tied up for action."[20] By contrast, there is ample historical evidence that white men ventriloquized the voices of black Caribbean women. Indeed, "Quasheba" was a familiar pejorative to denote black women among whites. "Quasheba," after signing her name to her letter adds as postscript, "but you can put any odder name you tink proper." The poem pointedly references Reverend Holt's status as a Baptist preacher, like that of the hanged black rebel Paul Bogle (who, like Reverent Holt, was also a farmer). Their Baptist ministerial credentials gave them both moral authority and middle-class credentials in a denomination that was associated with the blacks, a fact which

[18] A BLACK WOMAN, "Mr. Holt at the 'New Particular' Baptist Chapel," *Colonial Standard and Despatch* (November 19, 1866), partially reproduced here. Translation mostly my own, with thanks to Jean D'Costa and Dorothea Edmondson for clarifications on archaic Creole spelling and pronunciation.
[19] The first black author of Creole literature, Henry Garland Murray, describes black women as violently inclined in terms similar to those of the ventriloquist authors: "With our black girls, it's worse. They want to kick and bite you, and tear out your eye...." See Henry Garland Murray, *Brown Sammy In Search of a Wife* (1874), p. 19.
[20] See Jonathan Dalby, "Precursors to Morant Bay: The Patterns of Popular Protest in Post-Emancipation Jamaica, 1834–1865," pp. 99–129, in *Journal of Caribbean History* 50 (2) (2016), p. 104.

must have been especially galling to whites. Despite brutal suppression and a terrible economic recession, the black middle class was rising. That a black farmer could travel to England in search of new markets like a member of the plantocracy showed an ambition that surely must have been galling to the struggling white creole elite. The rise of the landowning black peasantry, combined with its increasing literacy, was a source of anxiety for the white population.

The increase in literary dialect in the latter half of the nineteenth-century anglophone Caribbean is connected to its increasing association with racial violence. Literary dialect proliferated at moments of social unease or political unrest. Just as the elite newspapers of the post-Emancipation period mirrored elite fears of the flight of black labor in the "overheard" conversations of black women cursing out black man for idleness, so too did the elite newspapers of the volatile 1860s, when British capital fled the Caribbean in search of global markets.[21] The anonymous writers of "Colour fe Colour" and "Mr. Holt" use black working-class women's angry voices to berate black men for their temerity in hoping for white wives[22] and, perhaps more pertinently, daring to try to make money from selling their crops abroad when white planters were struggling.

Both narratives feature explicit violent retribution against black men: jail ("bilbo room"), lynching ("dead like Paul Bogle"), flogging, flaying ("disarve to be tripped to him black 'kin"). Sexual competition and economic competition were very much linked. (A few decades after the Morant Bay trials Robert Love, the black publisher of *The Jamaica Advocate*, noted, "If a man is black, as soon as he has [money], he is declared white; if ignorant, he is declared learned, if vicious he is declared eccentric, if ugly he is declared handsome...The Remedy for the Black Man's Burden is *money*."[23]) The threat contained in the poem's references to the Rebellion leader, the Baptist minister Paul Bogle, as well as the Maroons and Colonel Fyfe, are particularly loaded in 1866. The Maroons and their Scottish commander Colonel Fyfe hunted and executed the rebels remorselessly, as well as other blacks who had not participated, gaining a well-earned reputation for extreme violence and bloodthirstiness. Governor Eyre, who had ordered the repressive measures, had recently been recalled to England by the displeased

---

[21] See Christopher Taylor, *Empire of Neglect: The West Indies in the Wake of British Liberalism* (Durham and London: Duke University Press, 2018).

[22] The theme of interracial marriage as a positive sign of racial advancement was taken up with an earnestness by black male writers in later Caribbean texts. See for example the Trinidadian novel *Rupert Gray* (1907), where the marriage of a black protagonist to a white creole woman is used to express nationalism and racial upliftment; and "A Negro's Christmas Message to His Race in Jamaica" (1899), where the writer, a black Jamaican, writes "We see the intermarriage of the black and white, and they [meaning black men] have shown themselves to be good husbands. There is not one single instance in which it can be proven that a black who has taken a white woman to be his companion has not only treated her with the same love and respect as any white man would.... We love our white friends, and time will come, when by the rapid growth of education, we shall make them like us."

[23] Robert Love, *Jamaica Advocate* (October 4, 1902), cited in Patrick Bryan, *The Jamaican People, 1880–1902* (Mona: University of the West Indies Press, 1991/2000), p. 83.

English government. Jamaican society was still reeling from the repercussions of Morant Bay. Why, at this particular time, would a poem reference the fearsome Maroons, the brutal Provost Ramsay, the relentless Colonel Fyfe, the terrors of the bilbo room, and other signposts of black oppression at the hands of the white elite? If it were declared to be authored by a white, such writing would likely not be considered amusing, even by elite white readers, given the seething racial tensions of the period. However, in the mouths of irate black women the story of Mr. Holt and his white-wife ambitions becomes burlesque, a black-on-black comedy that can be ridiculed and dismissed. Black men like Mr. Holt who aspire beyond their station are put in their proper place by their emasculating black women.

At the same time a complementary strategy to ventriloquizing black women's voices was the use of apparently positive black female images by the white elite. Narrative representations of robust, good-looking black peasant women did double duty. On the one hand they promoted pro-planter views in elite Jamaican newspapers in the post-Emancipation years. On the other they rebutted the lurking criticism that black women were the victims of white male violence. In May 1866, still on the heels of the Rebellion, the *Colonial Standard* published a rebuttal to a critique of its pro-planter politics by noting that the "well-shaped limbs" of black peasant women stood in contrast to the supposed starvation of the peasantry caused by the elite annexation of land.[24] That month the newspaper also published a pastoral account of a mountain hike, which featured a flirtatious encounter between the white correspondent and a saucy bunch of Negro women "with their bright bandannas...each holding herself straight as a dart under her head-load of fruits and vegetables:"

Has it not been said that negresses are ugly? Some may be—some are. But some have the face of the Sphinx, a sweet contemplative face, with dark, lustrous, flashing eyes, and such was the face and such were the eyes of the black mountain nymph, whose breast was now no longer disturbed...Her love token was a bit of chew-stick, with which the black people clean their teeth, and which she said would make mine whiter than her own. As hers glistened like ivory, of course I said that this was not possible; and then there was more merry laughing, and the nymphs went down...at a swinging walk, sending back any number of kind salutations.[25]

The pastoral images of saucy, dialect-speaking "black mountain nymphs" were potent weapons in the battle against the devolution of planter society and the rise of black men. These images refuted that of blacks as enslaved or oppressed victims of rape, brutality, and exploitation. They promoted the view of black women

---

[24] See Audi Alteram Partem, *Colonial Standard* (May 9, 1866).
[25] See A Special Correspondent of The Times, "A Mountain Ride," *Colonial Standard* (May 5, 1866).

as industrious beneficiaries of a bountiful land ably run by whites. They inferred black women to be willing agents in the suppression of traitorous black male agency. Two decades later English writer Anthony Trollope would frame the question of black suffrage in terms of black women's superior attributes: "If black suffrage is to be the rule in Jamaica, I would take it away from the men and give it to the superior sex. The women are the working bees of the hive. They would make a tolerable nation of black amazons, and the babies would not be offered to Jumbi [as in Haiti]."[26]

The poem "Mr. Holt" invokes a similar image of black women's supposed Amazonian fierceness. The smoldering reference to the Maroons is also gendered. Black Jamaican women are implicitly linked to them through the theme of remorseless revenge. (Jamaica's most famous Maroon is, perhaps not surprisingly, a woman: the legendary Nanny.) The Maroon Wars ended in 1739 when the Maroons made a pact with the British to aid the colonial authorities in returning escaped slaves to the plantation and play the role of a native militia. In the succeeding years the Jamaican Maroons were no longer feared by the whites, who now saw their untamed "African" savagery in the service of their own interests. The whites now admired the Maroons as organically moral Noble Savages who knew the true worth of whites and therefore stayed loyal to the colonial government—in contrast to the other blacks, who were not to be trusted.[27] Similarly, although fearless black women had been among the popular leaders of the Morant Bay uprising,[28] they were clearly regarded by whites as the lesser threat compared to black men. Why not set these savage women after upstarts like Mr. Holt, just as the Maroons were deployed to capture the upstart black rebels of Morant Bay? The humor here is very much an inside joke, which reveals the extent to which white creoles understood and spoke Jamaican Creole. The visceral appeal to violence combined with the increasingly dexterous use of literary dialect by white creoles in Jamaica laid the groundwork for the rise of Creole Literature as a black art form.

[26] James Anthony Froude, *The English in the West Indies, or the Bow of Ulysses*. (London: Longman's, Green, & Co., 1888), p. 198. Froude dwells on the image of Haiti as a cannibalistic society where babies are offered to "Jumbi."

[27] For example, the unnamed (but self-identified Jamaican) writer of the article on "'The Jamaican Maroons" in *The New York Tribune* uses heroic descriptions such as "remarkably free and independent carriage and general air," "contented savagery," and "valuable service" in describing the image and actions of the Maroons in the Morant Bay rebellion. See "The Jamaica Maroons," a *New York Tribune* article reproduced in *The Sacramento Daily Union* 96 (101) (November 30, 1898), p. 7.

[28] Royal Commission Report, quoted in Gad Heumann, *The Killing Time: The Morant Bay Rebellion in Jamaica* (Knoxville: University of Tennessee Press, 1993), p. xiii, and cited in http://blogs.princeton.edu/graphicarts/2009/10/album_covering_the_jamaica_reb.html, accessed November 25, 2013. Eyewitnesses said that a black woman named Letitia Geoghagan, whose son's arrest for trespassing on a (long-abandoned) plantation, led the march on Morant Bay and threw the first stone.

Conflict, Creolese, and Quow: The Case of British Guiana

Post-Emancipation British Guiana was in the midst of radical demographic transformation. Indentured laborers from India and China, Portuguese immigrants, black immigrants from Barbados and other Caribbean countries joined native-born blacks, browns, and whites, in addition to the large Amerindian population in the hinterland outside of the towns and villages. Whites were not sole artery of violence. British Guiana's sudden, lurching cultural pluralism gave rise to a constant and unremitting level of suspicion, violence, and social instability between and among the different ethnicities.[29] The society would be riven by a number of disturbances and incidents of civil unrest, sometimes pitting blacks against other non-whites, including the rebellion of indentured Indian laborers against the colonial elite at Leonora in 1869 and Devonshire Castle in 1872, in addition to a series of anti-Portuguese attacks by blacks culminating in the Cent Bread Riots of 1889.[30] The native-born blacks were called creoles and their language Creolese, both names suggestive both of their cultural distinctiveness from other ethnic groups and a recognition of the primacy of their cultural claim on the society. A creole was both someone without a nation—not African, European, or Asian—and the only person who truly belonged in the Caribbean.

Blacks and browns in British Guiana were, like colored populations elsewhere, making tremendous gains in education and ownership, some going for schooling in England. Indeed, the later decades of the nineteenth century saw an unprecedented surge in what might be called an inchoate form of black consciousness on the part of educated black men. This was also tied to a burgeoning activist working-class consciousness in the region, one that was distinctly in opposition to white interests. Black and brown newspaper publishers founded numerous pro-working class, black-and-brown-identified newspapers, such as British Guiana's *The Liberal*, *The Echo*, and *The Creole*; and Jamaica's *The Creole and Record*, and the *Jamaica Advocate*. Eschewing any literary projects that denigrated black people, these newspapers carried no stories, jokes or poems using Creole, although they made frequent use of Scottish and even African-American vernaculars as, perhaps, a form of cultural ventriloquism (*The Jamaica Advocate* articulated its creed of racial equality through its motto, a line from Robert Burns' dialect poem: "A man's a man, for a' that.")[31] Educated black men like Bahamian

---

[29] Brian L. Moore, *Cultural Power Resistance and Pluralism: Colonial Guyana 1838–1900* (Montreal and Mona: McGill-Queen's University Press/University of the West Indies Press, 1995), p. 11.

[30] "Indian Protests for Rights: Pre-Independence," *Guyana Times International* (May 25, 2012), accessed December 16, 2020, Indian Protests for Rights: Pre Independence—Guyana Times International—The Beacon of Truth; Nigel Westmaas, "Revolutionary Centennial: Guyana's 1905 Rebellion," *Against the Current: A Socialist Journal* 114 (January/February 2005), accessed December 16, 2020, Nigel Westmaas—Against the Current.

[31] See "Notice to Correspondents," *The Creole* (December 13, 1856).

Robert Love and British Guianese S. Powell Thompson travelled around the Caribbean spreading politically radical ideas of black empowerment through education and business opportunities through their lectures and newspapers.[32] Afro-Trinidadian John Jacob Thomas and Jamaica's Thomas Russell challenged the widely held perception that Caribbean dialect was just so much irrational gibberish by publishing the first philological studies of Creole ever seen in the Caribbean.[33] As Faith Smith frames it, Thomas sought to "tame" the working-class energies that radicalized his work and to bring them in line with modern conceptions of the nation.

In British Guiana the *Working Man* newspaper was established in 1872 primarily for a multiracial working class readership. Intended for "every person who was not an idler of all races, black, mixed and Indian, except whites," its editorial board asserted that its columns were open "to all without leaning to any,"[34] The other colored newspapers, *The Creole*, *The Daily Liberal*, and *The Echo*, all spoke out forcefully against the racism in the educational system and land distribution policies and urged blacks to vote.[35] Black men, former laborers on the estates, had bought abandoned plantation elites, thereby angering the former owners. The colored press, not shy about jumping into the fray, pointed out the inequity in the fact that while land purchases by white planters were subsidized by the government this was not the case with the former laborers, who were being "accused of industry" by what it regarded as the dissolute white elite.[36] A letter writer in *The Creole* condemned the editor of a white newspaper for arguing that the colonial government should "educate Quashie a little, but do not spend much money to give him fair learning... or Quash would use big language towards us and refuse to cut cane."[37] White and colored newspapers were the voice of their readers, and those readers were set in opposition to each other. The tension between blacks and whites in British Guiana mirrored conflicts on multiple levels of class, color, and ethnicity, as the old elite desperately tried to keep a lid on the rising tides of black and non-white cultural and economic power. Much of this tension played

---

[32] See "S. Powell Thompson—Lecturer and Teacher, from Guyana," which cites *Daily Gleaner* (December 28, 1870), accessed January 29, 2021, https://sites.google.com/site/moreinterestingjamaicans/s-powell-thompson.

[33] John Jacob Thomas, *Theory and Practice of Creole Grammar* (1869); Thomas Russell, *Etymology of Jamaican Grammar* (1868). While there is no evidence to suggest that Thomas was black or brown, my reading of his work in the Introduction suggests that this is likely.

[34] See Nigel Westmaas, "*The Working Man*: Profile of a 19th Century Working Class Newspaper" (February 26, 2002), accessed April 25, 2014, http://www.guyanacaribbeanpolitics.com/rodneyite/commentary.html. Westmaas notes that the *Royal Gazette*, associated with the white elites, was hostile to its arrival, and dismissed *The Working Man* as a soon-to-vanish upstart: "we will not congratulate this bantling [sic] on its birth, knowing well from the fate of several of its kindred what a wretched existence it is sure to have and how glad it will be, in the course of a few months to step aside and die."

[35] See Nigel Westmaas, *A Mirror of Social and Political Ferment: The Newspaper Press of Guyana, 1839–1899* (Ann Arbor: dissertation, 2006).

[36] Editorial, *The Creole* (January 24, 1857); Letter to the Editor, No. 7, *The Creole* (January 3, 1857).

[37] See COLOUR, "Education of Quashie," Letter to the editor, *The Creole* (February 17, 1882).

out through the interplay of Creolese and standard English. The broad spectrum of British Guianese society spoke or understood Creolese. Creolese would develop into a literary form against the backdrop of upheaval and instability that characterized post-Emancipation British Guiana.

Like its Jamaican counterpart, Caribbean scholars recognized early on that Creolese was a language in its own right.[38] As the Indian population became established in post-Emancipation society, Creolese acquired Indian dialect words (Bhojpuri, for example) and became the language of the Indo-Guyanese population as well.[39] Literary dialect indicated a few things for Guyanese readers, one of which it allowed them to gauge the level of assimilation of the new arrivals. Elite newspapers like the *Argosy* regularly featured Creolese-speaking Indo-Guyanese, Portuguese subjects (often stereotyped as shopkeepers named "Manny"), as well as Creolese-speaking "Barbajian" or native whites. Typically the immigrants were featured speaking Creolese in news items, but not in stories, cartoons, sketches, or other literary venues. Otherwise sober news reports of disturbances on the sugar estates or court proceedings strategically used Creolese to indicate the lesser intelligence or the violent inclinations of the participants, usually Indian laborers and blacks.[40] One such defendant, an Indian called Rughbur, threatened the overseer whose testimony convicted him by warning, "When I come out of jail whatever happen no body must be surprised!"[41] Another *Argosy* cartoon titled "A Paying Business" shows a "Manny" and his black customer bartering in Creolese (Figure 2.2).

Literary dialect was also used to comment, disapproving, on the inversion of traditional class distinctions. One cartoon, ominously titled "What is Approaching," highlights the impoverishment of the old sugar plantation elite via dialect (Figure 2.1). A vulgar, Creolese-speaking white "digger" refuses to hire the submissive, well-spoken plantation owner, telling him, "I like all my clerk with 'Honorable' befo' dem name."[42] But sometimes dialect was also used as a comeuppance of sorts to highfalutin white characters who spoke in standard English. Black women were almost inevitably the represented as the masters of the Creolese put-down. In one such cartoon, a black washerwoman curses her white female employer who has cheated her of wages: "only one ting I isn't hable to wash clean ma'am,

---

[38] J. Cruikshank, *Black Talk* (1916); pp. 6–12; J. van Sertima, *The Creole Tongue* (Demerara, 1905), pp. 4–5, cited in Brian L. Moore, *Cultural Power, Resistance and Pluralism, Colonial Guyana 1838–1900* (Montreal and Kingston: McGill-Queen's University Press, The Press University of the West Indies, 1995), p. 92, footnote 31; as well as Samuel Augustus Mathews, *The Willshire Squeeze* (1822), which features Creole proverbs from Demerara.

[39] Hubert Devonish, "Nature of African-East Indian Contact in 19th Century Guyana: The Linguistic Evidence," seminar paper, Department of History, University of the West Indies, Mona (1991); H. V. P. Bronkhurst, *Among the Hindus and Creoles of British Guiana* (London: T. Woolmer, 1888), both quoted in Brian Moore, *Cultural Pluralism* (1995), pp. 162–164.

[40] Entremets, *Argosy* (November 28, 1891).

[41] "Sweet Mouth," Court Reports Before the Docket, *Argosy* (December 26, 1891).

[42] Argus, "What is Approaching," *Argosy* (October 17, 1891).

WHAT IS APPROACHING.

Digger :—An' who is you ?

Applicant :—I am a poor man, Sir, owner of a lot of sugar estates, and I humbly ask you to give me a clerkship on one of your placers.

Digger :—Me placer full o' dem plantah a'ready, and now I does take only membahs ob de Co't o' Policy. I like all my clerk with 'Honorable' befo' dem name.

ARGUS.

Figure 2.1 Argus, "What is Approaching," *Argosy* (October 17, 1891).

and dat is *you charatah*."[43] Another common theme was fighting black women who cursed and threatened violence. ("'Jail! Look at me good! Me look like a ooman who'fraid de jail?'"[44]) As in Jamaica, in post-Emancipation black women were featured more than any other ethnic or gender group in local stories featuring Creolese-speaking characters. Beyond court reports and cartoons, the newspapers published long-form Creolese narratives that further ensconced Creolese as the national language. One of these was a clever comic short story written in

[43] Argus, "Settling with the Washer," *Argosy* (October 24, 1891).
[44] Argus, "No Indeed!," *Argosy* (August 29, 1891).

C.S. Argus

A PAYING BUSINESS.

Customer :—Manyell, I wants a jill salt-fish, and you muss gi'e me a bit of cheese, a few match, a taste of butter, and lend me you' baxe to cut me firewood. You knows I am reg'lar customah.

Manoel : Me Gad ! Before so I sa gie you the saltfish fa not'ing.

#459 in the National Archives Collection. Ca. 1891.

Selected from the series by an anonymous cartoonist (initials "C.S.", pen-name "Argus") which appeared in the Argosy newspaper from 1885 to the end of the nineteenth century.

Figure 2.2 Argus, "A Paying Business," *Argosy* (ca. 1891).

Image courtesy of the National Archives of Guyana. My thanks to John Rickford and Nigel Westmaas for reproducing this image from John Rickford, ed., A Festival of Guyanese Words (Georgetown: University of Guyana, 1978), p. 205.

the language of the King James bible but from the viewpoint of a Creolese-speaking "Ethiopian handmaiden" who opined such sentiments as "'look-he dey, he jumping like a jigga flea."[45]

Despite the multiracial Creolese speakers represented in its newspapers, in British Guiana as in Jamaica ventriloquist dialect was still the preserve of white authors intent on using literary blackface to opine on unsavory or racially sensitive subjects. Names of West African origin like "Beke" or "Quow" were popular handles for would-be literary gentlemen in the colony, who wrote either mostly or entirely in Creolese. "Beke" was, like buckra or backra, another African word for white. "Quow" was originally a common African day name which, in British Guiana, became a derogatory term for an albino or otherwise light-skinned black person.[46] Like their literary forebears elsewhere, these white writers also saw the "negro language" as a vehicle for their own literary ambitions, but unlike the ventriloquists of an earlier generation. X Beke, Quow and other white writers wanted their audience to know that they were white "Africanized" men. Dialect texts thus constituted a kind of bell-weather for white identity. Over the course of a century whites become with the idea of themselves as innately Caribbean, and not merely displaced British subjects. By the late nineteenth century these white authors of Creole narratives make no secret of their attempts at creative authorship through black speech. Their economic and political interests were often in conflict with that of the British colonial government. The search for an indigenous literary therefore mirrored white creole desires for political and economic autonomy.

The two most notable writers in this pseudonymous tradition are Edward Cordle of Barbados and Michael McTurk, the aforementioned "Quow," of British Guiana. As was consistent with the anonymous white authors of the pre-Emancipation period, both Cordle and McTurk chronicled black urban, not rural, life.[47] Blacks flocked to cities in the post-Emancipation era, but their presence in cities and not on plantations was also a source of tension with white elites. Whereas Murray maintained a gauzy focus on rural black and brown culture of

---

[45]   Argus, Entremets, *Argosy* (November 7, 1891).

[46]   See X. Beke, *West Indian Yarns* (Georgetown, 1884); Michael McTurk, *Essays and Fables in Prose and Verse, Written in the Vernacular of the Creoles of British Guiana* (Demerara/Georgetown: Argosy, 1877/1899). Paula Burnett explains the changing meaning of "Quow" in *The Penguin Book of Caribbean Verse* (1986), p. 375.

[47]   Edward Alexander Cordle, a white creole printer for the Bridgetown *The Weekly Recorder*, published his verse ballads throughout the 1880s. His anthology of poems, *Overheard*, was published in Barbados posthumously in 1903. Although he published under his own name, Cordle's poems feature no outside white narrator who "overhears" black speech: instead they feature two blacks, usually two women, discussing local issues or romantic conflicts, with the same accompanying cartoon image of two black peasant women gossiping. These are known as the "Lizzie and Joe" poems, Lizzie and Joe being the two black working class couple whose lives are chronicled through their own voices. Like the white writers before him, Cordle, a classics scholar, was clearly fascinated by the erotic lives of the black working class. Many of the Joe and Lizzie poems feature infidelity, jealousy, and violence. Their most salient feature, however, is the one that has become a staple of dialect poetry into the present moment: the use of the fictional narrator who is addressing a friend—usually a woman.

yesteryear, Cordle and McTurk dwelt at length on contemporary blacks in Bridgetown and Georgetown respectively. McTurk is the second anglophone Caribbean author, after Murray, to publish a work almost entirely in Creolese. His first book, *Essays and Fables in Prose and Verse, written in the Vernacular of Creoles of British Guiana*, first published in 1877, proved so popular it was re-issued two more times, in 1881 and 1899.[48]

Although English, Michael McTurk's family had a long history in British Guiana. His father had left England to work in the colony, and although he was raised in Liverpool, McTurk himself returned as a young man to the country and worked in various capacities: as a stipendiary magistrate, a geologist, and as a local commentator. He was already a well-known character in British Guiana before he became Quow. It is likely, therefore, that McTurk's readers knew Quow's real identity. The title of his obituary upon his death in 1915 emphasizes his ubiquity in national life: "End of an Extraordinary Career. Intrepid Bushman and Fearless Explorer. Hero of Boundary Dispute. Once Sentenced to Death. Story of an Adventurous Life."[49]

McTurk utilized the common literary device of two friends talking or corresponding to set up his Creolese verses. Quow pens a series of ballad-like letters to his friend Jimmis, usually discussing local affairs. The character of Quow is described as a white-haired old black man who frequently expresses exasperation at the errant ways of the younger generation. Through Quow, McTurk expresses his own views on the new dispensation for blacks as they acquire more education and more rights. He provides a gloss for several of the Creole phrases he uses. This suggests an elite white or "white enough" audience—the typical readership for a flagship newspaper in the late-nineteenth-century Caribbean. (Although the *Argosy* was likely read by all literate populations, there were several newspapers that catered to different ethnic groups.[50]) Although McTurk's target audience must have been familiar with Creole, its literary form was still fairly new. Or perhaps one of the affectations of the white and light-skinned elite was that it needed a gloss at all.

McTurk's work as a stipendiary magistrate meant, more so than other white ventriloquists, he needed a racial cover for his inflammatory views of the

---

[48] McTurk's 1877 edition was published under the title, *Essays and Fables in Creole English*; see "Mitchell's West Indian Bibliography," 11th edition, accessed February 8, 2021, Mitchell's West Indian Bibliography.

[49] "Death of Mr. Michael McTurk, CMG…," *Argosy* (January 8, 1915).

[50] Newspapers servicing the different ethnic groups of society proliferated in late-nineteenth century British Guiana. While the white elites had *The Argosy*, *The Chronicle*, and *The Royal Gazette*, the educated colored community had its own newspapers: *The Echo*, *The Daily Liberal*, and the *Creole*. The Portuguese community had its own newspapers as well. However, it is likely that the *Argosy* was also read by blacks, coloreds, and other non-white or non-elite segments of the community. See Nigel Westmaas, *A Mirror of Social and Political Ferment: The Newspaper Press of Guyana, 1839–1899* (Ann Arbor: dissertation, 2006).

population over which he presided. He was supposed to represent an objective judicial system at a time when the black and colored population complained of the biased treatment they received in the courts compared with other communities.[51] Under colonial law in Guyana public servants were forbidden from commenting on affairs of the government in the press. Consequently, the letters to the editor column was "weaponized" in British Guiana, as elsewhere in the Caribbean, by white civil servants whose monikers everyone knew.[52] By speaking as an elderly black man who might be forgiven his strong opinions on his own community, however, Quow would be allowed more latitude. The ventriloquizing device allows McTurk to discourse freely on volatile racial subjects in a humorous vein in a way that he could not as a magistrate.

With titles such as "Dem Wotless Gaagetown Nagah" ("Those Worthless Georgetown Niggers") and "Quow on the Degeneracy of the Rising Race," many of the poems express a disdain for, or more accurately an outright hostility towards, the new generation of socially mobile blacks. Young blacks are depicted as striving—vainly—for education and higher status. They are also depicted as violent and jealous of the industrious Portuguese, Chinese, and Barbadian immigrants, and—in a continuation of an old theme—foolishly obsessed with looking fashionable. Using his pseudonym to indulge in freewheeling social commentary and ridicule of non-whites, McTurk pokes fun at foolish "coolies" (Indians) and "Chinee," but never whites of any kind. He reserves his most acidic—and constant—criticism for blacks. He berates young black men for breaking into the Portuguese merchant stores (doubtless a reference to the continuing tensions between the two groups after the Cent Bread Riots of 1889[53]), falsely accusing the Chinese of "libbin' pon tief," and denigrating the Barbadians as "worthless niggers." Quow, writing in Creolese, makes a point of ridiculing the Barbadians for speaking in pompous, formal English even while carrying knives. Black women he dismisses as "dem wotloss 'oman a Gaagetown—dem call demse'f 'diamond gall'" ("those worthless women in Georgetown—who call themselves 'diamond girl.'") The native-born blacks are implicitly and explicitly contrasted to the hardworking

[51] Nigel Westmaas, *A Mirror of Social and Political Ferment: The Newspaper Press of Guyana* (2006), p. 84.

[52] See Nigel Westmaas, "'Dear Editor:' A Brief Social History of the Guyanese Newspaper Letter Column [sic]," *Starbroek News* (August 8, 2010).

[53] The Cent Bread Riots of 1889 erupted over black Creoles' grievances against the Portuguese merchant community, which were accused of routinely cheating black customers yet receiving more favorable treatment from the authorities than blacks. McTurk conveniently leaves out black accusations of Portuguese cheating, to focus on Portuguese accusations of black thievery. McTurk was published by the *Argosy*, which was known to be a vehicle for the conservative white plantocracy, and which provided very pro-Portuguese accounts of the riots. Very different accounts of the riots appeared under anonymous black-identified pseudonyms such as "Sambo" in *The Echo* and other colored newspapers. See Nigel Westmaas, *A Mirror of Social and Political Ferment* (2006), p. 84; and Odeen Ishmael, "The Cent Bread Riots," *The Guyana Story: From Earliest Times to Independence* (Xlibris, 2013), pp. 216–17.

immigrants, whose social or professional ambitions, or mere presence in the city, he does not question as he does with the blacks.

Urban black culture is specifically held up to ridicule: blacks ("creoles") are mocked as unable to handle farm tools, even as they strain to learn cricket and the piano. Quow laments to Jimmis that "when me an' you bin creole, Jim, awe no' bin a do like dat." ("When you and me act creole, Jim, we don't act like that."[54]) He is particularly hostile to educated or fashionable blacks, male or female, who pretentiously aspire to be more than they are:

> Dem boy can' handle shubble, an' cutlish da bista dem han',
> Dem gal can' handle hoe-'tick, an' none a dem wan' fo' l'arn,
> Dem boy a 'tudy crikit befo' dem prapah barn,
> An' dem gal a nack piana so têh dem fingah full wi' carn.

> Go take wa'k a Gaagetown Sunday, you sa' see somet'ing fo' full you yiye,
> Da fashin wa' dem a go on, dem creole gal an' boy
> …Dem a big-big lady an' gen'lman dem…
> Dem complexshun berry delicate, dem can' wa'k biout parasole,
> But dem face 'tan jus' like w'itewash 'pan tap piece fiah-cole,
> Big ring full 'pon dem fingah têh dem no hable ben' dem han'.

> Those boys can't handle a shovel, and a cutlass blisters their hand,
> Those girls can't handle a hoe-stick, and none of them want
> to learn,
> Those boys are studying cricket before they're proper born,
> And those girls knock on the piano until their fingers fill
> with corns.

> Go take a walk in Georgetown on Sundays, and you will see
> something to fill your eye,
> The fashion that they go on with, those creole girls and boys
> …They're such important ladies and gentlemen…
> Their complexion is very delicate, they can't walk without a
> parasol,
> But their face looks just like whitewash on top of a piece of
> fire-coal.
> Big ring full on their finger until they're not able to bend
> their hand.[55]

---

[54] Michael McTurk, "Quow on the Degeneracy of the Rising Race," in Michael McTurk, *Essays and Fables in Prose and Verse, Written in the Vernacular of the Creoles of British Guiana* (1877/1899), p. 39.
[55] Michael McTurk, "Quow on the Degeneracy of the Rising Race," in Michael McTurk, *Essays and Fables in Prose and Verse, Written in the Vernacular of the Creoles of British Guiana* (1877/1899), pp. 39–40.

McTurk makes a particular point of denigrating as effeminate what he views as black male affectations. Black masculinity is linked in inverse fashion to black education. He sneers at young, literate black men with desk jobs unconnected from physical labor as "dem pashuma-two-bit-nagah-boy wid pen behin' dem yase" ("those withered/weakling two-bit nigger boys with pens behind their ears") and "Aunty-men" (which McTurk glosses as "hermaphrodite" but means homosexual in the contemporary Caribbean). The virulence of the critique is pointedly linked to black men's earlier status as enslaved. Quow mockingly asks of young black men, "Dem bin drunk fo' make dem mannish so da time awe bin slabe?" ("Have they been drinking to make them so macho since the time we've been slaves?") The logic is contradictory but the vaguely threatening implication is clear: young black men with education ("pen behin' dem yase") are effeminate, and those without are merely acting tough with borrowed machismo. It was not so long ago that both kinds of black men, educated and not, were forced to be deferential.

Although Quow doesn't make distinctions between browns and blacks, his satirical "Repote ob de Meeting Ob de Kullad Gen'lmans Aglicultulal and Debating Society" ("Report of the Meeting of the Colored Gentlemen's Agricultural and Debating Society") is illustrative of the general theme that blacks, whether "colored" or otherwise, are being pretentious when they aspire to be more than laborers. The "colored gentlemen" are a set of pompous blow-hards who do not actually say anything but immediately start rejecting bills before they have been submitted.

A consistent thread in all of Quow's poetry is his declaration that colonial initiatives in educating the black majority would be better spent in putting them in prison and sending them back to the fields:

> [A] money wa' bacra da wase 'pon heddication, bettah dem put
> um 'pon Jail,
> Nagah no know bout heddication, but dem sabby 'bout lick 'pon
> dem tail
> ....A hope dem put cat 'pon ayou 'kin, an' gi'e um to ayou ha'd,
> ...mazaroni da ayou Englan', an' Jail da ayou callege,
>
> A deh ayou a get'n fo' l'arn ayou witless knowledge.
> The money that whites waste on your education, better they put
> you in Jail,
> Niggers don't know about education, but they know about licks
> on their tail.
> ....I hope they put the cat o'nine [whip] on your skin, and give
> them to you hard,

> ... [M]azaruni is your England, and Jail is your college,
> It's there that you'll get to learn your worthless knowledge.[56]

It is not hard to spot the source of McTurk's venom toward urban blacks. It is their flight from the plantations to the metropole, with all of its presumed benefits: wealth, education, commerce, white culture. Mazaruni, a remote rural area of the country, and England, the sophisticated metropole, are pointedly contrasted. This opposition is meant to underscore the glaring gap between where blacks *should* be, in McTurk's estimation, and where they *want* (and had already started) to go to further their educational and commercial prospects. The rhetorical violence of Quow's ballads, and the physical threats implied (jail, cat o'nine whippings) are not anomalies but rather a mirror of white hostility towards the emerging black professional class, whose rise threatened elite interests and hold on power.

Counterpoint: The Black "Africans"

Across the anglophone Caribbean, the destabilizing of black identity from rural to urban, from illiterate to educated, is marked by the increasing use of dialect by whites to criticize or even threaten the black community in the late nineteenth century. The black and brown middle class understood the rhetorical insults lobbed by Quow, Beke, and other white "Africans," and did not let them go unchallenged. In British Guiana, home to several newspapers owned by men of color, these rebuttals took the form of editorials and letters to the editor. With monikers such as "A Negro," "Africanus," "Quaco," and even "Sambo," men of color penned elaborate rebuttals to white insults in *The Argosy* in the most florid Victorian prose, their "Victorianese" itself a direct rebuttal of white ventriloquist dialect. By out-Englishing the whites, they implied that they, as men of color, were the authentic gentlemen of letters, not these white imposters hiding behind "black" voices.

One would-be letter writer, "Quaco," made the mistake of writing in dialect to make his point. This earned him a scolding from the editor of *The Creole*: "'Quaco.' If you will write in your own style and diction, your effusions may find a place in the paper, and your object, which we dare say is a good one, will be better served thus than by mimicking the ignorant."[57] The editor's assumption is that "Quaco" is an educated black or brown man imitating a poor black man.

Better received were the kinds of letter that displayed the kind of elaborate prose admired by Victorians across the Atlantic world. Displaying precisely this kind of "Victorianese" in a letter to editor of *The Echo* in 1892, "Negro" responds

---

[56] Michael McTurk, "Dem Wotless Gaagetown Nagahs," in Michael McTurk, *Essays and Fables in Prose and Verse, Written in the Vernacular of the Creoles of British Guiana* (1877/1899), p. 33. Translation is mine.

[57] Notice to Correspondents, *The Creole* (December 13, 1856).

to white denunciations of black culpability in a recent disturbance. He begins by deploring "fastidious individuals" whose "highest delectation is to disseminate aspersions of a people, whose simple crime is – being black:"

> The spirit…of negro slavery…is old, bed ridden and impotent. It has grown, thereby, irritable and malignant…convulsed by periodic nightmares at the phantasmal penumbra of some ill-treated, now long departed…venting up spleen at the expense of the children of a people it had wronged.[58]

Just as Quow pointedly mocked educated brown "gentlemen" through the dialect ("Repote ob de Meeting Ob de Kullad Gen'lmans Aglicultulal and Debating Society"), twenty-first-century readers may reflexively dismiss the grandiloquence of "Negro's" writing as an absurd imitation of the gentlemen of letters model. Brian Moore describes the black and brown middle class of the nineteenth-century Caribbean as in "cultural self-denial,"[59] but as Bridget Brereton points out, educated people of color were not wealthy, were not planters or landowners, had few businesses, no vote, and little political or economic influence. What they did have, however, was "one attribute which the mass of the population did not have, and which the society, as a whole, valued: and that was cultural and intellectual skills. They elevated 'culture' into a supreme value because…this was the only field in which they appeared at an advantage in the society."[60]

Understanding their use of language in the context of what their class lacked, therefore, we might re-interpret the supposed mimicry of the colored middle class as a kind of saturated imitation, its superfluousness a form of rebuttal in the war over literary dialect that was being waged, subtly or explicitly, across the region. Despite the increasing popularity of vernacular literary and musical forms of entertainment across all classes and ethnicities, browns and blacks remained suspicious of literary dialect's legacy of racial insult. The result of this legacy was that people of color policed the use of dialect within their own ranks. The question of who deployed literary dialect, and why, was paramount in determining its aesthetic value. A writer of color who wrote literary dialect for populations of color was navigating a minefield of assumptions. Although educated, the members of the black and brown middle class still viewed literary dialect as a weapon of the elite which could be used against their own community, even when written by one of their own. That assumption would change in the twentieth century, but the seeds of change were planted in the post-Emancipation era through vernacular popular culture initiated and promoted by people of color.

---

[58] Negro, Letter to the editor, *The Creole* (June 1892).

[59] Brian L. Moore, *Race, Power and Social Segmentation in Colonial Society: Guyana after Slavery 1838–1891* (Philadelphia: Gordon and Breach Science Publishers Inc., 1987), pp. 131–2.

[60] Bridget Brereton, *Race Relations in Colonial Trinidad, 1870–1900* (Cambridge: Cambridge University Press, 1979), p. 94.

3

The Charles Dickens of Jamaica

In 1877 Henry Garland Murray died from a recurring fever picked up in Panama a few years earlier. He was, according to the country's leading newspaper, "justly regarded as the 'Charles Dickens of Jamaica.'" Effusively eulogized, the all-round popular performer had electrified audiences across the island with his dialect stories.[1] Black, white, and brown, elite and not, everybody came to hear Murray. A highly educated "colored" man, as he described himself, Murray moved easily between the registers of the Queen's English and the most rural intonations of Jamaican dialect in a dazzling display of "bad" grammar.[2] No one had quite seen his like before, and he packed them in.

His fellow journalists loved him. "The truth is Mr. Murray's peculiar gift is that of genius—the highest a man can have," gushed one. "Absolutely unequalled," proclaimed another. Murray's work was lauded as both "peculiarly Jamaican" yet "universal" in appeal. Reviewers understood that they were witnessing the birth of a national literature.[3] Yet, despite his local celebrity, and the throngs of prosperous well-wishers who crowded his funeral, Henry Garland Murray died in absolute poverty. Subscriptions were taken up to aid his surviving widow and children, who faced destitution. It was a fate he had always feared.

Henry Garland Murray's life and work represents a critical juncture in the history of Creole literature and performance. A well-educated black man—for, despite his self-description, I conclude that he was likely black, not brown (at least not according to normative Caribbean categories)—Murray was born sometime around the end of slavery in Jamaica. He lived through the Morant Bay Rebellion in 1865; traveled to foreign countries to extend his craft; and, most importantly, authored the first Creole story with a colored narrator published in the anglophone Caribbean. The story of how and under what circumstances Murray labored reveals the genre's complex origins. An analysis of his stories uncovers his own difficult position and strategies as a non-white author who lived, precariously, by his craft. We gain insight into the desires of his multiple audiences, an

---

[1] Obituary, *Daily Gleaner* (January 30, 1877), p. 5.

[2] "Coloured" is an ambiguous term in this context, and could be dependent on social status. Although Murray implies that he is brown, it also could mean that he did not see himself as "guinea-black" (that is, an illiterate, poor, "uncivilized" black.)

[3] Review [*Brown Sammy*], *Daily Gleaner* (November 2, 1874); Obituary, *Daily Gleaner* (January 30, 1877), p. 5.

Creole Noise: Early Caribbean Dialect Literature and Performance. Belinda Edmondson, Oxford University Press.
© Belinda Edmondson 2022. DOI: 10.1093/oso/9780192856838.003.0004

assortment of classes, races, and even nationalities. Murray's trajectory brings together the many disparate thematic strands in the development of the Caribbean's Creole literary and performative tradition. His career reveals the influence of commerce, travel, and the looming presence of U.S. culture. It exemplifies the era's conflicts over racial tensions, racial stereotypes, and racial uplift. Taken together, Murray's life and work shines a light on the limits of education for black people in a society where "pure" or authentic blackness meant *lack* of education, illiteracy, and poverty, while inauthentic blackness—blackness in appearance only—meant the possibility of wealth and status.

Five years before he died, Henry Garland Murray packed his bags and left Kingston for a "flying visit" to Boston and the New England area.[4] Already a national celebrity in Jamaica, he hoped to take his show on the road. Murray wanted to reap more significant profits from his singular talent. He was in every respect the most prominent symbol of what black and brown people had achieved only a few decades out of slavery. His varied career illustrates his multiple talents. A son of a "respectable and worthy citizen" of Montego Bay, Murray was a gifted student whose ambition to write had started early: he had started his own newspaper as a child.[5] He embarked on a career that was a stepping-stone for many blacks, as a teacher at Kingston's prominent Mico School, founded for the education of the formerly enslaved. Murray was, according to his obituary, a teetotaler of "strict temperance principles" and a member of the multiracial Friendly Society Lodge in his native Montego Bay as well as other Masonic and benevolent orders in the capital of Kingston, where he socialized with some of the country's wealthiest men. From teaching Murray moved on to journalism, and became a reporter for Montego Bay's *Cornwall Chronicle*, then a reporter and editor of Kingston's *Morning Chronicle* and, finally, the publisher of his very own, albeit short-lived, newspaper, *Murray's Daily News*. A driven man, Murray moved consistently upwards in the small but growing ranks of the black and brown middle class. Unfortunately gentility did not guarantee financial security. Especially for black and brown people.

American Adventure: Mr. Murray Goes to Boston

Murray had to provide for his wife and five children. And as a performer he wanted to expand his horizon. Friends and patrons had encouraged him to audition for the Boston Lyceum. If he succeeded in procuring a contract, Murray

---

[4] William Wells Brown, *The Rising Son: or, The Antecedents and Advancement of the Colored Race* (Boston: A.G. Brown & Co., 1874), p. 548. Murray left sometime in September 1872, returning before November 1872. Reviews of his trip date from November 1872.

[5] Obituary, *Daily Gleaner* (January 30, 1877), p. 5.

would join the lucrative lecturing circuit on the eastern seaboard of the United States. More was riding on Murray's success abroad than his own financial security. The broad spectrum of Jamaican society had an interest in promoting a black performer's successful international career. Colored society for obvious reasons would wish to see its own reflection in the rarefied circles of international celebrity. Yet the white elite had its own investments as well. Jamaica's image abroad was defined by its impoverishment in the aftermath of sugar's dominance and the infamously brutal policies of the colonial administration during the international scandal of the Morant Bay Rebellion. The white elite constantly complained of the inaccurate portraits of the oppressed black peasantry trafficked in the international media.[6] Coming from a man of African descent, Murray's pastoral images of black peasant life during slavery were seen as particularly effective in combating these pernicious images. The white elite received these images as balm to recent foreign critiques. They hailed his readings as evincing a "deep vein of patriotic sentiment." Coming on the heels of the Morant Bay Rebellion, an oral narrative of black life by a black man, rendered in the language of the people, did a form of cultural welding in the riven society. It incorporated the slave past not as a vicious racial conflict but as a pastoral elegy of times gone by that nonetheless articulated the society's fundamental Africaneity; both whites and non-whites could enter into such a national narrative. The reviewers in the plantocratic *Colonial Standard and Despatch* suggested at various times that Murray's performances were precisely what was needed, both to "educate" the population into patriotism and thus make it virtuous and to administer "correct" views of the country abroad:

…[W]e also hope that at no distant day Mr. Murray may be enabled to enlighten other lands with correct views of Jamaica Manners and Customs, and he himself an example; that ability and genius are not quite extinct even in this distant and not over-rated Colony…[O]ne good result of an able and eloquent delineation of national character, will be to diffuse throughout the mass of our population stronger local attachments…a warmer and deeper feeling may well be looked for in a People's grateful breast as they experience, under the influence of such beneficient teaching, the stir and glow of that fervid patriotism which is the incentive to public virtue, and the basis of all real prosperity.[7]

As a journalist with performance credentials Murray was particularly suited for the Boston Lyceum. He was used to traveling for work. After the failure of his

---

[6] See "America," *Colonial Standard and Despatch*, (May 7, 1866); also Audi Alteram Partem, (November 19, 1866).

[7] Murray's performance was given as a benefit for the Kingston Reading and Literary Society. See "Mr. Murray's Lecture," *Colonial Standard and Despatch* (October 25, 1869). See also the review of Murray's earlier lecture in "Mr. Murray's Lecture," *Colonial Standard and Despatch* (April 26, 1869).

newspaper he had moved to the Isthmus of Panama sometime in the 1860s, where he had honed his elocutionary abilities performing for the migrant Jamaican population.[8] While his contemporaries gave "lectures," a description which emphasized their literary authority, Murray referred to his performances modestly as "readings."[9] The difference was telling. Nineteenth-century performers hoping for a well-heeled, educated audience habitually used the term "lecture" rather than performance, and yet these *were* performances—full of all the attributes of theater, but delivered in a format that was considered learned. Murray was a respectable member of a race that was always on trial, it seemed, for lack of gentility one way or another—intemperance, boorish behavior, bad language. A black man in the business of entertainment received more than ordinary disapproval. While an entertainer or performer might be considered someone not in the ranks of the genteel classes, in the mid-nineteenth century Caribbean, as in the United States and Britain, a lecturer was almost by definition an educator. The title of "lecturer" therefore had more than the usual resonance for people of color, in that it gave license to a black man to perform as an entertainer without descending in status.

Murray "lectured" on a wide variety of topics, usually amusing local customs of an earlier, often enslaved, generation, delivered with a comic angle and a proverb or a moral attached, such as "Spelling Bees in Olden Times" and "Muster Day in Olden Times." His performances combined vernacular and standard grammar prose, often focusing on African-derived customs or characters: "Eboe John," "John Canoes," "Anancy's Grave," "Feedin' Perrit [Spirit]: A Lecture Illustrative of Jamaica Mythology," "Cropover Rejoicings," "Congo Sammy," "Coromantee William," or "Captain Cuffy's Last Voyage." Although mostly comic, many of these had a sentimental, pastoral tone. For example, his description of the African Eboe John's love of his "green hillside" neatly straddles pro-slavery arguments that enslaved Africans were happy while acknowledging their alternate spiritual beliefs and deep yearnings for the African homeland: "But John loved the scenery...because it reminded him of that which had been the 'green spot of all the earth' to him— the home of his free boyhood in the far-off Eboe land....He believes he is going to the Eboe land...to be 'gathered to his fathers.' 'Come da Eboe country' he says to Dorinda, 'no go da Mandingoe...'"[10]

Such an ideological balancing act would appeal to all the ethnic and class divisions of stratified Jamaican society. Although Murray mostly satirized poor black peasants, he was also willing to poke fun at white or otherwise elite "buckras" and

---

[8] See Henry Garland Murray, "Two Weeks at Colon!," *Daily Gleaner* (December 20, 1876). Murray describes his visit to a "'Jamaica colony' at 'Monkey Hill'" in Panama. There were migrant workers from neighboring Caribbean countries on the Isthmus of Panama as early as 1849, brought in to work on the Panama Railroad along with several thousand workers from all over the world. See George W. Westerman, "Historical Notes on West Indians on the Isthmus of Panama," *Phylon* 22.4 4th Quarter (1961), p. 340.

[9] See Review [*Brown Sammy*], *Daily Gleaner* (November 2, 1877), p. 5.

[10] See "Mr. Murray's lecture," *Colonial Standard* (May 26, 1869).

"bushas."[11] This tactic was illustrated by his lectures "Sketches of Gordon, The Walkfoot Buckra," "Mass John, the Negro Buckra," and "Busha Sincox." He also delivered serious lectures commemorating the achievements of brown men, as in "Edward Jordon [sic]—His Life and Lessons," a reference to the famous attorney and publisher. Murray also gave speeches at churches and schools aimed at working class, usually black, Jamaicans, urging abstinence from alcohol. These moralizing lectures were given under the auspices of the Grand Division of the Sons of Temperance of Massachusetts from which he had obtained a diploma—"or whatever the instrument is called," as the *Daily Gleaner* snidely referred to it—while in Boston, which deputized him as the Grand Patriarch of Jamaica to lecture on the evils of drink.[12] It seems clear that the American temperance society made a tidy profit from these "diplomas," as did the financially struggling Murray, who likely used its authority to clear a profit from his proselytizing.

Although Jamaica had its own tradition of theatrical-style reading concerts that featured a broad array of mostly British literature from Shakespeare to Robert Burns, none combined erudition with the "low" humor of dialect comedy that Mark Twain helped to make a staple of the American lecture circuit.[13] And, undoubtedly, the Jamaican performance circuit could not pay anything close to what entertaining "lecturers" commanded in the United States. The Boston Lyceum was perhaps the best known of the popular lyceum movement during the mid-nineteenth century. Lyceums were essentially public lecture halls, and audiences tended to represent a broad spectrum of the community who paid a fee to hear the speaker. All manner of performances took place there under the banner of "lecturing," from serious philosophical disquisitions to popular entertainment in the form of comedy sketches, musical recitals, and dramatic scenes. The more popular the speaker, the higher the fee. The best speakers could discourse on a range of subjects, whether popular or esoteric. Founded just a few years earlier in 1868, the Boston Lyceum functioned as a kind of talent agency for performers of all kinds, sending its clients to venues along the Eastern seaboard. Its roster included luminaries such as Mark Twain, Charles Dickens, and Frederick Douglass.

---

[11] "Buckra" generally meant white, although there was a certain class element to the term which made it sometimes applicable to genteel or prosperous black men, according to the contemporary Thomas Russell, *Etymology of Jamaica Grammar by a Young Gentleman* (Kingston: De Cordova, MacDougall & Co., 1868), p. 15. "Busha" referred to the plantation owner, almost inevitably white.

[12] See Obituary, *Daily Gleaner* (January 30, 1877): "While [in] the United States he obtained from the chief Temperance authorities there a diploma, or whatever the instrument is called, as Grand Patriarch of Jamaica. We believe he addressed a few audiences in this city on Temperance, but we are not aware thus [sic] he succeeded in obtaining any proselytes." See also the *Morning Journal* May 5 and November 11, 1873; cited in Brian L. Moore and Michele A. Johnson, *They Do as They Please: The Jamaican Struggle for Freedom after Morant Bay* (Mona: University of the West Indies Press, 2011), pp. 331 and 516, footnote 53. For the class issues in Jamaica's temperance movement see Brian L. Moore and Michele A. Johnson, *They Do as They Please* (2011), p. 322.

[13] For a more detailed discussion of public reading performances in mid-nineteenth century Jamaica, see Brian L. Moore and Michele A. Johnson, *They Do as They Please* (2011), pp. 171–2.

This is the company Murray hoped to be in. Not content with local acclaim, he desired international celebrity. More importantly, he needed the money.

While in Boston Murray gave three audition lectures to appreciative audiences as well as a private reading to the celebrated temperance orator John B. Gough.[14] One of the lectures was "Life Among the Lowly in Jamaica." The title for the lecture was derived from the subtitle for Harriet Beecher Stowe's bestselling novel *Uncle Tom's Cabin*, which was a touchstone for many black performers across the Atlantic world. Murray's comic, dialect-inflected performance was part of a number of post-Emancipation cultural productions in the Caribbean, the U.S., and Great Britain featuring black performers that riffed on Stowe's best-selling abolitionist novel. *Uncle Tom's Cabin* had many incarnations as vernacular theater, including comic and melodramatic treatments in blackface minstrel shows.[15] Both literature and entertainment, highly moral and yet comic, *Uncle Tom's Cabin* was an ideal vehicle for a black Caribbean educator and performer like Murray, who needed to take roles that required a black body yet could not afford to risk his hard-won status as an educated black man. His status was, like those of other professional blacks, precarious.

Like his subject, Murray's Lyceum lecture/performance similarly walked the line between the didactic and the performative, the comedic, and the pathetic. A black man rendering black subjects in comic performance was not uncommon— many blackface minstrels in the US. were African American—but Murray was clearly aiming for an effect beyond minstrel laughter. The Boston audience may have been significantly African American, drawn from the ranks of Boston's black professional class and attracted to an educated black performer in their midst. In it was William Wells Brown, the author of the first African-American novel *Clotel* (published only nineteen years earlier), and himself a sometime lecturer on the Boston Lyceum circuit.

A pan-Africanist with an abiding interest in the global black community, Wells Brown was already familiar with Henry Garland Murray, and touted him as "the able editor of the leading newspaper in Kingston" (a bit of hyperbole—the leading newspaper was the *Gleaner*, a medium for the country's elite whites). He also made much of Murray's "fine personal appearance . . [his] smiling countenance

---

[14] Murray's three performances in Boston are described in *Falmouth Post* (November 26, 1872). The *Daily Gleaner* refers to Murray's private reading for Gough, during which Gough was "overcome by laughter" (Obituary, *Daily Gleaner* (January 30, 1877)).

[15] Eric Lott details the various uses of so-called "Tom shows" by abolitionist, pro-slavery, and comic blackface minstrel troupes in Eric Lott, *Love and Theft: Blackface Minstrelsy and the American Working Class* (Oxford: Oxford University Press, 1993), pp. 213–19. See also "*Uncle Tom's Cabin* Takes the Nation by Storm," The American Experience, PBS Television, accessed March 21, 2014, http://www.pbs.org/wgbh/amex/foster/peopleevents/e_cabin.html. Carlton Bryan of the Native Jamaica Choir also performed in an Uncle Tom's Cabin choir while touring in London in 1913. See Jeffrey Green, "The Jamaican Choir in Britain, 1906–1908," accessed December 8, 2020, 027: The Jamaican choir in Britain 1906–1908—Jeffrey Green. Historian.

beaming with intelligence," and his "air of a well-bred gentleman."[16] Wells Brown's tacit approval of Murray's gentility reflects the importance of this fact for an educated black audience, which, even as it desired to hear the vernacular voice of its community, would need to be reassured that a black, dialect-speaking Lyceum lecturer not be confused with his black, dialect-speaking characters.

More to the point, Wells Brown, himself no slouch as an orator, was impressed by Murray's performance:

> To be able to tell a story, and tell it well, is a gift, and not an acquirement; a gift that one may well be proud of....We had heard of Mr. Murray....[B]ut his great powers as a lecturer, we were ignorant of....He commenced in a calm, cool, moderate manner, and did not depart from it during the evening. Mr. Murray's style is true to nature, and the stories which he gave with matchless skill, convulsed everyone with laughter. He evinced talent for both tragic and comic representation, rarely combined. His ludicrous stories, graphically told, kept every face on a grin from the commencement to the end. For pathos, genius, inimitable humor, and pungent wit, we have never seen his equal. He possesses the true *vivida vis* of eloquence. Mr. Murray is a man of learning, accomplishment, and taste, and will be warmly welcomed whenever he visits us again.[17]

Yet, despite his virtuoso performance and Wells Brown's warm encomium, Henry Garland Murray was not hired by the Lyceum Bureau. John Gough, himself a Lyceum speaker, was enlisted to advocate on Murray's behalf, to no avail. The speakers' roster was all filled up for the year. He would have to wait until the next year, one manager told him; that is, unless he could pay the equivalent of 30 pounds to expedite matters. But Murray did not have the needed funds to grease the palms of the Lyceum Bureau management. *The Daily Gleaner*, an ardent champion of Murray's, attributed his failure in Boston to "a system of bureaucracy that prevails there, by a monopolizing clique...."[18]

Disappointed, Murray returned to Jamaica. He continued to perform, even turning his unsuccessful Boston experience into a lecture titled "What I Saw in America." Murray was still confident that he was on to a new genre, and that his vernacular performances were not merely a passing trend. The *Daily Gleaner* insisted that "the interest in them has in no way abated—it has rather increased" because Murray "has met a public want." Murray himself asserted that "interest in [his performances] has in no way abated" and that "[t]his sort of thing has been

---

[16] See William Wells Brown, Chapter 50 ("Representative Men and Women"), in *The Rising Son: or, the Antecedents and Advancements of the Colored Race* (1874).

[17] William Wells Brown, *The Rising Son: or, the Antecedents and Advancements of the Colored Race* (1874), p. 549.

[18] See Obituary, *The Daily Gleaner* (January 30, 1877).

unprecedented hitherto in our country."[19] Nevertheless, while still popular, his lectures were no longer reviewed by the Jamaican press as breathlessly as they had heretofore done.[20] Apparently a dialect-speaking black educator was no longer a novelty.

The Birth of Black Literary Dialect

It was at this moment when press interest in his oral performances faltered that Murray pursued what has become his most lasting achievement. As the lucrative possibilities of the American lecturing circuit diminished, Henry Garland Murray returned to his first love, writing. In 1874 Murray's *Manners and Customs of the Country a Generation Ago: Brown Sammy In Search of a Wife* was published by R. Jordan Printers, owned by the prominent brown politicians Robert Jordan and Robert Osborn. It was the first published story in the anglophone Caribbean written almost entirely in Creole.[21] Murray had already published his comic story *Tom Kittle's Wake* in 1869, which itself was a first by a colored author, featuring dialect-speaking characters framed by a standard grammar omniscient narration.[22] In the Preface to *Tom Kittle's Wake* Murray notes that he had always objected to the publication of his stories on grounds that the "native patois" is not "readable," anticipating a twentieth- century concern about the translation of the oral genre. Therefore, he concludes, "I have Anglicised the idiom for readers 'not to the manner born,'" an ironic phrase obliquely referencing European aristocrats (those "to the manor born.") Given that his readership is mostly local, either Murray is considering a foreign audience or he is implying that his local readership will need to translate Creole, as if they were foreigners to it—a perspective very similar to Samuel Augustus Mathews' declaration of white creoles' ignorance of dialect almost a century earlier.

And yet, it is clear that with the publication of *Tom Kittle's Wake* Murray aimed for a broad reading audience, which would mean a non-white one. Offered at the very affordable price of one shilling, the publication of *Tom Kittle's Wake* followed on the heels of Murray's many performances at Kingston schools. He had already

---

[19] Review [*Brown Sammy in Search of a Wife*], *Daily Gleaner* (November 2, 1874); Henry G. Murray, Preface, *Brown Sammy in Search of a Wife* (Kingston: R. Jordan, 1874).

[20] According to Errol Hill, a "distinct falling off occurs in the regularity of press reports on his presentations" after Murray returns from Boston. See Errol Hill, *The Jamaican Stage* (1992), p. 207.

[21] Michael McTurk, a white resident of British Guiana, runs a close second to Murray. Using the African day-name "Quow" as a pseudonym, in 1877 McTurk published a collection of prose poems titled *Essays and Fables in the Vernacular of the Creoles of British Guiana*, which was so popular it was re-issued in 1881 and 1899. Despite the mis-leading title, the "fables" are entirely works of McTurk's imagination.

[22] *Tom Kittle's Wake* (Kingston: De Cordova, October 1, 1869). The subtitle reads "The Second in a Series of Readings," suggesting that there may have been an even earlier publication, or at least an earlier set of readings prior to 1869.

begun writing a book of character sketches while an editor when he was encouraged to offer his first reading at the Wolmer's, a free school catering specifically to children of the colored middle class, in early 1869.

With *Brown Sammy*, Henry Garland Murray broke free of the constraints of standard grammar by the use of a Creole narrator. This was no small step. Genteel Jamaican society of the 1870s was continually on the watch for evidence of black middle class vulgarity and lack of erudition. And likely not just white elites either. A review of one of Murray's 1869 lectures at Wolmer's suggests that it might have been members of the colored middle class who were anxious that a dialect-speaking black man acting out stories of the peasantry would be a blight on respectable society. Perhaps with that in mind, initially Wolmer's administrators refused to grant him permission to lecture. This despite the fact that, as the *Gleaner* noted, it had granted permission to another organization to use the room. The *Gleaner* concluded that "[Murray's] case has been a hard one...We hope he will be supported liberally."[23] After a successful reading at Wolmer's the plantocratic *Colonial Standard* wryly noted the general enthusiasm among the respectable audience members for Murray's vernacular reading:

> We are glad to observe—as evidenced by the crowded Room on Wednesday evening—that certain silly misconceptions of the subject-matter of the lectures are now completely dispelled—*several timid, though well-meaning people having somehow or other at first entertained a notion that matter would be introduced of a nature not altogether agreeable to ears polite*. It is a mystery to us how any such misgivings, considering the position and character of the lecturer, should have ever existed...*it is pleasant to see that these foolish and somewhat uncharitable apprehensions are at last abandoned by the Community.*[24]   [emphasis added]

Murray's choice, not merely to perform but to write almost entirely in Creole, was a bold and far-sighted step, anticipating the Creole hybrid literary genre developed in the twentieth century. While dialect sketches had been published with increasing regularity since the late 1830s, *Brown Sammy* was the first fully conceived story, using all local sources and rendered mostly in Creole, from the point of view of a non-white narrator by an author of African descent. Even without the use of Creole, Henry Garland Murray appears to be the first published black or non-white fiction writer in the anglophone Caribbean.

The stories were apparently both popular and commercially viable, because *Brown Sammy* was followed two years later by a sequel, *Brown Sammy Gets*

---

[23] *Daily Gleaner* (January 27, 1869), cited by Karl Reisman, "Tom Kittle's Wake: A West Indian Classic," http://fadograph.wordpress.com/tom-kittles-wake-a-west-indian-classic-1877/, accessed October 18, 2013.

[24] See "Mr. Murray's Lecture," *Colonial Standard* (April 26, 1869).

Married and Finds Trouble, or 'Married Hab Teet'.[25] This first in the annals of Caribbean literature was shaped as much by pecuniary considerations as it was by the author's clear sense that this was an original work of art. Henry Garland Murray's need for money was constant and pressing. He fell ill after his return from Boston and a benefit had to be organized by prominent Jewish and white members of the community to pay for his expenses. In his gratitude he dedicated *Brown Sammy in Search of a Wife* to his benefactors even as, in almost the next sentence, he excoriated Jamaican society for not allowing him to make a proper living through his art:[26]

> Unfortunately, in this country, men who have done all for themselves, and toiled painfully, amid, and against discouragements of the most terrible kind, and made "a name and a fame"—must content themselves with such reward as is contained in the applause of their countrymen—a kind of thing that is very pleasant in its way, but which cannot supply the place of food and raiment to oneself, and one's family. There are rewards in the gift of POWER here, *but as to be born in Jamaica, seems a sin in their eyes, men like me, must be content to toil, and toil—till heart and flesh having failed—like overwrought horses, we drop down ingloriously, with our burdens chafing us to the very last moment.*[27]   [emphasis added]

His illness seems to have given Murray a glimpse of the abyss on the other side of the acclaim. Without property and power, even educated, talented men of color were just one personal misfortune away from poverty. Murray's anger at Jamaican society for his inability to make a comfortable living from his art seems distinctly raced and classed, as illustrated by his conspicuous and pervasive use of the images of hard labor linked to "men like me [black men or men of color] who "must be content to toil" until "like overwrought horses, we drop down ingloriously." He would publish more stories in the years to come, but in his preface to *Brown Sammy* Murray complains that he has not published more of his performances "on account of the necessity of having to pay Publishers beforehand."

Although he clearly relied on his white and light brown elite patrons for his livelihood, Murray's pointed complaint is evidence of the special burden of patronage for the colored artist. It is not incidental to the story that follows that Murray reserves his most impassioned critique for Jamaican society at large,

---

[25] See Henry G. Murray, `*Brown Sammy Gets Married and Finds Trouble, or "Married Hab Teet"* (Kingston: R. Jordan, 1876).

[26] *Brown Sammy in Search of Wife* is dedicated to "His Honor Mr. Justice Drake, John R. McNab Esq., George Levy, Esq., Kingston; Dr. John DeLeon, T.H. Sharpe, Esqr., S.J.P., Montego Bay, and D.C. DeSouza, Esqr., Falmouth. Active Promoters of Entertainments for my Benefit—ad the Ladies and Gentlemen, by whose aid they were rendered successful—this story is Dedicated with sentiments of esteem and respect by Their Grateful and obliged servant, etc." See Henry G. Murray, dedications page, *Brown Sammy in Search of a Wife* (1874).

[27] Henry G. Murray, Preface, *Brown Sammy in Search of a Wife* (1874).

which won't afford him a living as an artist. Rank-and-file Jamaicans, black people, won't pay up to allow him to be altogether self-sufficient, freed from the yoke of elite patronage and, perhaps, whatever artistic constraints it brings. This is where we get an indication of the stakes of Creole literature, not merely literary dialect, for non-whites in the nineteenth century. Literary dialect was not literature. And Henry Garland Murray wanted to write literature. Letters to the editor paid nothing. Live performances were lucrative but short-lived, not to mention "low art." With the exception of Samuel Augustus Mathews, most white creators of Creole stories were foreign observers or members of the West Indian propertied class; their stories could be considered a sideline. Murray, and the non-white practitioners who came after him, relied heavily on their artistic productivity to make a living. Here was a literary endeavor with financial possibilities, not simply a hobby or an amusement for one's friends. The production and performance of dialect literature becomes, with Murray, a middle-class pursuit, a career. Non-white practitioners such as Murray could not afford to treat it as a sideline when their tenuous class status was on the line.

Underscoring his focus on a non-white audience was Murray's sense that black people were an essential part of his artistic production. Black and non-white people were the bulk of his audience. Their enthusiasm and knowing laughter would be a key part of his live performances. Murray must have felt keenly their absence when he turned to the written word. Some contemporary scholars have asserted that Murray and his sons (who followed him into the business) were condescending, alienated black quasi-elites who performed their stories solely for the white and light elites who paid to see them "mimic" black working-class speech and who choked with laughter at degrading caricatures of black working-class speech and life.[28] I believe this is a significant mis-reading. At the very least, Murray appears to have a vested interest in creating a black and non-white audience for his art. His stories were priced affordably, clearly aimed at a mass market. A few years earlier, Murray's hybrid Creole-and-English serial story "Jim Purdy: A Tale with a Moral," was published in the *Jamaica Instructor*, a newspaper with a black readership.[29] In this majority black, increasingly literate, society, the financial considerations of mass market production were inevitably raced. The emergent black reading public, weaned on affordable newspapers, magazines, and oral entertainments, was going to determine the success or failure of Caribbean authors in the years to come.

---

[28] See Brian L. Moore and Michele A. Johnson, *They Do as They Please* (2011), p. 132.
[29] "Jim Purdy: A Tale with a Moral," ran in *Jamaican Instructor* between May 1871 and at least July 1873, when subsequent issues became unavailable. According to Hill, the story employed both standard English and Jamaican Creole; it appears to have been read and recounted in the country. See Errol Hill, *The Jamaican Stage* (1992), p. 214, quoting W. G. Ogilvie, "Many Faces, Different Streams" (unpublished manuscript), p. 20.

For black readers, inevitably short on money but eager to join literate society, affordable newspapers and pamphlets were just what they wanted. Indeed, eight years earlier—just four years before the Morant Bay Rebellion—the Kingston *Morning Journal* had warned against the influence of "cheap periodicals" from the U.S. on the emergent reading public:

> [F]or men who read the events of the day carefully, most infallibly find their prejudices undermined and learn to look with loathing on those panderers to popularity who employ their misdirected talents in heaping abuse on an Aristocracy the purest in the world and the sincerest friends of the struggling classes. *As all semi-educated persons obey their feelings rather than their reason, the mischievous consequence entailed by the cheap periodicals are most melancholy and the constant misrepresentation of the motives actuating the higher classes of society keeps open that wide gap which it is the true interest of all to close.*[30] [emphasis added]

Far from affirming white superiority, the *Morning Journal* article feared that popular literature incited the "semi-educated," emotional and irrational black/brown working-class populations to hate the Jamaican aristocracy, as it called the white elites ("the purest in the world and the sincerest friends of the struggling classes"). The newspaper argued that popular literature fomented class warfare by its "constant misrepresentation of the motives actuating the higher classes." This, from a newspaper sympathetic rather than not to the black majority (in succeeding years the *Morning Journal* would give enough unflattering coverage to the suppression of the Morant Bay Rebellion to provoke a British officer to assault its editor, Robert Jordan, and threaten murder).[31] Racial and class tensions were already rife in Jamaican society, and literacy for the "wrong" purpose was seen as more fuel to the fire. Given that the popular literature in question was coming out of the United States, it is doubtful that the newspaper was referring to any specific incitements so much as a popular sense of ownership of the word, and the power derived from possessing the means to criticize the elites, a strategy already evident in Caribbean popular music, as we have seen. Popular literature was a double-edged sword as far as the elites of nineteenth century Jamaica were concerned. On the one hand, popular representations of dialect-speaking black people tended to reaffirm white ideas about black inferiority. On the other, such popular fare did not seem to be overly concerned with the central colonial project of educating the folk into respectability. Popular literature's appeal could push out

---

[30] *Morning Journal* (September 24 and 27, 1861), cited in Brian L. Moore and Michele A. Johnson, *They Do as They Please* (2011), p. 132.
[31] See *Morning Journal* (November 10, 1866), reprinted by "History Weird," accessed January 31, 2021, http://historyweird.com/1866-gordon-ramsay-indecent-language/.

the didactic aims of "good" (inevitably English) literature to uplift the masses—or, to pacify them. Upliftment and pacification were not mutually exclusive projects in post-Morant Bay Rebellion Jamaica. Quite the opposite, they frequently operated in tandem.

Morant Bay and the Quest for a Native Literature

In his preface to *Brown Sammy* Henry Garland Murray adeptly navigates the racial and class minefields involved when an educated black man writes in dialect. At the forefront of his concerns is that *Brown Sammy* will provoke the severe disapproval of its black and non-white readers. Anticipating this Murray tries to head off the criticism with a rebuttal. His qualifiers are worth quoting at length. He starts off by noting that, although he is describing an earlier generation of blacks,

> but as the "Schoolmaster" is more extensively "abroad" now than ever, and as his labours cannot but result in changing the face of society; we must therefore expect that future describers of "the simple pleasures of the lowly train," will find a different kind of material to what has hitherto existed. *I think I may say, it will always require one born of the African, to delineate him correctly.* Others may know him in a general way; but it will be difficult, if not impossible, to felt in oneself [sic], its peculiar impulsions. *My theory is, that a coloured man, more than a white or black man will successfully delineate the character of the uneducated negro.* His advantage is that, standing so to speak, between two minds, he knows, by experience, what are the peculiarities of both—the others respectively being informed on only one side. There are one or two narrow-minded people, who set up to think it is a great SIN—something dreadful in the sight of God, and Angels, and good men such as they consider themselves to be—that I should give attention to illustrating the manners, customs and superstitions of the negro; but I am of opinion that future annalists of Jamaica, will find my books of considerable service to them in tracing the progress of the masses of our population. Even now they are being called into requisition elsewhere. I have seen "Tom Kittle's Wake" quoted approvingly, in a book that has been recently published in England, about Jamaica. I have been told of a paper in a leading New England Magazine, in which I have seen a similar article in a highly respectable Boston newspaper, with my Sarah Miller's song of the Ackee Tree; and one of my tales.   [emphases added]

Reading this extraordinary preface, it is inconceivable that any critic should dismiss Murray as merely a condescending elitist intent on ridiculing his own people. On the contrary, Murray is acutely sensitive to black and African-descended peoples' concerns and criticisms. Murray declares that only black or African-descended performers can authentically reproduce the sounds and signs of blackness. Just as importantly, he identifies himself as one "born of the African." This is a bigger moment than present-day readers might suppose. In the nineteenth-century Caribbean it was one thing to look like "one born of the African;" it was quite another to identify as one. In a society where, as we shall presently see, black men with enough money and education could in some sense turn "white," and had every reason to do so, Henry Garland Murray need not have highlighted his racial identity. Undoubtedly there was more than racial consciousness at play here; there was clearly a commercial benefit to singling out his particular performance of blackness as more authentic than that of white delineators. But Murray's advertising strategy does not tell the whole story of why he chooses, at this particular moment, to highlight his blackness.

Slavery had sputtered to an end in Jamaica and the rest of the English-speaking Caribbean in 1838, thirty-one years before *Brown Sammy* was written.[32] For the black and brown majority, African blood and its association with slave status was the "mark of Cain" from which there was every incentive, economic and otherwise, to dissociate. Yet black life at the dawn of emancipation is actually Murray's subject. The end of the slavery era is almost certainly the setting for *Tom Kittle's Wake*, since the eponymous hero "used to be owned by an old brown man named Marshall."[33] Murray himself was already a "young man" in 1845, a mere seven years later, so it seems that these dialect stories are the reminiscences of his youth. The characters of *Brown Sammy* appear to be almost entirely of the black peasantry. They are mostly free blacks, with one or two black characters appearing to be in some kind of servitude; also included are brown characters, usually a bit better off, one with a Scottish father (but who is still not quite well off enough to seduce the town beauty, a black woman); and mostly distant whites. Murray goes out of his way to tell amusing stories of an earlier generation precisely because, as he tells the reader, "the 'Schoolmaster' is more extensively 'abroad' now than ever," meaning that the black people who form the vast majority of the country's "lowly" class are rapidly becoming educated. Future descriptions of contemporary black society will, therefore, find "a different kind of material than has hitherto existed." By casting *Brown Sammy* as a nostalgia piece, Murray blunts the criticism of Christian-minded "good men"—no doubt the non-white educators and ministers of his acquaintance—that he is painting an inaccurate portrait of black people's educational progress. He insists that, far from being retrograde, *Brown Sammy* provides "future annalists of Jamaica" with a "service" in allowing them to "trac[e] the progress of the masses of our population;" that is, his publication will allow

---

[32] Slavery ended in 1834, after which the "apprenticeship" period ran from 1834 to 1838.
[33] Henry G. Murray, *Tom Kittle's Wake* (1869), p. 6.

future generations of presumably educated Jamaicans to illustrate just how far black people have come on the road to full equality with whites.

As with so much else, Murray likely had dual motivations in casting his story during the end of the slavery era. If on the one hand he hoped to show black progress, he also intended a reassuring portrait of pastoral Jamaican life where benign whites and unthreatening blacks and browns all lived harmoniously together. In fact recent events had shown that emphatically not to be the case. *Brown Sammy* was written a mere four years after the Morant Bay Rebellion of 1865.

As I have previously noted, the Rebellion was a cataclysmic event in Jamaican history. The multiracial Jamaica Assembly was abolished and Crown Colony rule instituted. The consequence of the Morant Bay Rebellion was that it effectively ended direct political participation by black and brown Jamaicans until the country gained independence in 1962. But it also highlighted the deep discontent of the black majority, and the push for more autonomy by the island's non-white population as a whole.

In October 1865 black farmers in the parish of St. Thomas-in-the East, chafing under heavy taxes, unemployment, the denial of universal suffrage, and most of all their lack of land, rioted, killing 33 whites. Governor Eyre in reprisal brutally suppressed the rebellion, indiscriminately murdering over 400 blacks either without trial or in kangaroo courts. He justified this brutality to the legislature by claiming that Jamaica was in danger of becoming "a second Hayti:"

> One moment's hesitation, one single reverse might have lit the torch which would have blazed in rebellion from one end of the island to the other; and who can say how many of us would have lived to see it extinguished? It is my duty to point out to you that, satisfactory as it is to know that the rebellion…has been crushed out, *the entire colony has long been, still is, on the brink of a volcano, which may at any moment burst into fury.* There is scarcely a district or a parish in the island where disloyalty, sedition, and murderous intentions are not widely disseminated and, in many instances, openly expressed…[34] [emphasis added]

Only nine years before the publication of *Brown Sammy*, then, Jamaica was "on the brink of a volcano." To the ruling class, the twin specters of the Haitian revolution and an independent black Jamaican state full of resentful, semi-educated blacks and browns weaned on cheap U.S. periodicals, were omnipresent. Eyre and other white elites particularly blamed "the seditious writings…of evil-minded

---

[34] Governor Eyre's speech to the Jamaica Assembly, November 7, 1865. Governor Eyre persuaded the members of the Assembly "to make a great and generous sacrifice for the sake of your country, and in immolating on the altar of patriotism the two Branches of the Legislature, of which you yourselves are the constituent parts, to hand down to posterity a noble example of self-denial and heroism." From *Annual Register: A Review of Public Events at Home and Abroad for the Year 1865* (London: Longman & Co., 1866), p. 270.

men of higher position and of better education…[and the] scurrilous, vindictive, and disloyal writings of a licentious and unscrupulous Press," by which they meant the few whites and Jews, as well as brown politicians like George William Gordon and black ministers like Paul Bogle, who spoke out against Eyre's cruel policies.[35]

Murray had been a witness to the effects of the Rebellion. More than this, as a journalist at the time for the *Jamaica Guardian* and one of eight members of the "upper classes" Murray had been called upon to testify at the trial of one of the accused instigators, a black shoemaker named Thomas Harry. Harry had supposedly made an "inflammatory" speech declaring that no blacks were employed in merchant stores, in the customs or at the post office, and that no provision was made for the education of black children.[36] As a black member of a profession excoriated by the Governor for its "seditious," "licentious," and "unscrupulous"[37] coverage of his policies, Murray must have been very much on his p's and q's. Because he was "not eminent as a political writer," Murray was probably a safe bet not to disturb the status quo.[38] It was just as well. An educated black journalist was already suspect.

Murray's creative labor also took place in a context in which both England and the U.S. cultural forms in one way or another were significant influences on both "high" and "low-brow" forms of Caribbean artistic production. U.S. popular culture in particular played a pivotal role in the charged atmosphere of Jamaican racial politics of the mid-nineteenth century, both in its written and performative mode, particularly blackface minstrelsy, of which more later. Jamaican theater was already a vibrant institution by this time, but founded on plays and oratory inevitably drawn from the English classics. At the time of Murray's achievement, Jamaica was already in the throes of severe Anglicization. Historians have noted the more overt manifestations of Victorian English culture in everyday Jamaican life in the second half of the nineteenth century.[39] English consumer and leisure culture was aggressively promoted to the emerging black and brown middle classes in particular. These heightened manifestations of Englishness are taken to

[35] Mimi Sheller notes the multiracial nature of 1865, including the activism of Jamaica's Jews. See Mimi Sheller, "Complicating Jamaica's Morant Bay Rebellion: Jewish Radicalism, Asian Indenture, and Multi-Ethnic Histories of 1865," *Sage Journals* (August 8, 2019), accessed December 8, 2020, Complicating Jamaica's Morant Bay Rebellion: Jewish Radicalism, Asian Indenture, and Multi-ethnic Histories of 1865—Mimi Sheller, 2019 (sagepub.com).

[36] See *Jamaica Disturbances: Papers Laid Before the Royal Commission of Inquiry by Governor Eyre, Reports from Commissioners* by Great Britain Parliament, House of Commons (London: George Edward Eyre and William Spottiswoode, June 1866), p. 327.

[37] See Governor John Eyre, speech to Jamaica Assembly, 1865, reported in *Annual Register: A Review of Public Events at Home and Abroad for the Year 1865*, p. 270.

[38] Obituary, *Daily Gleaner* (January 30, 1877).

[39] See Brian L. Moore and Michele A. Johnson, "Celebrating Christmas in Jamaica, 1865–1920: from Creole Carnival to 'Civilized' Convention," pp. 144–78, in *Jamaica in Slavery and Freedom: History, Heritage, and Culture*, edited by Kathleen Monteith and Glen Richards (Mona, Jamaica: University of the West Indies Press, 2002), p. 169.

be the consequence of the post-Morant Bay reassertion of empire by the colonial administration and elite white interests, threatened by both the creeping specter of black political power. Even as these respectable—and costly—activities were promoted, the old-time Christmas traditions of the black working class were clearly under fire. In December 1865, just months after the Morant Bay Rebellion, the authorities required that all Jonkonnu revelers first obtain a special license before going into the streets; the blowing of instruments or beating of drums in public was otherwise banned.[40] Clearly African-derived peasant traditions like Jonkonnu were considered to be a threat to institutional interests.

It was in this atmosphere of radically competing interests—racist suppression and black ambition, increasing Anglicization and American-style blackface minstrelsy—that Murray wrote *Brown Sammy*. Someone of his educational standing might have been expected to make his performance debut orating Shakespearean sonnets, given that, as Gauri Viswanathan aptly puts it, "[t]he English literary text functioned as a surrogate Englishman in his highest and most perfect state."[41] Instead Murray chose to perform as the thing he was both close to and far from: an uneducated black man. Was he, like his contemporaries, a kind of racial ventriloquist, a black professional man ventriloquizing a working-class black man? It is a question that is never asked of black authors who reproduce black vernacular speech but, given the history of racial ventriloquism in the anglophone Caribbean, it is worth asking. By 1872 ventriloquism was a characteristic attribute of Caribbean writing. And certainly, emulation and mimicry were two powerful concepts that structured Murray's life. He worked within the confines of both as a respectable colored man aspiring to maintain and even extend his status; and as an artist striving to fulfill his talent and artistic vision. Also, beyond its obvious financial appeal, the popular U.S. minstrel tradition, with its overt racial humor, offered opportunities for mimicry that could be read both ways. By inhabiting a "black" voice, a black performer could exploit but invert a common vehicle for racial commentary. Inversion, the dialectical relationship between white and black modes of performance, was already a feature of Jamaican music and popular discourse. Before Murray wrote *Brown Sammy* he performed it as a "reading," complete with "songs and musical accompaniments."[42]

Apparently Murray's emulation of American burlesque performance modes required explanation. Even Murray's enthusiastic supporters in the press felt the need to justify what were perceived as his American inclinations. One opined that "though barren of pecuniary results" the Boston visit had beneficial effects for

[40] See Brian L. Moore and Michele A. Johnson, "Celebrating Christmas in Jamaica" (2002), p. 158. Jonkonnu is an African-derived masking tradition.

[41] Gauri Viswanathan, "The Beginnings of English Literary Study in British India," pp. 376–80, in *The Postcolonial Studies Reader*, edited by Bill Ashcroft, Helen Tiffin, and Gareth Griffiths (New York: Routledge, 2006), p. 380.

[42] See "Course of Popular Lectures," *Daily Gleaner* (April 8, 1873).

both Murray and other Jamaicans: "It served to clear away the mists of prejudice against the Americans, which it is almost impossible for the *untravelled* Jamaican not to entertain, and to enable him to judge more justly, and think more kindly than he had been taught of a great and enterprising people."[43] [emphasis added] Murray himself seems sensitive to the perceived line between British highbrow and American low. In his preface he notes that his stories have been "quoted approvingly" in a book published in England, and in the United States by a "highly respectable" newspaper (unlike, presumably, the other disreputable periodicals with which the U.S. was associated in the Caribbean). If the English and the Americans thought his work acceptable, what right had Jamaicans to complain?

Clearly Murray hoped to appease his critics by appealing to the pervasive Caribbean desire for foreign, presumably white, approval. It could not have hurt that he was supported by the Reverend John Radcliffe, a progressive Scottish resident in Jamaica and himself an author of the 1869 locally published volume, *Lectures on Negro Proverbs*. Radcliffe believed that while "[w]e have no National Literature in Jamaica (since it has no race that can be regarded as native)" nevertheless "we have the Literature of…the negro race.…"[44] The fascination with folklore and philology that was the legacy of Britain's Romantic period here found fertile ground in the reforming spirit of liberal British educators and ministers like Radcliffe, and was extended by the work of Caribbean linguists like John Jacob Thomas in Trinidad and Thomas Russell in Jamaica, both of whom published the texts on Creole grammar in the Caribbean.

The search for a native literature, like that of a native language, was extant in the English-speaking Caribbean, nowhere more so than Jamaica. Educated blacks and browns advocated for a Creole literature written and performed by Jamaicans, not foreigners, particularly in the aftermath of the Morant Bay Rebellion. In one such example Robert Jordan, the brown editor of the *Morning Journal*,[45] in 1868 penned a disdainful editorial excoriating the attempts of foreign authors, Radcliffe among them, to render "pure" Creole speech in written form:

> In a recent number of a contemporary journal there appeared what was called a negro Sermon.… [The author] is not a *Creole* whatever he may be, or he would hardly have ventured to put forth such a thing as that, expecting it to pass muster for Creole. Of course it is not his fault if the thing is defective, because the Creole dialect is really a sealed book, to one who has not lisp'd it from his earliest

---

[43] Obituary, *Daily Gleaner* (January 30, 1877).

[44] John Radcliffe, *Lectures on Negro Proverbs* (Kingston: M. De Cordova, McDougall & Co., 1869), vii [forward]. Radcliffe attended Murray's lectures, and Murray thanks him for "the generous manner in which [he] came forward, identified himself with my effort, and bespoke the favour of the public for me." See Henry G. Murray, *Tom Kittle's Wake* (1869), preface.

[45] Errol Hill identifies Robert Jordan as the editor of the *Morning Journal* in *The Jamaican Stage* (1992), p. 213.

years. We opine that this so called creoline collection has been imposed upon him by some creole who is only enough so to make a muddle of it. With regard to the "Sermon" under review, we have known only two men that could render it with real *classical* purity. One of them is dead. We know another who renders it only passably—*he is apt to mix up with it English words and Kingston Slang. Pure Creole* is a thing hard to be found now-a days. The 'march of civilization' is fast driving it into out of the way corners, whence before the lapse of many years it will be dislodged altogether. Mr. Radcliffe has tried to do something for Creole literature, but his 'nancy stories' like the sermon of our contemporary, are far from being *pure*. In a late paper of his...he...gave expression to the wish that some one would make a collection of them. This idea is a good one, but if the work be attempted by any other than a *Creole*, and one who goes about it *con amore*, it will prove a *failure*.[46]

Jordan's advocacy of a "pure" Creole literature implies a "pure" ethnic Jamaican subject whose cultural expression is the sole ingredient of Jamaican identity. Anticipating Murray by a few years, Jordan inserts educated brown Jamaicans into the national conversation on Jamaicanness by arguing that "the march of civilization" is making "pure Creole" a thing of the (slave) past, then goes on to offer his own expertise in Creole, as one innately "qualified" to do so by virtue of his black blood. He offers himself in pointed contrast to Radcliffe or other would-be Creole writers ("The writer of this knows any quantity of 'set songs,' 'mule songs,' 'shasha songs,' 'myal songs,' etc. which he would have no objection to furnish to anyone coming *qualified* for the task of putting them together....")

Jordan's boundary policing of Creole literature is instructive for what it tells us about the struggle to claim the cultural territory in Jamaica during this period. At a time when white foreigners were on both sides of the ideological divide—Governor Eyre and his supporters on one, Radcliffe and other white progressives on the other—Jordan carves out a third space that delimits the interventions of foreigners in the creation of a Jamaican cultural identity. He articulates a form of creole essentialist nationalism when he emphasizes the importance of the "purity" of Creole expression that can only be rendered by an actual creole who loves the language and culture, despite his claim that "pure" Creole is a dying language.

Ironically, this occurred at the very moment that the region was consumed with desire for all things British and fear of all things African, even as black political and social power was emerging. The schism between the interest in an authentic native Caribbean literature and the desire for Englishness, with its corollary fear of African expression, was linked to the tense dynamic operating between liberal and conservative British views on culture and politics. In Britain,

---

[46] See editorial, *Morning Journal* (November 2 1868).

both liberals and conservatives saw Jamaica and its colonies as the weather vane for the future direction of Great Britain itself.[47] This contradictory dynamic found an expression in the local review of *Brown Sammy*, which meditated on the need for "our own fruits" in its appraisal:

> The gift of Mr. Murray [is] *thoroughly indigenous to our soil* as were the productions of Hellenic genius to that favoured country and more so than most of those of modern Europe.... [ ] *these lectures of Mr. Murray are the first contributions to a truly local literature.... Hence Mr. Murray's popularity with all classes.*
>
> ....
>
> We think that the very fact that Mr. Murray's genius is so... of the soil, so peculiarly Jamaican, would ensure for his works favourable reception and appreciation wherever literature is prized. If this seems paradoxical we would illustrate it by analogy. Our own fruits, which are the natural production of the country, gratify the palate everywhere, while exotic European fruits grown here would be universally condemned by those who know the taste of the genuine growth of Europe. In the same way a genuine native literary production would be far more satisfactory to European critics than any sickly imitation of their own literature could possibly be. *And though these lectures are intensely local in their characteristic and colouring; they are universal in their sympathies.*[48]   [emphasis added]

The reviewer's assertion that Murray's dialect narratives are on par with those of the Greek masters in their sheer originality and universality is an extraordinary bit of nationalist rhetoric at a time of ubiquitous denigration of black culture by the elites. (One wonders if, given the reviewer's concerns with producing a local literature, he may not have been Radcliffe himself.) More to the point, the reviewer understands that a watershed moment in Jamaican—and Caribbean— literature has arrived by the advent of a "truly local literature." To "grow" English literature on Jamaican soil, he argues, would simply result in a poor emulation, or "sickly imitation," not an original contribution to culture. The reviewer inverts the imitation paradigm by suggesting that it is Europe which is not original in that it imitates ancient Greece. Jamaica, on the other hand, has transcended the emulation altogether to achieve an original literature. Murray asserts as much himself in his promotion of his own work.

Murray's most revealing assertion, however, concerns his own racial qualifications to write an all-Creole story, and one with a colored narrator at that. Murray claims that a "coloured man, more than a white or black man will successfully

---

[47] For a thorough account of the liberal and conservative positions in England on the Caribbean see Catherine Hall, "The Economy of Intellectual Prestige: Thomas Carlyle, John Stuart Mill, and the Case of Governor Eyre," *Cultural Critique* no. 12 (Spring 1989): 167–87.

[48] *Daily Gleaner* (November 2, 1874), p. 5.

delineate the character of the uneducated negro" because, "standing between two minds, he knows, by experience, what are the peculiarities of both." In so declaring Murray is responding to John Radcliffe's quest for to identify a Jamaican national literature by declaring that he, as a brown man, *is* the sought-for native of Radcliffe's and the British liberals' Romantic imagination: I believe, however, that Henry Garland Murray was in fact black and not the brown man that he declares himself to be.

Echoing Jordan's advocacy of a "pure" Jamaican subjectivity, Murray's assertion reflects the extent to which black and brown Jamaicans were becoming aware of their own cultural and political power. His declaration is noteworthy for several reasons. First, if we take it to mean that Murray was a member of the brown, or mixed race, community, then it is one of the more unusual moments in Caribbean discourse when a brown author highlights his own sensitive racial status, not simply that of his subjects. While brown Caribbean men did indeed declare their mixed race status through political advocacy, like Trinidadian Jean-Baptiste Philippe's *Free Mulatto*, or penned stories with brown heroes like *Emmanuel Appadocca*, in nineteenth- century Jamaica elaborate depictions of the habits and proclivities of brown people were inevitably non-fiction, and authored by whites.[49] Second, the vagueness of Murray's assertion is mirrored in the vagueness of the titular character Brown Sammy himself, an illiterate character who can be read as either brown or black. Murray refers to Brown Sammy as "negro" in the preface, but the hero's racial status seems to shift throughout the narrative, and so may be predicated on his class, not racial, status. As the Jamaican grammarian Thomas Russell reminds us, in Jamaica racial terms were also classed, such that the Creole term for white—"buckra"—could also mean a black man with money.[50] Foreign whites produced most of the extant narratives on Jamaican culture and used humor as a way to affirm the inferiority of non-whites. Murray's declaration of his suitability to delineate black characters may therefore be read as a desire to be both close to and far from the object of his story: he wishes to supplant the dominant foreign narrative with what he clearly sees as a more authentic account from an educated man of African descent—brown, but not black—who will not be mistaken for his protagonist. Finally, although Murray's stated aim is to "delineate the character of the uneducated negro," he also claims to know the "peculiarities" of white men. This implies that Murray is also invested in defining white people too, yet without actually naming them as the object of his humor. To laugh at white people was a far riskier undertaking than laughing at black people.

Clearly it was part of Murray's agenda to delineate the multiracial character of Jamaican society at large. His claim echoes the evolving view of brown people as

---

[49] See Belinda Edmondson, Chapter 2 ("Brownness, Social Desire, and the Early Novel"), in *Caribbean Middlebrow* (Cornell, 2009).
[50] See Thomas Russell, *Etymology of Jamaican Grammar*, p. 15.

uniquely positioned to be cultural interpreters of the larger Jamaican population. Brown Jamaicans were identified so closely with an intrinsic "Jamaicanness" that a few years later in 1888 the black Jamaican journalist J. H. Reid would declare them to be "the most intensely Jamaican of the whole population."[51] On the other side of the color spectrum, the white Jamaican journalist William Livingstone observed in 1900 that "The coloured members of the population....are, as a rule, hostile to the British official system, their motto being, 'Jamaica for the Jamaicans,' by whom they mean themselves."[52] In this brown Jamaicans were adopting the view that the hybrid nature of Caribbean creole culture was the only true native culture of the Caribbean, and therefore Creole was the only native language.[53]

The Racial Strategies of *Brown Sammy*

Although putatively a story of an earlier, possibly enslaved, generation, *Brown Sammy* rehearses a theme common in the post-Emancipation Caribbean: black aspirational desires for literacy and social status. Under the pretext of comedy it also examines, in-depth, Jamaican intra-racial and class distinctions. The illiterate hero pretends to be educated in his quest to find love, with predictably hilarious results. His grand-sounding real name, "Samuel Williams Jeames Jinkins, Esquire," reflects the familiar dissonance between the façade of cartoonish upper-crust Englishness, what colonial society determines he should aspire to; and his lived Creole reality. At one point Brown Sammy recalls his childhood upbringing "up at Gully"—a poor neighborhood—alongside a "whitey whitey" Sammy and a "black guinea boy," also named Sammy. The humor revolves around the divergent ways in which the three Sammys are called home: "So sometime you hear de white head boy moder da call like a young puss; 'Sammie,' den we say *white* Sammy da you, an him go; den tay bambye you hear fe me moder da bawl, tell you tink him neck tring da go bruck 'Sammee!' den we da *Brown* Sammy—an I go; den tay bambye you hear ola massa Pulies call out 'Where's dat fella Sammy! *Black* Sammy go."[54]

---

[51] J. H. Reid, "The People of Jamaica Described," in *Jamaica's Jubilee: Or What We Are and What We Hope To Be* (London: Partridge and Co., 1888), p. 88, quoted in Bryan, *The Jamaican People: Race, Class and Social Control* (Mona: Univ. of the West Indies Press, 2002), p. 81.

[52] See William Livingstone, *Black Jamaica: A Study in Evolution* (London: S. Low, Marston & Co., 1900), p. 281.

[53] Ironically, white Americans appeared to entertain the opposite view; that only "pure" blacks could speak "pure" dialect. See African-American writer Charles Chesnutt's complaint that white authors of dialect fiction inevitably used "full-blooded blacks" with "dog-like fidelity" to whites for dialect speech. See Charles Chesnutt to George Washington Cable, June 1890, cited in Richard Broadhead, ed., Introduction, *The Conjure Woman and Other Tales* (Durham and London: Duke University Press, 1993), p. 14.

[54] "So sometimes you'd hear the white boy's mother call him like a young cat: 'Sammie.' Then we'd say white Sammy that's you, and he'd leave; then by and by you'd hear my mother bawl out until you'd

The public demeanors of white and non-white women are distinguished here: the white mother calls out to her son "like a young puss" (kitten), or in more delicate tones than the non-white mother, who strenuously "bawls" out until her "neck strings" look like they will break. Thus far the distinction between white and black behavior confirms the stereotypes about white and black women, that the former is genteel while the latter is loud and unladylike. This would suggest that "Brown" Sammy is, culturally speaking, black. Yet the black boy is called home not by his black mother but rather by his presumably white master (suggested by the titles "Missa" and "Massa" Pulies) calling him back to work. Black Sammy, unlike Brown Sammy, is linked to slave status and the adjective "guinea" (meaning African) is part of his racial description. Still, although Brown Sammy has "currill hair (curly hair),"[55] both he and his mother think he has "teeth in his nose"—in other words, that his nose is overly large—because "My [D]addy come from Guinea Coast!," meaning that Brown Sammy's father is African, and therefore clearly enslaved. The story's other acknowledged brown character, William Christie, has a Mandingo, Obeah-practicing grandfather on one side and a Scottish father on the other. So African blood, and all the cultural attributes that come with it, is highlighted even for the brown characters. Brown Sammy, therefore, may be considered brown or black depending on his social context; he may be what Murray describes in the story as a "Madagascar," "a child of parents, Sambo on one side, and Black on the other."[56] (Sambos were one-quarter white, but classified as black by the census.[57]) The story reveals that, for black people in 1870s Jamaica, "real" black was *African* black.

This raises the intriguing possibility that in the mid-nineteenth century the term "brown" had already gained a certain elasticity, used similarly to the earlier term "free colored" which encompassed free blacks as well as browns: in other words, to denote class status as much as color.[58] Black Sammy's blackness is connected to Africaneity, to servitude and slavery. By contrast, although Brown

---

think her neck string would break, 'Sammee!' Then we'd say that's Brown Sammy—and I'd leave; then by and by you'd hear old Mister Pulies call out 'Where's that fellow Sammy!' Black Sammy would leave." Henry G. Murray, *Brown Sammy in Search of a Wife* (1874), p. 7.

[55] Henry G. Murray, *Brown Sammy in Search of a Wife* (1874), p. 19. Sammy is described as the object of envy, "wid him long boot, an him currill hair, an him brass chain."

[56] Henry Garland Murray, *Brown Sammy in Search of a Wife*, p. 15. The description of the "Madagascar" pertains to the character of Sally, the village beauty. A Sambo is a black person who is one-quarter white.

[57] According to H.G. de Lisser, "There is a considerable element of the Jamaican population which is known as 'sambo,' an element with about one-fourth of white blood; this Caucasion or Semitic mixture shows itself plainly in their color or their features, and they should, strictly speaking, be classed as 'coloured.' But very few members of this section of the people have so classified themselves in the census.... the term coloured, having by custom come to be applied to persons of a distinctly brown or clear complexion." See H.G. de Lisser, *Twentieth Century Jamaica* (Kingston: The Jamaica Times Ltd., 1913), p. 44.

[58] Jamaican linguist Jean D'Costa notes that even contemporary uses of the term "brown" are vexed, having shifted with social and economic change. They might be used to mark class differences among as well as shades of color within a family. Email to author, September 26, 2013.

Sammy may be poor and perhaps black, he's still got a mother who calls him home, and he's no slave—hence the use of the term "brown," to denote Brown Sammy's more "civilized," or less African, form of blackness. There are two possibilities here: either Murray is assigning blackness to poor brown people based on their lower social status than their phenotype suggests, *or*, more likely, he is assigning brownness to black people based on *their* not-African, or creolized, form of blackness. "Black" was clearly a pejorative descriptive term in the mid-nineteenth century, as it continued to be in the twentieth.

The indeterminate nature of brownness found here, both in the brown author's positioning of himself as a cultural interlocutor between blacks and whites, as well as in the murky nature of Brown Sammy's brownness (or blackness), points to an emerging formulation of creolization in Murray's story. That this working-class manifestation of brown culture in the nineteenth century takes the cultural form of literary dialect, a genre associated with black Jamaica today, suggests that if on the one hand brownness was associated with social mobility and aspirational whiteness, so too did it provide a foundation for what is now identified as a specifically black Jamaican cultural practice.[59] Murray's acceptance of Creole culture as part of his own racial community, not simply a feature of the black majority, illustrates one response of educated colored men to the "problem" of culture.

In 1859 brown author Richard Hill wrote that in the pre-Emancipation era brown men, like himself educated in England, "looked upon themselves as blasted trees,—'barkless, branchless, and blighted trunks upon a cursed root,'" because of their indeterminate social and political status on the island.[60] By contrast, the locally educated Murray clearly felt that his erudition, far from alienating him from local society, actually gave him an advantage in parsing it. By so doing, Murray anticipated the reification of Creole literature to nationalist symbol in the twentieth century.

Brown Sammy's intermediate position in the story echoes that of Murray's own social standing. Just as Brown Sammy stands between White Sammy and Black Sammy, so too does Murray himself occupy the intermediary racial position with his declaration that a "coloured" man is best equipped to "translate" the manners and speech of whites and blacks. But what, exactly, does Murray mean by "coloured?"

As I have indicated, racial categorizations in the nineteenth-century Caribbean were slippery. To assign one race or "color" to someone who might be trying to downplay their African origins—or play them up, depending—is, in many ways, a futile endeavor. Contemporary critics have referred to him as either black or

---

[59] See Belinda Edmondson, "'Most Intensely Jamaican:' The Rise of Brown Identity in Jamaica," pp. 553–76, in *Victorian Jamaica*, edited by Timothy Barringer and Wayne Modest (Durham and London: Duke University Press, 2018).

[60] See Richard Hill, *Lights and Shadows of Jamaica History: Being Three Lectures Delivered in Aid of the Mission Schools of the Colony* (Kingston: Ford and Gall, 1859), p. 104.

brown because Murray plays up his African origins, but do not analyze the significance of the intra-racial distinction.[61] Jamaican historical linguist Jean D'Costa observes that "[a]sking Jamaicans to give definitions of racial characteristics... was always problematic....The physical markers of class are so involved with race that black men turn white, and some white men turn 'ole naygah'."[62] As early as 1868 the Jamaican grammarian Thomas Russell indicates that black men with money and education were often called "buckra," or white.[63] Money and color were therefore intimately aligned in the nineteenth century Caribbean.

There are no surviving photographs of Henry Garland Murray. His sons, Andrew and William Coleman who succeeded him in the dialect performance business, are described as "negro" in the Jamaican press, a description not accorded to professionals who were known to be brown, like Edward Jordan, George Stiebel, or Richard Hill.[64] Further, William Wells Brown takes pains to describe the coloring of all of the other light-skinned black personalities that he chronicles in *The Rising Son* ("Mr. Lynch was of a brown, or coffee color;" "Mr. Talbot is a dark mulatto;" "Mr. Smith is a mulatto.") However, in his description of Henry Garland Murray, Wells Brown mentions everything *but* his subject's color—usually a sign that the person is not noticeably light-skinned.[65] This suggests that, to American eyes, Murray's "brownness" might not have been particularly visible. Murray's own claims to a "coloured" identity (particularly if he were himself "sambo" or "Madagascar" like his protagonist) were therefore perhaps as much about class as physiognomy.

Why is the racial status of Murray and his protagonist so central to the story's significance? As we have seen, countless traveler writers have noted since the eighteenth century, the entire spectrum of Jamaican society, from the white upper class to the black working class, speak some version of Creole at least some of the time. Yet nineteenth-century representations of dialect speech by regional authors almost inevitably tended to single out blacks as the sole representatives of "bad" grammar. If Murray, as a brown man, utilized a poor brown character as vehicle for dialect speech, this would have been a radical gesture for Jamaican society of the Victorian era. It would be an acknowledgment that brownness is

[61] Errol Hill, Brian Moore, and Michele Johnson refer to Hill as "black," while Jean D'Costa and Barbara Lalla refer to him as "brown." Hill and Moore/Johnson see Murray's apparent blackness as significant for different reasons; Hill sees Murray as the first instance of authentic black literary production, Moore/Johnson sees Murray as an egregious example of black mimicry of white racism. D'Costa/Lalla do not comment on the meaning of brownness for Murray, although they discuss the use of "mesolects"—intermediate shadings of creole and standard grammar—in the representation of mixed-race characters in Jamaican narratives. See Errol Hill, *The Jamaican Stage* (1992); Brian L. Moore and Michele A. Johnson, *They Do As They Please* (2011); and Jean D'Costa and Barbara Lalla, *Language in Exile* (1990).
[62] Jean D'Costa, email to author, September 26, 2013.
[63] Thomas Russell, *Etymology of Jamaican Grammar* (1868), p. 15.
[64] See Errol Hill, *The Jamaican Stage* (1992), p. 210.
[65] See William Wells Brown, *The Rising Son* (1874), p. 510.

indistinguishable from blackness except as a marker of class stratification. In the early twentieth century phenotypically brown authors such as Henry MacDermot ("Tom Redcam") and H.G. de Lisser (a brown man passing for white) would write novels utilizing dialect for brown characters as well as black, but that moment was still far away.[66] However, if Murray as a genteel *black* man used a working-class black creole character as his dialect vehicle, then the story would still emphasize class status as the primary marker of difference among black Jamaicans, but not otherwise disturb the society's racial classifications.

Murray's views on racial equality are on display in his short story, "The Origin of Woman."[67] The main character black Lizzie and her husband are arguing about the role of black women. They resort to the biblical story of Adam and Eve to illustrate their position. Her husband insists that "when minista' read 'bout dat rib's bone, him must mean buckra ooman, becasin so dem white, so de bone white. Ef you mek de same, you' 'kin would a ben white." ["When the minister lectured on woman as issuing from Adam's rib, he must have meant a white woman, because just as they are white-skinned, so is Adam's rib white. If you had been made in the same way, your skin would also be white."] Lizzie, clearly the smarter one, is dismissive: "'Cho...ef you been open you' ears, you would a hea' de minsta' say de 'kin notin', but de blood, da de ting, becasin in de book say, dat white-o, brown-o, black-o, all mek de same blood; you eba' see white blood an' black blood?' "[68] ["Really...if you had been listening, instead of asleep, you would have heard the minister say that the color of one's skin is nothing, but it's the blood that's the thing, because in the bible it says that white, brown, black, all have the same blood; have you ever seen white blood and black blood?"]

"The Origin of Woman" is one of those moments, frequent in nineteenth-century Caribbean dialect literature, where the author's views manifests through that of a dialect-speaking character. In a society where political discourse on the subject is volatile, using humor to make a point about racial equality, is a disarming strategy. Dialect humor is a great equalizer, in many respects; everyone, regardless of class and race affiliation, can laugh; whether from a sense of distance—that's familiar but it isn't me—or from a sense of identification—yes! that's how we are!—all segments have a stake in its representation. Henry Garland Murray's investment in racial equality on display here is subtle but unmistakable. Using this lens to interpret the racial logistics of *Brown Sammy*, it is more likely that the character of Brown Sammy represents not necessarily browns, but rather, creole blacks. Though not as sophisticated as the author, they, like Brown Sammy,

---

[66] See Tom Redcam, *One Brown Girl And*—(1909); and H.G. de Lisser, *Jane's Career* (1913). In both novels brown characters of higher social status than working-class blacks are shown speaking dialect.

[67] Henry G. Murray, "The Origin of Woman." The provenance of "The Origin of Woman" is unclear, but it is reproduced by William C. Bates in *Journal of American Folklore* 9–10 (32–3) (April–June 1896), pp. 124–5, cited by Jean D'Costa and Barbara Lalla, *Language in Exile* (1990), p. 169.

[68] Henry G. Murray, "The Origins of Woman," *Journal of American Folklore* (1896).

are at least on an equal footing with the poor whites and African-identified blacks, those White and Black Sammys with whom as children they play down by gully. If class distinctions are made visible through the different language and parenting practices of the mothers, they are also elided through the indistinguishable nature of the Sammys' behavior, and name. "Sammy" seems to have connoted a generic sameness for ordinary men in the nineteenth century anglophone Caribbean, similar to saying "John Brown" or, in the contemporary U.S., "Joe Blow." As Brown Sammy himself says elsewhere, "[b]rown-o, white-o, black-o, it's all the same."[69]

This is not to say that representing children of different races on an equal footing at play is, in and of itself, a radical representation of progressive racial politics. It can also suggest the opposite; that whereas all children are delightfully indistinguishable, by adulthood the "natural" distinctions among them inevitably surface to establish an essentialized racial hierarchy. However, if Murray's dialect stories reveal anything about racial difference, it seems to be that racial difference signifies only in working-class black people. The text consistently elides the difference between race and class. Working-class brown people appear indistinguishable in language and habits from working class blacks, and the genteel of all races are unmarked by color. In the following passage Brown Sammy explains to brown "Mass Tom" that jealousy afflicts women of all races equally, but that men must deal with black women differently than genteel women:

Jalous is a nasty ting....It gie you a broke wing and fainty, fainty, and mek you chupid and good fe nuttin. When it hold woman it worse. White-o, brown-o, black-o, it's all de same. I sorry fe de gentleman dem....So dem sit down straight up, and a so dem put dem mout (purring up.) Den you hear the poor gentleman dem. "O my dyar, I is bery sorry you bex." Den you hear de lady, "Go away from me, Tam [sic], I don't want to speak to you? [sic]["] Some o'dem when de hexation take dem, them trow it 'pon de piano. Ploom, aloom. Dey hear the poor gentleman [,] "My [d]yar" "ploom, ploom" "My dyar, I is speaking to you", "ploom ploom." Dey will go on so the de poor gentleman, beg all de pardon, and will kiss her foot bottom, bufo she will please. *Wid dem, fe we black gals its worse. Dey want fe come buck you and bite you, and tear out you eye, dat ef you don't hab a trong heart they will beat you. De way da do wid dem, dis hold dem and hux off dem mout, an bung up dem eye, den you wi' settle dem....*

[Jealousy is a nasty thing. It breaks your wings and makes you faint-hearted, and makes you stupid and good for nothing. When it gets hold of women it's worse. White, brown, black, it's all the same. I'm sorry for the gentlemen....So [the women] sit straight up, and put their mouth like this (pursing up). Then you hear the poor gentleman say, "Oh my dear, I am sorry you are vexed." Then

[69] *Daily Gleaner* (November 2, 1874), p. 5.

you hear the lady: "Go away from me Tom, I don't want to speak to you." Some of them, when the vexation takes them, they take it out on the piano. Ploom, ploom. Then hear the poor gentleman: "My dear." Ploom, ploom. "My dear, I am speaking to you." Ploom, ploom. They will go on so until the poor gentleman has begged all the pardon and kissed the bottom of her foot, before she will be satisfied. *With our black girls, it's worse. They want to kick and bite you, and tear out your eye, [so] that if you don't have a strong heart they will beat you. The way to deal with them, is to just hold them and smack their mouth, and bang up their eye, then you will settle them....]*[70]   [emphasis added]

Contemporary readers will be struck by the familiarity between Brown Sammy's description of combative black women who try to overpower their men, and the black male characters' description of equally combative black women who will knock out men's "jaw teeth" and "wade in solid rock up to [their] hip pockets" in Zora Neale Hurston's 1937 classic, *Their Eyes Were Watching God*. In both instances, black women are contrasted to more genteel women: in the latter, to light-skinned African-American women who merely cry when they are beaten; and in the former, to genteel women of any racial group. Genteel Jamaican women are like genteel women anywhere: in this vision, their generic sameness functions to highlight the spectacular, hilarious difference of black women. Working-class black women are a flashpoint in Murray's formulation of race and class distinctions in dialect literature, as they were in early African-American representations of the "folk." Their supposed innate physical strength and fighting spirit makes them comically unfeminine. In a society where color and class distinctions constantly shift, working class black women provide a stable determinant of difference that does not come at the expense of ambitious black men. More broadly, blackness and working-class status here are completely aligned, so that to say "black" is to say "working-class" or "uneducated," even in a society where the middle-class, educated blacks were an increasingly familiar entity. This focus on the attributes of the black working class, particularly its women, as a signifier of both racial difference and cultural authenticity is one that obtains for other dialect stories across the Caribbean from the nineteenth century into the present.[71]

The Legacy of Henry Garland Murray

Henry Garland Murray's innovative merging of Creole performance and literature was to launch a black Jamaican tradition, starting with his own family. After he

---

[70]   Henry G. Murray, *Brown Sammy in Search of a Wife* (1874), p. 19.
[71]   See the "Lizzie and Joe" poems of Alexander Cordle of Barbados in *Overheard* (published 1903 but written in the 1880s); the "Suzie and Sambo" newspaper stories from 1930s Trinidad; and the "Auntie Roachy" stories of Jamaican Louise Bennett through the mid-to-late-twentieth century.

died, Murray's sons Andrew and William Coleman went into what became the family business, publishing and performing dialect stories into the early twentieth century. Both made a good living, particularly William Coleman. Known as "Funny Murray," William Coleman was seen as his father's true heir. Like his father Funny Murray also worked as a reporter, and bought and edited a newspaper, the *Cornwall Herald*. Also like his father, he understood that his depictions of black life would cause offense. Recycling his father's rationale, Funny Murray defensively argued that

> it is surely possible to depict the peculiarities...either of individuals or of communities, in language which, if slightly satirical, is wholly untinged by an ill-humour, any offensive suggestion, any word or thought which is likely to cause a moment's pain. Such at any rate has been my aim....Every race has its characteristic traits; those of the Anglo-African race are too well known throughout the West Indies to need enlarging upon...It may be, in fact it must be, that the growth of education will make a wide difference between the coming and the past generations of Jamaicans; but no amount of education...will, to my mind, quite atone for the loss of the quaintly quipped or unduly elongated words, the quick and often utterly illogical repartee, the strangely apt and frequently far-fetched similes and allusions which characterize the conversation—or shall I call it the chatter?—of such men...They are types of a generation that is passing away.[72]

William Coleman's eulogizing of the "quaint" and "illogical repartee" of the black working class in the face of mass education suggests that he fears the subsumption of black particularity within a class-bound sameness. In this his vision is similar to his father's elision of race and class differences, but unlike his father it seems motivated by anxiety over his own position as a black middle-class man who is able to laugh at the peculiar and irrational utterances of the black working class. Without the class distinction indicated through speech, black middle-class particularity itself disappears, and blacks become merely—black. Without class, race is more visible as a distinguishing characteristic from whiteness, or brownness. Perhaps this is why Funny Murray publicly condemned the notion of a free education beyond basic elementary instruction for the island's majority population. Instead he advocated trade and farm schools for poor Jamaicans.[73]

But times had changed since 1874; black dissent was no longer entirely silenced, and the black middle class could now express its opprobrium in print.

[72] W.C. Murray, Introduction, *A Day with Joe Lennan, the Rosewell duppy doctor, and Tommy Silvera or Suck o' Peas Sil* (Kingston: Vendryes and Co., 1891), quoted in Patrick Bryan, *The Jamaican People, 1880–1902: Race, Class and Social Control* (Mona: University of the West Indies Press, 2002), p. 200.

[73] Robert Love, *Jamaica Advocate* (August 13, 1898), quoted in Errol Hill, *The Jamaican Stage* (1992), p. 209.

Dr. Robert Love, editor of the black nationalist newspaper the *Jamaica Advocate*, articulated his contempt for Funny Murray in a scathing editorial. He dismissed "the stupid objection made in a paper edited by a Negro in Savanna-la-Mar that the State who kept the Negroes in absolute ignorance whilst they were slaves, should not educate them freely now they are free men and citizens."[74] Love saw a link between Funny Murray's views on free education and his popular dialect performances, of which Love also disapproved: "For ourself, we cannot say that we enjoy these lectures for the simple reason that in them, our race is held up to ridicule and lampooned. When this is done by a member of the more fortunate race it makes us angry; when done by one of our own race, even the humour does not take away a feeling of sadness from us." Love's critique of Murray voices the objections of the larger African-descended community towards those who represent it yet may not have its best political interests at heart. In this Love anticipates the eviscerating political critiques of Marcus Garvey of black authors of dialect literature in the decades to come.

Knowledge of the origins of *Brown Sammy* and its brown/black creator is essential to our understanding of Creole literature, then as now, and what impels it forward. The story of Henry Garland Murray and his singular achievement reveals dialect literature to be as much a production of black middle-class values and desires as the representation of "authentic" working class, or peasant, culture. Not simply entertainment nor altogether a proto-nationalist form, vernacular literature from its inception was a complex mix of intellectual, political, artistic, and commercial elements, inseparable from its non-working class performative mode, which "birthed" it; from the commingling of African storytelling traditions with American minstrelsy and British/Scottish dialect literature; from the financial needs of its creators; and from the political desires of black or African-descended people of all classes in the Caribbean and beyond.

---

[74] Robert Love, *Jamaica Advocate* (August 13, 1898).

4

Travelling Dialect

Dialect is a paradox. Bounded by its geographic and cultural specificity, it is, by definition, insular and local, the product of limited interactions; its literary concerns fleeting and dated, not universal, cosmopolitan, or of lasting value. And yet dialect narratives and musical traditions have been global fixtures for hundreds of years. Chaucer's *The Canterbury Tales* is written in a medieval London dialect, while Mark Twain's dialect classic *Huckleberry Finn* is continually mined for its "universal" themes. Both are on classroom reading lists all over the world. American music has a particularly lengthy list of globally popular songs in various American vernaculars, and in recent years the rise of the explosively popular reggaeton, the Puerto Rican musical genre steeped in "Spanglish," has transcended all national boundaries to claim one of the largest international audiences in modern music. Still, even as dialect narratives race across the globe it is largely accurate to assert that dialect literatures tend to be unpalatable to international audiences: or even to regional audiences beyond the originating locale.

That languages travel we all understand. The connection between language, commerce and empire is, at this point, self-evident. English, the most powerful language in the world, is the best example of this relationship, its elite status predicated on an imperial history still shrouded in the depoliticized mythmaking of its own inevitability. By contrast dialects, English or otherwise, are not associated with the global currency of imperial languages. This has something to do with the values associated with standard English compared to dialect: the former linked to intelligence, command, and moral virtue; the latter to stupidity, social inferiority, and moral obliquity. As an imperial tool, dialect is hardly ideal. Unsurprisingly, it remains associated with stasis.

And yet. It is precisely dialect's local origins that gives it global appeal. Dialect texts that travel, whether song lyrics, theater, novels, or other forms of narrative, carry the same tension between the particular and the universal. Postcolonial scholars like Gauri Viswanathan have noted the global reach of imperial cultures through texts. British literature, she asserts, as the backbone of the colonial curriculum functioned as a form of socio-political control in England's colonies, a point that Kenyan writer Ngũgĩ wa Thiongo underscores when he describes how a brilliant high school classmate was made to fail all his exams, despite distinctions in

Creole Noise: Early Caribbean Dialect Literature and Performance. Belinda Edmondson, Oxford University Press.
© Belinda Edmondson 2022. DOI: 10.1093/oso/9780192856838.003.0005

every other subject, because he failed English.[1] Those gatekeeper texts of the imperial mission are represented as High Culture, an embodiment of universal truths that conveniently emanate from an imperial center. This representation usefully erases their earlier status as local objects, made for a local or nationally bounded audience. Yet it is their cultural particularity, their boundedness that, paradoxically gives imperial texts their cultural power. The odd familiarity of a foreign vernacular, its appeal to quotidian local culture, obscures its mission of social control. Ensconced within the protective apparatus of state authority, the imperial text instructs us to see its vernaculars as part of the Everyman appeal of truly universal art when read as part of a colonial curriculum, not as an expression of a discrete culture at a discrete moment.

The archives of Caribbean literature reveal that literary dialect, both imported and local, was in the vanguard of both the imperial mission and its antithesis, the nationalist agenda. Travel, as a mode of its transmission, was central to that duality. The imported nature of dialect literature and performance was, and is, both visible and hidden; hidden in that, as transnational vernacular modes were assimilated and adapted to local Caribbean cultures over time, their foreign origins were obscured; but also visible, in that part of the initial attraction of these transnational dialects was that they also represented a kind of vernacular cosmopolitanism, a way to be Caribbean, black, and modern in the post-slavery world. My aim here, then, is to illustrate the centrality of travel to the development of the Caribbean literary dialect tradition, and to illuminate dialect's trans-local aspect as symptomatic of its role as both a tool and a destabilizing agent of the colonial enterprise.

In the seventeenth and eighteenth century Caribbean countries changed colonizers and official languages so frequently that even today the official and unofficial languages do not always align. Trinidad and St. Lucia, for example, have been English-speaking countries since the early nineteenth century, yet their vernaculars remain stubbornly French-inflected. Creole literary dialects—for there were more than one—of the late eighteenth- through early twentieth- centuries were spawned by a swirling cacophony of both regional and international dialects. Out of these the Caribbean literary dialect tradition was born. Vital to its birth was both the presence of actual travelling populations as well as that of "travelling" literary dialects via imported periodicals from England and, most particularly, the US. The cultural traditions of indentured laborers and working-class whites from Scotland, Ireland exerted considerable influence. So too the popular Irish and "Yankee" dialect sketches performed by American elocutionists throughout

---

[1] Gauri Viswanathan, *Masks of Conquest: Literary Study and British Rule in India* (New York: Columbia University Press, 2014); Ngũgĩ wa Thiongo, *Decolonising the Mind: The Politics of Language in African Literature* (London: Heinemann, 1981/1988), p. 12.

the nineteenth century.[2] Then there were British theatre troupes who performed blackface and "negro" comedy routines alongside Shakespearean scenes, including the legendary Shakespearean actor Charles Kean, who wowed Jamaican audiences in the 1860s with dialect-saturated performances such as "Wallack's Negro Comic History of England in 199 chapters with stirring local hits introducing the whole of the Jamaican oddities."[3] The welter of Caribbean emigrants who migrated from Barbados, Grenada, and other "small islands" to British Guiana and Trinidad in the late-nineteenth century also contributed a pan-Caribbean element to the rich stew of dialects in the region.

Dialect also circulated throughout the region via the travel writing, music, academic discourse on folk culture and other written documents that disseminated among the reading public of the Caribbean. This was especially true in the waning decades of the nineteenth century, as nationalist interest in folk and native culture grew out of an emerging sense of Caribbean singularity. Textual versions of dialect disseminated within the Caribbean through English travelers, and, as I have discussed earlier, a multiracial range of local performers who also disseminated a kind of pan-Caribbean or trans-Atlantic literary dialect through their travels. As I have discussed, white Kittitian Samuel Augustus Mathews traveled frequently from his native St. Kitts to Antigua, Dominica, Barbados, and finally, to Demerara, British Guiana, where in 1822 he published his final book. Similarly, black Jamaican performer and author Henry Garland Murray traveled as far away as Panama and New England to perform his dialect sketches in the 1860s.

As interest in folk cultures grew in the late nineteenth century, philological tracts on Caribbean folk proverbs and phrases were popular both within and without the Caribbean, emerging in places as varied as the Demerara-based academic journal *Timehri*, which published "Jamaica Proverbial Philosophy" in 1890; in London that same year, a collection of Anansi tales published under the title *Mama's Black Nurse Stories*; and in the Sunday editions of the *New York Herald*, a regular sampling of Anansi stories.[4] In particular, Jamaica's distinctive patois became associated with a kind of homogenizing pan-Caribbean "literary dialect" tradition in the nineteenth century. It seems fair to speculate that Jamaica, because of its size, relative wealth, and prominence, became an easy shorthand, a one-size-fits-all version, for writers who wanted to illustrate how black creole communities sounded in the Caribbean. In a parallel development, Ghana's

---

[2] American elocutionist Mary Webb's tour of Jamaica in 1858 is noted in *Daily Advertiser* May 6, 12, and 15 (1858), cited in Errol Hill, *The Jamaican Stage* (1992), p. 191.

[3] *Colonial Standard* (May 18, 1867), cited in Errol Hill, *The Jamaican Stage* (1992), p. 199.

[4] See the Reverend D. J. Reynolds, "Jamaica Proverbial Philosophy," *Timehri: A Journal of the Royal Agricultural Society* 4 (Demerara, 1890): 47–55; Mary Pamela Milne-Holme, *Mamma's Black Nurse Stories* (London: William Blackwood & Sons, 1890); Sunday editions of the *New York Herald* in the 1890s, cited in Izett Anderson and Frank Cundall, *Jamaica Negro Proverbs and Sayings*, 2nd edition (Kingston: Institute of Jamaica, 1927); *Daily Gleaner* (February 4, 1899); also Charles Rampini, *Letters from Jamaica. . .with Negro Proverbs* (1873).

Concert Party Theatre, an art form that emerged under colonial rule in urban Ghana in the early twentieth century until the 1990s, used pidgin as its common language so that its performers could tour multiple African states. (Pidgin, like Caribbean Creole, is a transnational African dialect that functions as the region's lingua franca.)[5] In the same vein, it seems that one common Caribbean language was surely easier to render than the many variations, not to mention the idiosyncrasies of individual transcribers who heard different sounds, well, differently. This homogenizing tradition may have been one result of so-called "dialect leveling," where dialects in proximity to each other become more similar over time,[6] or perhaps it was because the original vernaculars of the anglophone Caribbean sounded more like than different due to the relatively similar ethnic make-up of the inhabitants prior to large-scale Asian and other migrations. But it also seems clear that travel, whether textual, performative or migratory, accounted for this homogenizing tradition.

Arguably the most lasting effect of travel on Caribbean Creole, however, are two features which are fundamentally linked. In the late-nineteenth century dialect transformed from a signifier of a fundamentally rural Caribbean identity to a mostly urban one; and it expanded from an almost entirely performative language to a literary one. The ugly reality of slavery elided, blackface could be rationalized as a represention of unsophisticated rural black culture, not literate urban black communities. Rural to urban, oral to literary: both transformations merged in the performance and dissemination of American-style blackface minstrelsy to the theatre-going publics of the Caribbean. The dialect-laden, comedic "plantation songs" of blackface performers were reframed as upscale events by a succession of travelling black choirs, first among them the Fisk Jubilee Singers. As folklorist Roger Abrahams notes, "black dialect" books and stories in the United States were a by-product of the popular blackface minstrel shows of the nineteenth century, and those texts were often written by minstrel performers or producers, or compiled by the members of the respectable classes, among them judges, doctors, and professors.[7] In the Caribbean a similar phenomenon occurred; blackface minstrelsy became the impetus for a slew of related cultural products—stories, lectures, song-and-dance performances—absorbed by an increasingly literate multiracial audience hungry for global imports that were both funny and familiar.

Increased travel without and within the Caribbean coincided with the increasing urbanization of Caribbean society in the late nineteenth century. Cities were

---

[5] See Jesse Shipley, *Trickster Theatre: The Poetics of Freedom in Urban Africa* (Indiana University Press, 2015); and David Donkor, *Spiders of the Market: Ghanian Trickster Performance in a Web of Neoliberalism* (Indiana University Press, 2016). My thanks to Jesse Shipley for alerting me to the pidgin tradition in Concert Party Theatre.

[6] My thanks to Professor Lindsay Russell of the University of Illinois for alerting me to this linguistic phenomenon.

[7] Roger D. Abrahams, ed., *Afro-American Folktales: Stories from Black Traditions in the New World* (New York: Pantheon Books, 1985), pp. 11–13.

also the sites of most theaters, newspapers, and educational institutions. So it is not surprising that, although many of the early nineteenth-century dialect sketches are of urban scenes, it is only at the end of the century that the urban dimensions of Caribbean Creole are fully explored; white creole Michael McTurk's dialect poems are about Georgetown, British Guiana, in the 1890s; Alexander Cordle's were written in Bridgetown, Barbados in the late nineteenth century; and Claude McKay dedicates his *Constab Ballads* to the policemen of Kingston, Jamaica in 1912. This ultimate turn towards the city at the inauguration of the twentieth century cemented the connection between Caribbean Creole and the larger Atlantic world. It was here, at the site of white power and black ambition, that turned outwards to the wider world, both as the language of colonial harmony as well as the language of a more troublesome black modernity.

Early Influence: African-American Dialect in the Caribbean

The pivotal importance of African-American literary dialect to the development of anglophone Caribbean dialect as a written form is, by now, self-evident. Much of this influence has to do with the explosive popularity of blackface minstrelsy in the Caribbean in the latter half of the nineteenth century. As Louis Chude-Sokei persuasively argues, "The struggle to claim vernacular culture in the Caribbean revolves around the definitional tensions of the minstrel figure: as naïve producer of native song and sound, and as comic blackface stereotype in a global economy of racial masquerade in which vaudeville, burnt cork, American racial spectacle and carnival became linked through a transnational movement of black dialects."[8]

Nineteenth-century African-American minstrel styles have influenced black vernacular cultures globally, in places as far away as Accra, Ghana, or Cape Town, South Africa.[9] The ubiquity of popular American blackface minstrel troupes in the nineteenth-century anglophone Caribbean is a fact that scholars are exploring in more depth.[10] Famous American minstrel troupes such as Christy's Minstrels and the Georgia Minstrels toured the region, including relatively faraway British Guiana, almost as soon as they became popular in the United States. They also toured Britain, and the British, despite—or perhaps because of—their abolitionist views, conceived such a passion for blackface minstrelsy that they produced their

---

[8] Louis Chude-Sokei, *The Last Darky: Bert Williams, Black-on-Black Minstrelsy, and the African Diaspora* (Durham and London: Duke University Press, 2006), p. 154.

[9] See Edmund John Collins, "Jazz Feedback to Africa," *American* Music 5 (Summer 1987), p. 180, quoted in Louis Chude-Sokei, *The Last Darky* (2006), p. 146. See also Catherine M. Cole, *Ghana's Concert Party Theatre* (Bloomington: Indiana University Press, 2001) for research on Ghana's blackface "Concert Boys;" as well as Jesse Shipley, *Trickster Theatre: The Poetics of Freedom in Urban Africa* (Bloomington: Indiana University Press, 2015).

[10] For two well-known examples see Errol Hill, *The Jamaican Stage* (1992), and Louis Chude-Sokei, *The Last Darky* (2006).

own version of it, which *their* theater troupes then took on tour to the Caribbean.[11] By the end of the eighteenth century there is already evidence of the minstrel tradition in American literature; at least ten plays of the period included dialect to portray African-American characters as contented slaves or comic figures.[12]

The central influence of African-American dialect on nineteenth-century Caribbean popular discourse is revealed in its early dissemination. Americans, particularly African Americans, were of significant interest to Caribbean populations, black and white, and the consumption of African-American dialect reflected that interest. The United States was both a beacon of solace as well as a source of anxiety to white slave-holding creoles in the Caribbean. Slavery was still reassuringly legal in the United States when it was not in the post-Emancipation Caribbean. Newspaper accounts of the white plantocracy's plan to import African Americans in the 1860s after the loss of black Caribbean labor were contradictory in their assessment. On the one hand, the plan to import African Americans could engender "revolutionary" sentiments in the black population, suggesting that whites feared an even larger black majority in the region. On the other, the plan was a welcome rebuttal to the British, those "old women in chairs" who dictated Caribbean labor policy.[13] African Americans were, therefore, certainly within the purview of elite Caribbean society.

The presence of African-American speech, albeit in the distorted form of minstrel dialect, reflects the focus on African Americans in Caribbean newspapers from as early as 1839, barely a year after Emancipation was declared across the region. Two examples from early Trinidadian newspapers illustrate its influence on the narrative rendering of anglophone Caribbean dialect: "Look Here Sambo" and "New Government Buildings."[14]

In 1839 *Trinidad Standard* published "Look Here, Sambo," an "overheard" conversation between Cuff and Sambo, two African-American men:

> DIALOGUE—"Look here, Sambo, you got dat quarter dollar you owes me?"
> Sambo—"La! Cuff, no; money so scarce, so many stopperages in Mobile, their

[11] According to Errol Hill, British theatre troupes regularly staged plays using African-American minstrel figures; see Errol Hill, *The Jamaican Stage* (1992), chapters 9 and 10. The abolitionist novel *Uncle Tom's Cabin* was a bestseller in England and a popular subject for plays. The novel's reliance on African-American stereotypes may explain the British fixation with blackface minstrelsy.

[12] See Alfred Bendixen and Steven R. Serafin, eds., *The Continuum Encyclopedia of American Literature* (New York and London: Continuum, 1999), p. 644.

[13] See Gentleman in New York, "American Immigration," *Colonial Standard* (March 3, 1868); and Audi Alteram Partem, *Colonial Standard* (March 20, 1868). In the former, the writer suggests that "Americanizing" the West Indian colonies is a risky venture, because the black population may be influenced to "revolutionary" sentiments by the Americans due to the American "individuality of character." In the latter, the editorial page asserts the plan is a welcome stab at independence by the Jamaicans against the nagging British and their "old lady" concern for the blacks.

[14] See Anonymous, "Look Here Sambo," in *Trinidad Standard* (September 13, 1839), p. 2; and EAVESDROPPER, "New Government Buildings," *Port of Spain Gazette* (1844), reprinted in Lise Winer, "Six Vernacular Texts from Trinidad, 1838–1851," p. 75, in Edgar W. Schneider, ed., *Englishes Around the World: Studies in Honour of Manfred Gorlach*, vol. 2 (Amsterdam: John Benjamins, 1997).

[sic] ain't no money in circumlation." Cuff—"Oh sho, Sambo, what de nashum you got to do with Mobile? Nigger, pay up! pay up!" Sambo—"Well, look here, Cuff, me hear Massa tell more dan twenty men dat same tale; and I ain't see no gentleman treat him like you me. Act like a gentleman if you *is* a nigger."[15]

As linguist Lise Winer notes, there is no local Trinidadian content in "Look Here, Sambo," only references to Mobile (Alabama) and quarter dollars, which lead her to conclude that this was an import from the United States. Moreover, white creoles, who constituted the readership of *The Trinidad Standard*, were already familiar with actual African Americans through immigration. African-American veterans of the War of 1812, the so-called "Merikins," who fought alongside the British were given acres of land in Trinidad and settled in several "Company" villages. There is also evidence of other African Americans who visited as sailors or free coloreds, and perhaps stayed in the region.[16]

The chief source of humor in "Look Here, Sambo" lies in the dig at indebted white gentlemen who would never be so vulgar as to ask their debtors for their money. Here, dialect serves as a marker of the authentic: it is the truthful counterpoint to the evasive genteel discourse haunting the margins of the joke, a model of the compelling dialectic between the vulgar and the respectable that remains part of the Caribbean Creole tradition today. Dialect as social satire of genteel discourse utilized by "Look here, Sambo" is in keeping with the Trinidadian newspaper writing tradition that evolved during the nineteenth century. However, this suggests even more imbrication: having digested African-American dialect forms through reproductions like "Look Here, Sambo," white creoles appear to have used them as a template for rendering written forms of their own, Trinidadian, dialect.

In 1844, a few years later, both African Americans and black Trinidadian creoles are the targets of satire in "New Government Buildings," another "overheard" conversation printed in the *Port of Spain Gazette*.[17] The African American is a "buddy," or man; the Afro-Trinidadian is a "sissee," or woman. The likely white creole author sneers at the idea that they could be considered gentility, or equals: "The 'lady', I beg to premise, was a creole of the colony—to the marrow bone—the 'gentleman', one of the Immigrants of North America." The two characters are speculating on the new government buildings being erected in Port of Spain. The

[15] Anonymous, "Look Here Sambo," *Trinidad Standard* (September 13, 1839), p. 2; reprinted in Lise Winer, "Six Vernacular Texts from Trinidad, 1838–1851," p. 75, in Edgar W. Schneider, ed., *Englishes Around the World: Studies in Honour of Manfred Gorlach* (Amsterdam: John Benjamins, 1997).

[16] See John McNish Weiss, "The Corp of Colonial Marines: Black Freedom Fighters of the War of 1812," accessed January 23, 2014, http://www.mcnishandweiss.co.uk/history/colonialmarines.html.

[17] See EAVESDROPPER, "New Government Buildings," *Port of Spain Gazette* (1844), reprinted in Lise Winer, "Six Vernacular Texts from Trinidad, 1839–1851," pp. 75–6, in *Englishes Around the World: Essays in Honour of Manfred Gorlach*, edited by Edgar W. Schneider, vol. 2 (Amsterdam: John Benjamins Publishing Company, 1997).

African American opines that they are intended to be a penitentiary, which is, he asserts, a place for "people as is too good to be put in a gaol." The source of the humor is the pretensions of the African American to a cosmopolitan identity and learnedness because, as he puts it, he has had "the advantage of travel . . . and it is travel makes the Gentleman after all." Travel is both the sign of elite status and the proof of universal black inferiority—at least as far as the (presumably) white creole author is concerned—because it reveals that black people, whether from the United States or the Caribbean, are equally inferior. The African American condescends to the creole ("The ignorance of these West Indian colored people makes me feel proud of my American edication. . . . But I might as well talk to a horse—this woman dont understand a word I'm saying") even as he mangles standard grammar pronunciations and shows his own ignorance of the world. For her part, the Afro-creole woman is unaffected in her honest ignorance; she is in awe of this learned black man. The narrative depends on the readers' familiarity with what we think of as an Americanracial stereotype of the Zip Coon, a "citified" or otherwise socially ambitious but stupid black man who puts on grandiloquent airs and attempts to rise above his station. Zip Coon was a staple character in American minstrel shows in the 1830s, but is most associated with the post-Civil War United States. That this Zip Coon-like manifestation appears in 1844, six years after Emancipation in the anglophone Caribbean, reflects white creole anxieties about freed blacks, particularly men, who might also wish to "rise above their station" through travel and the acquisition of knowledge.

Blackface Minstrelsy and Literary Dialect

Renderings of African-American dialect were part of the explosion of dialect narrative and performance that proliferated in the Caribbean as blacks emerged from slavery to claim land, advocate for education, and press for political power. Imported reproductions of the African-American vernacular mode, in the form of poems and comic dialogues, continued to appear in Caribbean newspapers throughout the nineteenth century.[18] American dialect sketches and performances appealed to a wide cross-section of Caribbean society, across class and race lines. Blackface minstrelsy was a particularly striking vehicle for multiracial harmony, given its unflattering depiction of blacks. Blackface minstrelsy was directly tied to modes of "bad" black speech. Blackface performances raged across the Caribbean including in Cuba, where the Zip Coon stereotype manifested in the dialectical relationship between the *bozal* and the *catedrático*.

---

[18] See "This, That and the Other," *Jamaica Advocate* (October 1, 1899), pp. 2–3. Afro-Bahamian publisher Robert Love's newspaper carried a humorous story, in the African-American vernacular, of "an old colored woman in Washington" who, when asked if she really believed what the Bible said, that people are made out of dust, replied, "'Yes sah! The Bible says dey is, and so I b'lieves it.' 'But what is done in wet weather, where there is nothing but mud?' 'Den I s'pects dey make infidels an' sich truck.'"

The *bozal* was an African-born black, usually a slave, who remained hopelessly out of sync with Cuban—or modern—life. He spoke an "African" dialect of Spanish, filled with distortions of Spanish grammar and pronunciation. The *bozal* was inevitably paired with the *catedrático*, or "negro professor," according to Jill Lane, "whose vain efforts to feign education and social status produce nothing more than a ludicrous parody of refined speech and aristocratic manners."[19] Although Lane argues that the Cuban blackface tradition precedes that of the United States,[20] the *catedrático*'s remarkable similarity to Zip Coon, and his invention at a time when white Cubans were similarly concerned about abolition, suggests that this character may be part of a circulation of types in the region. Errol Hill refers to an episode in Jamaica during the nineteenth century when a group of Cuban men raised money for widows and orphans of one of the Cuban wars of independence by staging three minstrel shows in Kingston with names like "The Wise and Refined Negroes" and "The Essence of Virginia: A Grotesque Performance," as well as "the celebrated breakdown" dance.[21] The triangulation of cultures in evidence here—Cubans acting as African Americans for the entertainment of Jamaicans—reinforces the paradigm of circularity in the dissemination of African-American typologies. African-American minstrel characters were constantly revised, reconstituted, commingled with local archetypes, and returned to circulation within the region.

Blackface minstrelsy swept through the anglophone Caribbean well into the twentieth century, but it was in Jamaica where the American blackface minstrel tradition grew strong local roots.[22] The country already had a thriving theatre scene throughout the nineteenth century, well-attended by Jamaicans of every racial and ethnic description. In 1840 local amateurs staged the burlesque *Jim Crow in London; or, The Creole Ball*, as an afterpiece to Irish playwright Sheridan Knowles's *The Hunchback*, suggesting a circuitous route via London of American-style minstrelsy into Jamaica. The next year a visiting actor sang and jumped Jim Crow. Then, in a clear appeal to non-elites two years later a local theater company offered "popular-type entertainment consisting of...Negro songs, and dances at bargain prices" at the Royal Victoria Theatre.[23] Later that same year another local company presented a popular farce called *The Virginny Mammy; or, The Liquor of Life*, that was revived in the succeeding years. In 1849 there is evidence of yet another local production of minstrelsy; according to Errol Hill, one "Mr. Cassares,

---

[19] Jill Lane, "Blackface Nationalism, Cuba 1840–1868," *Theatre Journal* 50 (1) (March 1998), p. 21.
[20] Jill Lane, "Blackface Nationalism, Cuba 1840–1868" (1998), p. 23.
[21] Errol Hill, *The Jamaican Stage* (1992), p. 267.
[22] Trinidad also shows evidence of an enduring local blackface tradition. Donald Hill notes that in the early twentieth century black-and-whiteface routines were incorporated into Trinidad's carnival and the performers were called minstrels, or the Yankee band. See Donald Hill, *Calypso Callaloo: Early Carnival Music in Trinidad* (Gainesville: University Press of Florida, 1993), p. 157. John Cowley also notes the influence of blackface minstrelsy in Trinidad carnival in John Cowley, *Carnival, Canboulay and Calypso: Traditions in the Making* (New York and Cambridge: Cambridge University Press, 1996).
[23] Errol Hill, *The Jamaican Stage* (1992), p. 90.

assisted by resident music professors and amateurs, presented a concert at the New Court House in Kingston that included Ethiopian songs and glees."[24] By 1855 the "true Ethiopian minstrel style" of African-American singing was a commonplace feature of Jamaican society: a Kingston bookshop advertised "Negro and Ethiopian melodies with choruses" for sale.

A comprehensive understanding of the effect of American-style blackface minstrelsy on a Caribbean audience relies on our understanding of theater as a popular culture phenomenon in the anglophone Caribbean. The theater-going public represented almost every racial group of the society: white, black, brown. The theater space itself provided a form of what Elizabeth Dillon calls a performative commons, where people come not simply to watch but to represent themselves.[25] The theater, then, functioned as a relatively democratic space in an otherwise profoundly stratified society. And, in Jamaica at the very least, blacks were not just in the audience: Errol Hill finds evidence of black Jamaican amateur theatre groups from as early as the late 1840s.[26] Add to this the perception by the elites that whites who performed in front of these racially mixed audiences were in some sense tainted by their performative labor—the Jamaican governor's wife Lady Nugent complains of a respectable white creole who "exposes himself in that way to the public"—and it becomes clear that in Jamaica theatre was, if not a democratizing cultural force, at the very least a place where racial and class relationships were under continual negotiation.[27]

Jamaicans had already ingested and localized their own meanings of minstrelsy by 1865, the year of the Morant Bay Rebellion, when the first actual blackface minstrel troupe arrived in the country. The timing was perfect. In a year of explosive racial tensions, blacks, whites, and browns enjoyed the visiting blackface minstrels who, as foreign (not native-born) whites were well-suited to relieve boiling black resentment at the white plantocracy. It would be a mistake to assume, however, that the American blackface minstrel tradition in the Caribbean always consisted of whites parodying blacks. Although the ventriloquist renderings of African-American speech by white creoles might lead one to think otherwise, West Indians across the color spectrum were taken with African-American voices and cultural ideas (or white approximations thereof). Just as blackface minstrelsy enjoyed popularity among whites and blacks in the 1860s Caribbean, so too were its performers both white and black. In 1869, four years after the first blackface minstrel troupe made its appearance in Jamaica, the Original Georgia Minstrels visited the country: most likely it was Hicks' Georgia Minstrels, the first

---

[24] Errol Hill, *The Jamaican Stage* (1992), p. 268.
[25] Elizabeth Dillon, *New World Drama: The Performative Commons in the Atlantic World 1649–1849* (Durham and London: Duke University Press, 2014), p. 2.
[26] Errol Hill, *The Jamaican Stage* (1992), p. 91.
[27] Maria Nugent, *Lady Nugent's Journal of Her Residence in Jamaica from 1801 to 1805*, edited by Philip Wright and Verene Shepherd (Mona, Jamaica: University of the West Indies Press, 2002), pp. 147–8.

African-American blackface minstrel troupe.[28] Over the next decades other blackface minstrel troupes such as Christy's Minstrels would make the region, Jamaica in particular, a regular port of call.[29] American-style blackface minstrelsy had arrived in the Caribbean.

Nineteenth century attitudes towards African Americans in the Caribbean were therefore a contradictory mix of elements. On the one hand, the derisive "overheard" conversations in the Trinidadian newspapers suggest that the white elites there saw African Americans as "uppity," ignorant, or both. On the other, post-Emancipation efforts by white Jamaican planters to replace black creoles with still-enslaved African Americans were motivated by the view that African Americans were more docile than Afro-Caribbean people. Even the freed African-American population was considered tamer than the blacks in post-Morant Bay Jamaica.[30] At an 1852 meeting convened by Edward Jordan, the brown mayor of Kingston, a resolution was passed inviting African Americans to settle in Jamaica, presumably as a response to the Fugitive Slave Act that was passed in the United States two years before that threatened free African Americans living in northern states.[31] Edward Jordan was also the editor of *The Watchman*, a newspaper for coloreds whose political positions were consistently set against that of the Jamaican plantocracy. Jamaicans clearly felt a special kinship with prominent African-American "agitator" Frederick Douglass, who briefly visited the island in 1871. Gushed the conservative pro-planter *Daily Gleaner*, "The name of Frederick Douglass in America is like that of Edward Jordan (of blessed memory) in Jamaica...Frederick Douglass has special claims upon the 'people' of Jamaica; and we welcome him in the name of that people—embracing the vast intelligence and wealth of the island—on his arrival among us."[32]

The varied responses to African Americans came at a time when Jamaica was inflamed by tensions over land and colored rights culminating in the violence of

---

[28] Errol Hill, *The Jamaican Stage* (1992), p. 103; also Bernard L. Peterson Jr., *The African-American Theater Directory, 1816–1960* (Westport: Greenwood Press, 1997), p. 95. While Hill's account doesn't specify that the Original Georgia Minstrels were African Americans, Peterson's account of the troupe reveals that they were indeed an African-American-organized troupe, hugely popular with southern African-American audiences, who toured Panama and New Zealand, among international venues.

[29] Errol Hill, *The Jamaican Stage* (1992), p. 103. The first performance rendered entirely in "the Negro dialect" was by a quartet of blackface minstrels from New York in 1865, who sang and danced the number "To Walk in Central Park," dedicated to the people of Kingston, Jamaica. Christy's Minstrels travelled to British Guiana as well, and appeared onstage in Georgetown on October 18, 1880, according to the *Argosy* newspaper. See Frank Thomasson, *A History of Theatre in Guyana, 1800–2000* (London: Hansib, 2009), p. 69.

[30] See Governor Edward Eyre to Newcastle, July 5, 1862, "Despatches from the Governor of Jamaica," in "Correspondence respecting the Emigration of Free negroes from the United States to the West Indies. Confidential." CO 884/2/15, National Archives, Kew, England; cited in Tim Watson, *Caribbean Culture and British Fiction in the Atlantic World, 1780–1870* (New York and Cambridge: Cambridge University Press, 2008), pp. 188, 189 footnote 7; for comparisons of post-Morant Bay Jamaican blacks with African Americans, see Our Special Correspondent, "America," *Colonial Standard and Despatch* (May 7, 1866).

[31] See Errol Hill, *The Jamaican Stage* (1992), p. 104. [32] *Daily Gleaner* (March 13, 1871).

the Morant Bay Rebellion, as I have discussed. Black and brown Jamaicans were challenging the white elite in almost every area. The economic crisis on the island had made poverty endemic. Social tensions were particularly fraught: "Kingston and its vicinity must be fast verging [on] barbarism," moaned one commentator.[33] The emergent economic power of browns was deliberately crippled by whites with laws designed to keep them "impoverished and dependent."[34]

The volatile racial climate was both mediated and deflected by the arrival of American-style dialect performances. American racial typologies, deployed constantly in dialect performances, proved a useful tool for social control. Theatre companies from the United States and Great Britain travelling in the region seem to have been aware that Jamaica came with its own social challenges. They sought to localize their offerings by introducing topics that were relevant to the Jamaican situation, even incorporating Jamaican dialect into their shows. As I indicated earlier, legendary British actor Charles Kean wowed Jamaican audiences in the 1860s with his skit, "Wallack's Negro Comic History of England in 199 chapters with stirring local hits introducing the whole of the Jamaican oddities."[35] The title suggests that British Kean's "negro" take on English history was rendered in African-American dialect (the stand-in for the "negro" voice in England at this time), with some Jamaican dialect passages to cover the "Jamaican oddities." Either way, what we have is a confluence of African-American and Jamaican voices, or an "African-American" vocal narration of Jamaican history.

Derogatory stereotypes of blacks, particularly black men, proliferated in the decades after Emancipation in the Caribbean and the United States. This was the case in Britain as well: the Scottish writer Thomas Carlyle (a prominent supporter of Jamaica's disgraced Governor John Eyre during the Morant Bay Rebellion controversy) placed the post-Emancipation failure of the sugar industry in the Caribbean squarely at the foot of "Quashee." Quashee was, like the American "Sambo," the given name for the stereotypical black male creole. Carlyle describes Quashee as essentially lazy, gorging himself on pumpkins, and refusing to work, while sugar cane rots in the fields. In his infamous "Discourse on the Nigger Question," Carlyle further elaborates on Quashee's essential nature:

I decidedly like poor Quashee; and find him a pretty kind of man. With a pennyworth of oil, you can make a handsome glossy thing of Quashee. . . A swift, supple fellow; a merry-hearted, grinning, dancing, singing, affectionate kind of creature, with a great deal of melody and amenability in his composition.[36]

[33] *Morning Journal* (July 13–14, 1882).   [34] *The Anti-Slavery Reporter* 9 (1) (1861), p. 20.
[35] *Colonial Standard and Despatch* (May 18, 1867), quoted in Errol Hill, *The Jamaican Stage* (1992), p. 199.
[36] Thomas Carlyle, "Occasional Discourse on the Nigger Question," in *Critical and Miscellaneous Essays*, vol. III (London: Chapman and Hall, 1888), p. 471.

The stereotypes that Carlyle deploys in defense of the neo-slavery conditions of post-Emancipation conditions mimic the binary stereotypes deployed by white Southerners in the United States during Reconstruction. Antebellum blacks were Sambos: gullible, mindless creatures who loved nothing more than to sing, dance, and eat watermelon while lazing under a tree. Post-Emancipation blacks were uppity Zip Coons, still with a lazy disposition but now also with dangerous aspirations.

These stereotypes were reinforced by visual representations of blacks on stage, which then migrated to Britain via American blackface minstrel shows. Carlyle's stereotyping of the black Jamaican Quashee appears to be a condensation and Caribbeanizing of an American binary of black male stereotypes. Quashee is a countrified, Sambo-like simpleton unless he gets aspirations from his newfound independence, after which, like Zip Coon, he becomes citified—and dangerous. The blackface dialect performances staged in Jamaica and elsewhere in the Caribbean utilized these stereotypes to appeal across ideological, racial, and class lines in the region. African-American-style dialect performances managed signif-icant ideological work in welding together a fractious, riven society.

Rise of the Black Choirs

The later nineteenth century would bring more African-American performers to the Caribbean who sang black songs in a "serious," non-comedic performative mode. This was a significant development in the theatrical and musical traditions of the black Atlantic, as Paul Gilroy has shown, not least because here was the moment when black performers performed blackness onstage for black, not just white, people.[37] The Fisk University (or Tennessee) Jubilee Singers played to packed houses on a world tour in 1889, which included "Australasia" and the West Indies. In actuality highly trained from African-American singers from the urban Northeast, they were neither from Tennessee nor affiliated with Fisk University,[38] to the disgust of some of the white listeners who were expecting "authentic" performances of ex-slaves. Wrote one Australian reviewer,

> The sacred bottom is at last knocked out of that sorrowful nigger entertainment known as the Fisk Jubilee Singers...a show which is no different to Hicks' Black Minstrels in the sight of the gods...That most of the nigs must have been born

[37] See Paul Gilroy, pp. 87–93 ("The Jubilee Singers and the Transatlantic Route"), in Paul Gilroy, *The Black Atlantic: Modernity and Double Consciousness* (Cambridge: Harvard University Press, 1993).

[38] One of the Fisk Jubilee choir members explained to an interviewer, "I, myself, have never been to Tennessee as yet." See W. H. Pierce, interviewed in *Indianapolis Freeman* (June 15, 1888), cited in Lynn Abbott and Doug Seroff, *Out of Sight* (2009), p. 50.

after Emancipation Day was overlooked when they were warbling their tommy-rot about Stealing Away, &c.

Now they stand revealed as a secular crowd of *more or less cullud* pussons who never were the slaves of anybody except showmen…Hallelujah![39]

[emphasis added]

The hostility of the Australian reviewer towards the now-legendary Jubilee Singers is indicative of white audience expectations that they were witnessing a kind of neo-slave performance in "authentic" black dialect, hence the reviewer's sarcastic reference, rendered in pseudo-dialect, to "*more or less* cullud pussons," implying that these unpleasantly well-educated performers were not quite black. Yet, 44 years later, African-American author Zora Neale Hurston makes a similar criticism of the Jubilee Singers:

> In spite of the goings up and down on the earth, from the original Fisk Jubilee singers down to the present, there has been no genuine presentation of Negro songs to white audiences. The spirituals that have been sung around the world are Negroid to be sure, but so full of musicians [sic] tricks that Negro congregations are highly entertained when they hear their old songs so changed. They never use the new style songs, and these are never heard unless perchance some daughter or son has been off to college and returns with one of the old songs with its face lifted, so to speak.[40]

Zora Neale Hurston's critique is that the Jubilee's rendering of "Negro songs" is a collegiate version, cleaned up to appeal to whites. She implies that African-Americans understand this, because they know the original songs. The Australian reviewer's critique is that those "original" versions are just the same as the blackface minstrel songs that had already made the rounds in Australia and across the globe. These educated blacks, therefore, are charlatans trying to pass themselves off as poor southern blacks barely out of slavery when they are anything but. In the schism between these two critiques lies the Caribbean response, itself a complex amalgam of multiracial viewpoints.

The Jubilee Singers' tour of the Caribbean was a phenomenon not seen before in the region. They "swept the Carribbeans [sic], and illustrated the wonderful strides and progress which is being made by the Coloured Race of America,"

---

[39] See *Sydney Bulletin* (May 11, 1889), cited in Lynn Abbott and Doug Seroff, *Out of Sight: The Rise of African-American Music, 1889–1895* (Jacksonville: University of Mississippi Press, 2002), p. 25.

[40] Zora Neale Hurston, "The Characteristics of Negro Expression," in *Negro: An Anthology*, edited by Nancy Cunard (New York: Ungar Press, 1933/1970), p. 31. Hurston is also dismissive of W. E. B. DuBois' reading of the Jubilee Singers, arguing that his characterization of their music as "sorrow songs" was predicated on principles of Western music that didn't apply to them.

according to one poster.[41] Overflow crowds packed concert halls to see them in Jamaica, Trinidad, Barbados, British Guiana, Dutch Guiana (Surinam), St. Kitts, and Panama (itself home to a population of anglophone Caribbean blacks since the mid-nineteenth century). In Kingston alone the Jubilee Singers had 42 performances, at one of which 60 policemen were required to control the crowd. The Singers performed to a "crowded, rapturously enthusiastic," "spell-bound" house, which encored every song. "[T]he Singers gave powerful expression to the...sweetly plaintive melodies which gladdened the souls of the tenants of the mud cabins of the South in the olden time," rhapsodized the reviewer in the *Colonial Standard*.[42]

The Fisk Jubilee Singers had return engagements in 1889 and 1890, playing to multi-racial audiences across the Caribbean, as one of the singers told the African-American press.[43] The Fisk singers were bemused by what they perceived to be the differences among the various races and ethnic groups in the audience ("Creole Spaniards like a noise, but the [coloreds] like the solos and secular music [while]. . . .the low class . . . are particularly fond of the humorist, and a man does not have to be much of a comedian to set them wild.")[44] The choir's popularity, like that of the blackface minstrels, crossed racial and class lines, as apparently did the audience for any touring group from abroad that featured black culture. This appeared not to be the case with all African-American audiences. In the United States the original choir "encountered the ambivalence and embarrassment of black audiences unsure or uneasy about serious, sacred being displayed to audiences conditioned by the hateful antics of Zip Coon, Jim Crow, and their odious supporting cast," according to Gilroy.[45] (Class and intra-regional differences may have something to do with this response within African-American populations: the all-black Hicks' Georgia Minstrels were, according to one account, as popular among southern African Americans as they were with West Indians.[46])

From the extant Caribbean press reviews of the Jubilee Singers it is clear that their popularity with Caribbean audiences seems to have been precisely the feature which so irked Zora Neale Hurston: their singular blend of classical training

[41] *New York Age* (March 23, 1889), cited in Lynn Abbott and Doug Seroff, *Out of Sight* (2009), p. 32 The poster refers to the "Tennessee Concert Company," not the Jubilee Singers, but this is the same group.

[42] See "The Tennessee Jubilee Singers," *Colonial Standard and Despatch* (August 15, 1888).

[43] See Florence Williams, "A Singer's Triumph—Laurels Won by Madame Mathilda S. Jones in the West Indies and Central America," *New York Age* (February 16, 1889), cited in Lynn Abbott and Doug Seroff, *Out of Sight* (2009), p. 31.

[44] See interview with W. H. Pierce, *Indianapolis Freeman* (June 15, 1888), cited in Lynn Abbott and Doug Seroff, *Out of Sight* (2009), pp. 50–1.

[45] Paul Gilroy, *The Black Atlantic: Modernity and Double Consciousness* (1993), p. 89.

[46] According to Ken Padgett, the popularity of African-American blackface minstrel Billy Kersands, who first started with the Original Georgia Minstrels, was "unsurpassed" with Southern African-American audiences in the late nineteenth and early twentieth centuries, even as African-American audiences watched his performances in a theater where half the audience was white (seated in the whites-only section). See Ken Padgett, "Billy Kersands, 1842–1915," Blackface!, accessed December 30, 2020, http://black-face.com/billy-kersands.htm.

and an "African" performative mode. The same Jamaican reviewer who spoke of the "melodies of the mud cabins of the South" also praised the group's singing as a "masterpiece of correct musical interpretation and trained vocalization."[47] The *Daily Chronicle* of British Guiana noted that "The bodies of the singers sway in time with the music and...they put their whole heart and soul into it" and declared the choir to be "a living protest against modern namby-pambyism."[48] Trinidad's *Port of Spain Gazette* reviewer enjoyed the "exhilarating effect...of the happy expression of quaint, vigorous, original African feeling controlled, harmonized and refined under the powerful influence of civilized musical science....In listening to and seeing the movements of the singers we find the spicy originality of negro-minstrelsy, made fit for the educated eyes and ears of the refined occupants of the drawing room."[49]

Original African feeling. Civilized musical science. Spicy originality of negro-minstrelsy, made fit for the educated eyes and ears of the refined occupants of the drawing room. In these potent phrases we find the key to the popularity of the Jubilee Singers in the Caribbean. Just who are these "refined occupants of the drawing room" whose "educated eyes and ears" might be shocked by "spicy," "original African" music? African-American minstrel songs were popular across the racial spectrum in the Caribbean, and particularly popular with the plantocracy: it seems wrong-headed to assume that these "refined occupants" are whites whose delicate sensibilities need such careful handling. The comment does, however, assume that undiluted "spicy negro minstrelsy" could be a problem for some listeners. Given the changing racial composition of the Caribbean middle class in the 1880s, it seems clear that this comment alludes to non-white gentility. Educated black and brown people would undoubtedly be more sensitive than whites to viewing a performance associated with slavery, a trauma still within living memory for African-descended communities.

Enslaved or no, black culture clearly exerted a powerful pull on the black and brown middle classes of the Caribbean. The Jubilee Singers' synthetic, or hybridized form of the African-American "negro song" was clearly a draw, whose aspiring non-white inhabitants would see in this "collegiate version" of black music a way to reconcile the supposedly primitive, but somehow unshakable, cultural singularity of dialect performative modes with the refined training of the white-identified classical tradition. The disjuncture between "grotesque and incongruous" on one hand, and "tender sentiment and melodious expression" on the other, neatly parallels the rough-hewn authenticity of Hurston's original spirituals paired with

---

[47] See "Tennessee Jubilee Singers," *Colonial Standard* (August 15, 1888).

[48] *Daily Chronicle* (December 15, 1888), cited in Lynn Abbott and Doug Seroff, *Out of Sight* (2003), p. 50, footnote 21.

[49] *Port of Spain Gazette* (December 5, 1888), cited in Lynn Abbott and Doug Seroff, *Out of Sight* (2003), p. 50, footnote 20.

the critiqued "collegiate" versions. Here, then, was the ideal melding of Africaneity and modernity. Here was dialect as upliftment.

As Errol Hill notes, the influence of the Jubilee Singers in Jamaica was long-lasting: "Jamaican performers developed two branches of the minstrel tradition, both originally retaining blackface makeup. The singing troupes, however, soon dropped the mask as they began to add native folk songs to their repertoires. The comedians, however, kept it as they paired off into a string of duos [in the twentieth century...], illustrated by the popular blackface Jamaican comedy duo Bim and Bam, who performed comic sketches such as "Duppy Biznizz" in Kingston well into the 1950s"[50] (Figure 4.1).

The melding of the two American minstrel traditions in the Caribbean can be gauged by viewing the popular twinned images of the white Christy's minstrels, where they appear both as dignified white men and then as riotous "blacks." The black Jubilee Singers were only photographed in dignified choir pose, but the duality exhibited in the photographs of the Christy's minstrels is similarly illustrated in the dual and dueling images of the Kingston Choral Union, also known as the Native Jamaica Choir, during their tour of Great Britain in 1906–1907. Like the competing images of the white minstrels in and out of blackface, the Native Jamaica Choir photos viewed altogether suggest a binary, almost schizoid combination of formal Western society and "true" black peasant Jamaican life (Figure 4.2).

The first photo projects the solemn dignity reminiscent of their African-American parallels, the Jubilee Singers: black Jamaicans of various hues in formal evening attire, sitting with legs crossed, not touching. The second photo of the Native Jamaica choir ("straw hats") is in distinctly more relaxed poses, with members in peasant or "native" costume, some sitting or lying on the ground, women with arms akimbo in a visually more "typical" stance associated with black Caribbean women (Figure 4.3).

The all-black (or, more accurately, black-and-brown) Kingston Choral Union, established in 1882, was the best-known of a welter of Jamaican choral groups that proliferated in the wake of the Jubilee Singers' Caribbean tour. (Other groups included the Montego Bay Coloured Concert Troupe, and the Spanish Town Choral Union.) Later renamed the Native Jamaica Choir, the Kingston Choral Union was the most popular choir in a society that adored choir performances (Figure 4.4). These choral performances were a harbinger of the theatrical vernacular performances so popular in the Caribbean in later decades right into the present. To judge from the reviews of the time, the audience had a similar sense of familiarity and ownership towards the performances that contemporary audiences have towards vernacular performers. A choral competition in Kingston in

---

[50] Errol Hill, *The Jamaican Stage* (1992), p. 269.

BIM & BAM

Says:—
"It's Eerie,
Spookey,
Spine-Chilling !!"

It's Another Smashing Stage hit . . .

"DUPPY BIZNIZZ"

Starring: Hyacinth Clover & Danny Boy

At The WARD THEATRE

On Wednesday 1st August 10 A.M.

The mysterious stone throwing and money disappearing did not bother Mrs. Tiny Martin much . . . But when her 3 yrs. old son vanished from the bed that was too much for her. Then it was that the ever popular Mother Banner was called in to solve the mystery. You will howl . . . scream, rock, with laughter at the awe-inspiring cymballing of the mother as she drives her Flocks to the Rhythm of the Pocomania Drums.

Supported by a Galaxy of Popular Stars:

Count Lasher & his Calypso Band, Minto, Roy (Mule Train), Shirley Foster, George Nelson, Yvonne Francis, Wonder Brothers, A. B. Racca, Carlton Barker, Viris Barracks, Sylvia Brown.

TRENTON SPENCE & his Orchestra

PRICES: Gallery 3/-, Parquette 4/-, Dress Circle 5/-
(Tax included)

Doors 8 A.M. — Curtains 10 A.M.

(Be Early and avoid the Rush)

Figure 4.1 "Duppy Biznizz," *Daily Gleaner* (July 22, 1956). My thanks to Kenneth Bilby for sharing this image from his collection.

Figure 4.2   Fisk Jubilee Singers, Prints and Photographs Division, Library of Congress.

1895, modeled on British choral performances and held supposedly for its "enno-
bling influence on the people," drew an overflow crowd which let out "loud guf-
faws" and engaged in "hissing" when the performers were considered lacking. The
Kingston Choral Union won the competition by mixing classical pieces like
"Come Where the Lilies Bloom" with what were called "plantation" or "jubilee
songs," clearly African-American songs, with names like like "Talk About Your
Moses."[51] The Kingston Choral Union was also notable for its performances of
Jamaican folk songs. Actually, it might be more accurate to call some of these
popular music: at least one was actually a popular dialect song of the period. On
June 6, 1895, at the height of "Bedwardism," they performed the now-classic "Dip
Dem Bedward in de Healing Stream," about the Afro-Jamaican revivalist healer
Alexander Bedward, accused of sedition against the government that April and
found guilty by reason of insanity:

> Dip dem Bedward, dip dem
> Dip dem in de healin' stream.
> Dip dem sweet but not too deep
> Dip dem fe cure bad feelin'.

The Kingston Choral Union's performance was accompanied by a skit by comedian (and son of Henry) W. C. Murray, popularly known as "Funny Murray," who
sang "Bedward in the 'Sylum" and danced himself off stage.[52] This suggests that

---

[51]   See "The Choral Competition," *Daily Gleaner* (August 23, 1895), p. 7.
[52]   See review in the *Jamaica Advocate* (June 8, 1895), cited in Patrick Bryan, *The Jamaican People:
Race, Class and Social Control* (Mona: University of the West Indies Press, 1991/2000), p. 198. The

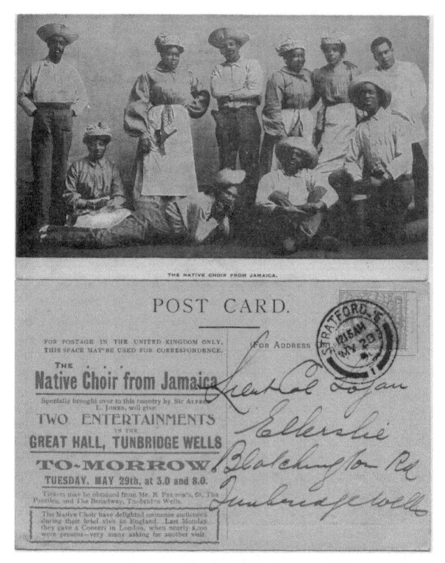

Figure 4.3 *The Native Choir of Jamaica*, Liverpool, England, 1906. Postcard image courtesy of Leon Robinson of Positive Steps, London, with the assistance of Jeffrey Green.

Daily Gleaner advertised the concert as a three-way bill, featuring C. T. Mosely ("The Great American Prince of Song") and the Kingston Choral Union singing together, among these "Tennessee Jubilee gems," as well as "Funny Murray." The subtitle reads, "Free funeral expenses…should you laugh to death." See *Daily Gleaner*, "New Moonlight Parade" (June 1, 1895), p. 2. See also Brian L. Moore and Michele A. Johnson, *Neither Led Nor Driven: Contesting British Cultural Imperialism in Jamaica, 1865–1920*(Mona: University of the West Indies Press, 2004), p. 79, for an account of Bedward's 1895 trial and the lyrics to "Dip Dem Bedward." The now-classic folk tune was re-made as a mento-reggae hit in 1976 by Stanley Beckford, titled "Dip Dem Jah Jah," accessed January 9, 2021, https://www.last.fm/music/Stanley+Beckford/Stanley±Beckford+Plays±Mento.

NATIVE CHOIR FROM JAMAICA (TWELVE COLOURED ARTISTES)
Sole Managers—Messrs. H. E. Jones & A. Douglass. Liverpool.

Figure 4.4 *The Native Choir of Jamaica*, Tunbridge Wells, England, 1906. From the collection of Rainer Lotz, Bonn, Germany.

the Kingston Choral Union performed a kind of contemporary social commentary when they chose popular music as part of their repertoire. All of this changed when English shipping merchant Alfred Jones re-named the group The Native Jamaica Choir, and sponsored their tour of Great Britain. As international representatives of a generic version of blackness, The Native Jamaica Choir was a popular and commercial success. Dressed both in classic Western formal as well as "native" attire, the sophisticated singers of the former Kingston Choral Union were billed as "real coon singers and dancers" by the British press—the same press which also described them as "remarkable musicians and vocalists," "well-educated and well-trained."[53] Similar to their Kingston performances, they utilized a varied repertoire of nostalgic plantation music, from supposedly African-American vernacular songs like "Keep Down de Middle of de Road," "De Water Melon on de Vine," and "If the Man in the Moon (was a Coon);" to sacred choral music in the English tradition. With this combination the Kingston Choral Union successfully melded, through music, the two competing visions of the African-American experience disseminated in the Caribbean, that of the plantation fantasy and the racial uplift ideal. Both visions were dependent on a rendering of the African-American vernacular: the comic dialect of blackface minstrelsy, and its serious, "collegiate" version. The Native Jamaica Choir also performed "Jamaican street songs" for their British audiences, although there are

[53] See *Worthing Observer* (August 5, 1906), cited in Jeffrey Green, "The Jamaican Choir in Britain," accessed March 11, 2014, http://www.jeffreygreen.co.uk/the-jamaican-choir-in-britain-1906-1908.

no reviews of these.[54] African-American-style musical forms were mish-mashed together with Afro-Jamaican ones. It did not matter which was which. It was all the same. And the British public was delighted.

The appeal of these unlikely combinations was not limited to foreign white audiences. To judge from the extant reviews, the elites and emerging middle class of the late-nineteenth century Caribbean were uncomfortable with the stultifying nature of what they called "civilized culture," at least as it played out in their own societies. They too yearned for the "spicy originality" of the dialect culture that was being left behind in their quest for modernity and equal status in the West. American Negro music could be a soundtrack for their own aspirations for independence and equality in the late nineteenth century, without the shackles of racial identification. Whites in the Caribbean embraced and identified with dialect performance, seeing in it an affirmation of themselves as Caribbean subjects. Blacks and browns also were drawn to the form. American-style Negro spirituals presaged a kind of modern black Atlantic identity, as Gilroy has famously noted, Negro songs that were *theirs*—that is, African American—yet, sort of, ours too.

The distinction, as well as the similarity, is crucial. The Jubilee Singers' invention of the dignified Negro Song was a precursor of the now-ubiquitous subgenre, the dignified calypso, in the mid-twentieth century. The blackface minstrel musical performances, however, helped to effect the transmission of calypso within and without the Caribbean. It is worth emphasizing that blackface as a performative strategy was not simply about blacking one's face: the peasant costuming, the vernacular voice, all were part of the blackface minstrel tradition that both concealed and revealed a complex Caribbean cultural identity. Together, the blackface minstrel tradition and the dignified Negro spiritual tradition provided a template for the circulation of musical entertainments, and a pan-Caribbean form of dialect, in the succeeding decades of the late nineteenth century Caribbean.

Calypso, Carnival, and Dialect

The calypso, like the African-American musical forms that preceded it, circulated both regionally in the Caribbean and even further afield in the United States very early in the twentieth century. Also like African-American musical forms, the calypso was a carrier of regional dialects, and its circulation unmistakably followed the itinerary of calypsonians. Initially the music of poor blacks, calypso came to represent an essential Caribbeanness produced and consumed by people of all races and classes even in the early twentieth century. The shadow of

---

[54] See advertisement in *Western Daily Mercury* (August 17, 1908), cited in Jeffrey Green, "The Jamaican Choir in Britain," accessed March 11, 2014, http://www.jeffreygreen.co.uk/the-jamaican-choir-in-britain-1906-1908.

American minstrelsy, as well as the movements of performers and migrants within the region, foregrounded calypso's evolution.

The pre-Lenten festival of carnival in the Caribbean was indissociable from the production of indigenous musical forms, particularly calypso in the twentieth century. The pan-Caribbean version of calypso originated in the parallel movements of carnival and calypso around the Caribbean. The yin/yang of respectability and anarchy, standard grammar and dialect that was a key feature of blackface minstrel shows and the later performances of all-black choirs from the U.S. and Caribbean, was also evident in the competing Pierrot and Pierrot Grenade (or Grenadian Pierrot) carnival characters in Trinidad from the nineteenth century. Although Trinidadian calypso was originally sung in French patois, with intra-regional migration from Venezuela, Barbados, and Grenada the Trinidadian calypso increasingly reflected a nominally anglophone, pan-Caribbean sound and style. Several of the early twentieth century calypsonians in Trinidad were schoolteachers or otherwise members of the emergent black or brown middle class. The immigrant calypsonians from the "small islands" like Grenada were looked down upon as uneducated by the Trinidadians, and good grammar became a site of contestation in the early calypso "wars," triggering lyrics like "I hate to tell you this but I must / Your nonsensical oration fills me with disgust."[55] The dialectical tradition of the voluble Pierrots was a way of incorporating characteristics of the society that seemed to be in opposition to each other. The distinction between the proper, urban, English-speaking native Pierrot and the "bad-talking," rustic immigrant Pierrot Grenade mirrored the social tension in Trinidadian society between black Trinidadians and black immigrants from Grenada and St. Vincent, considered unsophisticated and countrified. The "English" Pierrot would recite orations from Shakespeare and classic English literature, while the Grenadian Pierrot would hold his own, speaking in Creole and discourse on contemporary topics, often satirically. The dueling Pierrots would then descend into battle.[56]

The vaudeville acts of then-British Guiana in the early twentieth century similarly eased tensions between different classes and traditions. This was largely achieved through vaudeville calypso; and the language of calypso was dialect. Moreover, the dialect of British Guiana apparently was easily transferrable to the Trinidadian and other Caribbean stages, further streamlining and leveling a pan-Caribbean Creole syntax for regional consumption. Calypsonians were an integral part of the vaudeville acts that proliferated on the stages of Demerara and

---

[55] See Lise Winer, "Socio-cultural Change and the Language of Calypso," pp. 113–48, *New West Indian Guide*, vol. 60, no. 3/4 (1986), p. 117; calypsonians Atilla the Hun and Roaring Lion, "Asteroid" (calypso, 1934), lyrics quoted by Lise Winer, "Socio-cultural Change and the Language of Calypso" (1986), p. 118.

[56] See Helen Tiffin, "The Institution of Literature," in *A History of Literature in the Caribbean*, edited by A. James Arnold, vol. 2 (Amsterdam: John Benjamins, 2001), pp. 53–4.

Georgetown as the twentieth century commenced. Many of the Caribbean vaude-villians had been influenced by legendary blackface performer Bert Williams, who though based in the United States was of Bahamian descent.[57] The old American-inspired vaudeville shows were now very much local Caribbean affairs. The acts included singers—generally calypsonians—as well as dancers and elocu-tionists. Instead of theater houses, vaudevillians in Georgetown performed in cinemas prior to the beginning of a silent film. Cinema owners had decided that a good way to increase revenue was to incorporate live acts into the film experi-ence, and vaudeville provided the perfect complement to it. They were, in essence, the film's opening act.[58]

The vaudevillians reflected the multi-ethnic cultures of British Guiana: there were brown performers such as calypsonian Phil Madison, who visited Trinidad as early as 1908, and took his vaudeville troupe there in 1912, as well as white, black, and Indian ones. In the succeeding decades Indo-Guianese musicians Charlie and George Muttoo, known as the Muttoo Brothers and their Calypso Orchestra, continued the tradition of importing British Guianese music and per-formance into Trinidad. They popularized Bhagee (or Shanto) music in Trinidad through their frequent trips. Another pivotal British Guianese performer was Portuguese-Guianese performer Sidney Martin, who would perform his "dialect playlets" before silent film audiences of the 1910s, and even published a collection of them in a now-lost book. Martin's performances are a significant, if overlooked, event in the development of the Creole literary tradition, in that Martin was a white but non-British immigrant sharing equal billing with black and brown men.

The British Guianese vaudeville performers were pivotal in reconciling middle class and elite Trinidadian audiences to calypso—and with it the vernacular—as an expression of Trinidadianness. The British Guianese vaudeville acts were doubly displaced—they were from British Guiana and therefore not "local" Trinidadians; moreover, their use of blackface and the vaudeville form itself iden-tified them as Americanized, if not American. Because of this double displace-ment they were not judged by Trinidadian society's rigid standards of gentility. Consequently, middle-class audiences on the island were enthusiastic. A few decades later Trinidadian carnival masqueraders adopted the blackface routines

---

[57] For a detailed analysis of the influence of Bert Williams on Caribbean vaudeville performers, see Louis Chude-Sokei, *The Last "Darky"* (2006).

[58] Several sources note the multi-racial origins of anglophone Caribbean vaudeville shows on the silent film stages of British Guiana in the early twentieth century. See Errol Hill, Martin Banham, and George Woodyard, *The Cambridge Guide to Theatre* (Cambridge: Cambridge University Press, 2005), p. 463; Frank Thomasson, "Vaudeville" section of "Theatre-at-Large, 1900–1950," in *A History of Theatre in Guyana 1800–2000* (London: Hansib, 2009), pp. 106–12; Vibert C. Cambridge, "The Muttoo (Mootoo) Brothers Calypso Orchestra," accessed March 11, 2014, http://www.ecaroh.com/profiles/muttoobrothers.htm; Joel Benjamin, "The Early Theatre in Guyana," *Kyk-over-Al*37 (December 1987): 24–44; and Roaring Lion (Raphael de Leon), *Calypso from France to Trinidad: 800 Years of History* (General Printers of San Juan, Trinidad and Tobago, 1985).

of the vaudeville performers in so-called "Yankee" bands, where performers in black-and-whiteface would play the banjo and sing American folk or popular tunes. (An interesting counterpoint is the use of black-and-whiteface in contemporary Ghana which, it has been argued, reflects not disjuncture as one might assume, but racial harmony.)[59] The modern calypso was thus established in Trinidad. With it, a distinctive pan-Caribbean voice was born; modern yet local, easily adaptive, a voice that would come to represent the region, diffusing out into the larger Caribbean and beyond.

The dissemination and solidifying of textual and performative Caribbean Creole into a kind of *lingua franca* of the region in the latter decades of the nineteenth through the early twentieth centuries was effected through a multitude of sometimes competing influences: African-American dialect, as rendered by both European- and African Americans; working class British dialects; intra-Caribbean migrations; textual reproductions within and without the region; and the increasing association of Creole with an urban, working class sensibility that would come to define the anglophone Caribbean more consistently in the succeeding decades of the twentieth century.

From the strategic deployment of African-American style minstrel shows by the British navy post-Morant Bay in 1866 all the way to the amalgamated repertoire of African-American and Jamaican dialect songs by the Native Jamaica Choir in 1906, the invocation of both Caribbean and African-American vernaculars served to reinforce the harmonious coexistence of African and European culture under colonial rule for both local Caribbean and foreign audiences. The dueling English conceptions of black Caribbean people as either eager students of Western culture or happy savages found a solution in the hybrid musical form. Through their dialect lyrics and accompanying "native" costumes, the Native Jamaica Choir projected the Caribbean as an ordered, pleasant place full of docile blacks who strove to sing in the great white Western choral tradition even as they struck more "relaxed" poses when singing dialect songs. The language of dialect was, in this instance, unequivocal. It was the language of an essential and unchanging "native" culture in the face of major social change: in this interpretation dialect was, in essence, the language of empire.

It would be a mistake to conclude, however, that the deployment of dialect narrative produced by black and brown people was therefore *always* the language of imperialism. It would be similarly erroneous to conclude that, when untethered from the demands of white elites, its deployment was necessarily in *opposition* to the colonial project. At the turn of the nineteenth century the true legacy of

---

[59] For a discussion of the use of black-and-whiteface in contemporary Ghana see Catherine M. Cole, *Ghana's Concert Party Theatre* (Indiana University Press, 2001), p. 34. See also Donald Hill, *Calypso Calaloo: Early Carnival Music in Trinidad* (Gainesville: University Press of Florida, 1993), Chapter 8, particularly pp. 157–9; as well as Louis Chude-Sokei, *The Last Darky* (2006), p. 148.

transnational dialect was the legacy of ambiguity. Dialect was the language of empire. It was the language of black uplift. It was the language of the unrecon-structed savage. It was the language of an emergent Caribbean modernity, nostalgic and profane by turns.

The ambiguous nature of blackface vernacular performance by African Americans laid the foundation for a similarly ambiguous dynamic at work in the vernacular performances in the Caribbean. The "spicy originality" of the vernac-ular was performed simultaneously with its "refined" version—a combination which I have referred to elsewhere as a middlebrow cultural aesthetic.[60] The terms "original" and "refined" carry obvious class and generational distinctions—the voices of the poor and enslaved, next to the voices of the middle class and eman-cipated coloreds—as well as vaguely racial and geographic ones. "Pure" dialect was associated with authentic rural blackness, whether or not its speakers were actually black. By the same logic, "refined," homogenized, diluted, or otherwise mediated dialect was linked to a multiracial urban culture. So the journey sug-gested by "travelling dialect" is not merely an external, geographical manifesta-tion of culture. It is also an internal movement that signals a shift in the way that black Atlantic vernaculars are perceived, and received. The shifting meaning of the vernacular in the Caribbean accompanied questions of who can and cannot speak Creole, who should or should not. These were meaningful debates in an era when the "natural" order of people was shifting: Indian musicians played in vaudeville bands, black men wrote novels and grammar books in the Queen's English, and Portuguese vendors conducted their business in the Creole vernacular. The twentieth-century dialect narrative tradition would synthesize these different voices, and give rise to the more oppositional modes of the musical and literary vernacular tradition. But it still needed to make yet another outward journey. It was in Harlem, the Caribbean's northernmost city, that Caribbean immigrants—authors, performers, political agitators—shaped literary dialect's most enduring form.

---

[60] See Belinda Edmondson, Chapter 3, "Gentrifying Dialect," in *Caribbean Middlebrow* (2009).

5

Home to Harlem

Trinidad coming like a New York Town.
  Atilla the Hun and Lord Beginner, "Iere Now and Long Ago," 1935[1]

In 1929 the popular calypsonian, sometime Garveyite, and well-known blackface comedian Sam Manning penned "Deep Harlem," a series of four articles for his hometown newspaper, the *Trinidad Guardian*. Writing in an ethnographic vein, Manning provided his Trinidadian audience with both an insider's and outsider's view of Harlem. This was a travelogue with a difference, however. For one, as resident in either locale, Manning was "native" to both Trinidad and New York. Second, the Caribbean and New York were not as exotic to each other as one might have supposed. Trinidad, as the calypsonians Atilla and Lord Beginner note in their New York-produced hit, "Iere [Trinidad] Now and Long Ago," was swiftly becoming a modernized urban center, full of motor cars, electric lights, radio programming, new buildings and even an oil refinery in a formerly obscure part of the country.[2] And local calypso was also transforming the New York cultural landscape. As early as 1912 Trinidadian musical groups such as Lovey's Trinidad String Band were touring the United States and making records in New York, sparking a two-way flow as music company representatives visited Trinidad in 1914 to record local music. Well-known calypsonians from Trinidad and British Guiana travelled back and forth from the Caribbean to New York to record their calypsos on vinyl, then sold them in both the Caribbean and the United States. Some settled in New York and became known for their recordings of African-American songs.[3] Either way good money was being made on both sides of the Atlantic. Calypsonians were turning a profit.

---

[1] Raymond Quevedo (Atilla the Hun), and Egbert Mo-ore (Lord Beginner), "Iere Now and Long Ago," accompanied by Gerald Clark's Caribbean Serenaders, New York City, New York (March 22, 1935), Matrix 39451-A: release Decca 17264. I thank John Cowley for the full lyrics and citation to "Iere Now and Long Ago," which he kindly reproduced from his forthcoming CD collection on early calypsos.
[2] "The South has changed up entirely, / San Fernando is a beautiful town to see, / Point-A-Pierre, which was lost in obscurity, / Now possesses a giant oil refinery." See Atilla the Hun and Lord Beginner, "Iere and Long Ago" (1935).
[3] John Cowley, "West Indies Blues: An Historical Overview 1920s–1950s—Blues and Music from the English-speaking West Indies," pp. 187–263, in *Nobody Knows Where the Blues Came From: Lyrics and History*, edited by Robert Springer (Jackson: University of Mississippi Press, 2006), p. 1, accessed January 7, 2021, https://sas-space.sas.ac.uk/3080/1/Cowley_WIBtext.pdf. See also Donald Hill, Chapter 9 ("Selling Calypso in the United States"), *Calypso Calaloo: Early Carnival Music in Trinidad*

Creole Noise: Early Caribbean Dialect Literature and Performance. Belinda Edmondson, Oxford University Press.
© Belinda Edmondson 2022. DOI: 10.1093/oso/9780192856838.003.0006

In the Caribbean, in the meantime, the black middle class had distanced itself from calypso as "common" and low class. With its themes of sex, violence, immorality, urban poverty, and dialect, calypso was retrograde, an atavistic symptom of an Africanesque primitive culture from which respectable blacks sought to escape. C. L. R. James reports that as a studious black child in early twentieth century Trinidad, he "was made to understand that the road to the calypso tent was the road to hell."[4] Despite this, in the 1930s James and the multiracial members of the literary avant-garde Beacon Group of Trinidad, in their conception of the urban realist genre "yard" fiction would focus on exactly the same themes established in the calypso genre: sex, violence, poverty, and dialect. The difference was in who was "speaking:" the educated literary author, or the working-class performer.[5] The working-class-narrated calypso came first: middle-class-authored yard fiction followed.

But if calypso was reviled by respectable Caribbean blacks intent on aligning themselves with civilized culture, it was embraced in that beacon of black modernity, New York. The disjuncture between low status at home and high status abroad was so striking that Atilla the Hun noted, "when you sing calypso in Trinidad / You are a vagabond and everything that's bad / In your native land you're a hooligan / In New York you're an artist and a gentleman."[6] These New York-recorded calypsos, laden as they were with the dialects, patoises, and vernacular languages of the Caribbean, were a major vector in the circulation of dialect throughout the Caribbean. Their imprint on Trinidad's watershed yard fiction genre ensured the endurance of calypso's themes as a feature of Caribbean literature; further, when translated into written lyrics calypsos themselves became another form of literary dialect. New York, Harlem in particular, is therefore inescapably tied to the history of Creole literature in the Caribbean.

Trinidadians and other Caribbean nationals harbored a keen fascination with the New York "Mecca," as Manning called it, despite the discrimination against West Indians by native-born Americans, white and black. Manning asserted that New York was especially attractive because of what he perceived to be its egalitarian racial culture—no small feature for the "pigmentocratic" societies of the Caribbean:

I have seen them, high and low, rich and poor, fair and dark, rub shoulders in [a] common struggle for existence. There is no colour question in Harlem. There

(Gainesville: University Press of Florida, 1993); Errol Hill, "The Caribbean Connection," pp. 273–306, in *A History of African-American Theatre*, edited by Errol G. Hill and James V. Hatch (Cambridge: Cambridge University Press, 2003).

[4] C. L. R. James, *Beyond a Boundary* (London: Hutchinson, 1963), p. 26.

[5] See Leah Rosenberg, "Calypso War: Yard Fiction as Class and Ethnic Struggle," pp. 133–43, in Leah Rosenberg, *Nationalism and the Formation of Caribbean Literature* (New York: Palgrave Macmillan, 2007).

[6] Atilla the Hun, "History of Carnival," Decca Records (March 14, 1935), New York.

everybody is classed as one. If you are not white you are coloured; and black and coloured are just the same. If you have money you can have a fairly good time. If you have no money—well, you just haven't got it and no one has any time to spend with you, be you light coloured, brown or black.[7]

That a black man could footnote the spectacularly racist segregationist policies of the United States could be footnoted in favor of a Darwinian "colorblind" ideal must be perplexing to a contemporary readership unless it is understood in terms of what race meant to a black and non-white readership living in the colonial societies of the Caribbean in the early twentieth century. The black-white binary of the United States functioned as a kind of racial leveler. This means that intra-racial distinctions of class and color so crucial in the Caribbean were, in the United States, effectively leveled into just one class and color: black. This new conception of race coincided with an emerging radical racial identity, forged in the context of the egalitarian ideals and racist realities of the United States. Alain Locke summarized this newly emergent black identity in his masculinist manifesto of the New Negro ideal, *The New Negro* (1925). Locke envisioned the twentieth century as a "spiritual coming-of-age" for blacks, as he put it, in which the subaltern, second-class status of blacks that characterized earlier generations would be erased in the modern era with a muscular demand for equal rights. "We shall let the Negro speak for himself," he famously declared, a sentiment that Manning echoes in his assessment of the attraction of Harlem blacks for Trinidadians "at home:"

They are to-day asking alarming questions which would make the heads of people in a British colony like Trinidad ache with worry as to the future. . . . *the negro in America and elsewhere is being educated to think himself the equal of any man.*[8]   [emphasis added]

The "alarming questions" being raised by these troublesome, educated new blacks challenged the racial and social hierarchies of the black Atlantic. (One is reminded of the panic of the white racists in *Invisible Man* when the narrator, his mouth filled with blood, accidentally gives a speech on "social equality.") Manning's portrait of Harlem illustrates the appeal of the United States not just for West Indian immigrants in New York but also for Caribbean people in the Caribbean. Harlem, in Manning's telling, is a place where one might be a "race man" and also, in Atilla's elegant phrasing, "an artist and a gentleman." Its location at the center of gravity of both the intellectual and entertainment worlds of the United States ensured both elite and popular audiences for Caribbean artists. Harlem was a

---

[7] Sam Manning, "Deep Harlem: Mecca of the 'Big Bluff,'" *Trinidad Guardian* (June 26, 1929).
[8] Sam Manning, "Deep Harlem: Humorous Religion," *Trinidadian Guardian* (June 29, 1929).

symbol of how to be simultaneously black and modern, a space that was thoroughly American, thoroughly black, teeming with high- and lowbrow culture, seeing no contradiction in either.

As literary dialect transformed into Creole literature, it became, increasingly, the choice for black authors in both the Caribbean and the United States to chronicle the black experience in the twentieth century. The black writers of the Caribbean were inevitably part of a multiracial group of writers intent on show-casing a similarly "real" Caribbean, by which was meant working-class or peas-ant, and primarily although not entirely black. Caribbean writers, poised figuratively between the United States and Great Britain, showed the influence of both in early-twentieth-century Caribbean fiction. Leah Rosenberg notes that the cultural nationalism of Caribbean countries at the turn of the century combined with the appeal of Realist and Romantic genres for its writers who sought a model for establishing a politicized national literature. The quest for a national literature was so much a part of public discourse at the turn of the century that, when he visited Jamaica in 1911, famously anticolonial vernacular British playwright George Bernard Shaw was asked by a reporter what he thought Jamaica needed to develop a vibrant national culture. (Shaw's answer: First "you want a first rate orchestra giving performances at least once a week of the works of the great mas-ters of modern music, from Sebastian Bach to Wagner and Richard Strauss. When a Jamaican knows Beethoven's Ninth Symphony as well as he knows the ten com-mandments and feels hungry if he does not hear it well played fairly often, then he is to that extent no longer a colonial."[9]) If British influence on the Caribbean's developing national literatures is well established, America's is not. Literary dia-lect was not simply an outgrowth of American popular culture influence. It was now the language of the folk, and folk aesthetics were the foundation of a revolu-tionary national literature that was yet connected to the canonical texts of the colonial world.[10] The confluence of both, coupled with the rising resulted in the so-called "yard" fiction of Trinidad's multiracial Beacon Group and the "new primitivism" of McKay's popular dialect poetry, published in Jamaica. In the Caribbean what welded both traditions together, the folk aesthetics of Britain's Romantic tradition and American Realism (or Primitivism), was the focus on black culture.

In Trinidad, Sam Manning, as a published New York playwright, black nation-alist, and half of a popular Caribbean blackface comedy duo, is one vector of what I call the vernacular axis of the Caribbean, the means by which Caribbean literary dialect, enriched by its associations with American blackness, moved back and

[9] Interview with George Bernard Shaw, *Daily Gleaner* (January 12, 1911), quoted in Stanley Weintraub, "A High Wind to Jamaica," vol. 5, *Shaw Abroad* (1985), p. 37.

[10] Leah Rosenberg, Chapters 4 and 5 ("The New Primitivism" and "The Realpolitik of Yard Fiction: Trinidad's *Beacon* Group"), in Leah Rosenberg, *Nationalism and the Formation of Caribbean Literature* (2007).

forth across the Atlantic. Manning is a particularly visceral example because he forces the contemporary reader to consider that blackface minstrelsy and black nationalism were not necessarily incompatible, an unwelcome contradiction in a welter of contradictions that is the history of Creole literature. Other embodiments of the vernacular axis include Marcus Garvey himself, as a kind of anti vernacular counterpoint; and Claude McKay, the Jamaican author of dialect verse who rose to international fame in New York during the Harlem Renaissance of the 1920s. Although Garvey's ex-wife and Manning companion Amy Ashwood Garvey plays a significant role, the story of how literary dialect transformed into Creole literature, a vehicle for the black masculine voice, is very much a story of black men's lives.

This chapter takes its title from McKay's best-selling 1928 novel, *Home to Harlem*. I chose McKay's novel to highlight the double entendre embedded in the declaration of Harlem as a home for blacks in the United States. The story of the friendship between an African-American war veteran and an educated black Haitian immigrant, *Home to Harlem* suggests that Harlem is a figurative as well as a literal transnational blackspace, a symbolic and literal black home for race pride that features the wide contours of the black experience. Harlem is also, in this reading, an outpost of the Caribbean. Here I explore the emergence of Creole literature into a transatlantic genre through its main vectors: Garveyism and New Negro politics in New York; Claude McKay's journey from local Jamaican dialect poet in the early 1900s to internationally recognized dialect novelist of the Harlem Renaissance in 1920s New York; and, finally, the career of Manning himself, whose journey from calypsonian to comedian to playwright parallels the transformation of calypso dialect into literature.

"Literary Prostitutes:" Garveyism, *Home to Harlem*, and Dialect

A dusky tribe of destiny seekers, these brown and black and yellow folk, eyes filled with visions of their heritage—palm fringed sea shores, murmuring streams, luxuriant hills and dales—have made their epical march from the far corners of the earth to Harlem. They bring with them vestiges of their folk life...their quiet, halting speech...telling the story of a dogged, romantic pilgrimage to the El Dorado of their dreams.

W. A. Domingo, "The Tropics in New York," 1925

Marcus Garvey hated dialect fiction. Specifically, Garvey hated the kind of fiction that reproduced—or distorted—the actual voices of working-class Jamaicans and African Americans. He rejected any literary attempt to channel the voices of the people whose welfare was his life's work. Indeed, Garvey's United Negro

Improvement Association featured lectures on the "abuse" of dialect, among other cultural offerings.[11] The belief that, in the new century, the so-called Negro dialect could be the language of black affirmation was anathema to Garvey. No doubt, the Negro must speak for himself. But not in that "quiet, halting speech" of the Caribbean immigrants of fellow Jamaican W. A. Domingo's imagination in the above quotation. And emphatically not in the "broken English" of the African-American vernacular. Either way, the very act of rendering black speech affirmed every racist supposition of whites who, to Garvey's mind, fed so avidly at the trough of black self-abasement.

The appealing vision of hardworking black immigrants dreaming of "palm fringed sea shores" was not congruent with the emerging image of the New Negro of the new twentieth century. The New Negro of Harlem intellectuals' imagination of the 1920s was an urban African-American man, an economically independent, politically assertive, culturally original citizen of the United States and the world. He was vocal. The romanticized black Caribbean immigrant, appealing for equality in the well-modulated tones appropriate to the worthy supplicant to the American Dream, could hardly be equated with the vigorous, declarative voice needed to articulate the New Negro's advocacy of black rights in the new era.[12]

Himself an assiduous (if pedestrian) poet, Marcus Garvey was a particularly potent example of the New Negro. A man both dramatically internationalist and local in his appeal—Garvey is, to this day, associated with the culturally distinctiveness of Harlem—through him it is possible for us to witness the diffusion of Caribbean Creole literature and performance to a pan-Caribbean, diasporic practice. Garvey provides the tipping point for the vernacular axis that operated between the Caribbean and the United States via Harlem. His particular brand of populist black consciousness, coupled with his emphasis on the arts as a form of racial upliftment, brought into view the peculiar balance of art and politics that galvanized the spread of Creole literature and performance in the new century.[13] A brilliant speaker associated with crowd-moving orations from Kingston to Harlem, Garvey advocated for a transnational black literature that would rival the English canon. The exiled Pan-Africanist founder of the Universal Negro Improvement Association did not believe that the black vernacular could ever be

---

[11] See *Daily Gleaner* (January 5, 1915), which describes a lecture given by H. A. L. Simpson at an early U.N.I.A. meeting in Jamaica titled "The Abuse of the Jamaican Dialect," cited in Beverly Hamilton, "Marcus Garvey: Cultural Activist," in *Jamaica Journal* 2 (3) (August–October, 1987), p. 21.

[12] See Alain Locke, Introduction, in Alain Locke, ed., *The New Negro* (1925); also, Henry Louis Gates, Jr., "The New Negro and the Black Image, from Booker T. Washington to Alain Locke," accessed September 14, 2015, http://nationalhumanitiescenter.org/tserve/freedom/1917beyond/essays/newnegro.htm; see also Booker T. Washington et al., *A New Negro for a New Century* (Chicago: American Publishing House, 1900).

[13] John Cowley connects the rise of Garvey's U.N.I.A. to the development of a Caribbean–African-American musical hybrid form that relies on vernacular traditions of both communities in his essay "West Indies Blues" (2006), p. 191.

the basis for a great black literature. He considered most literary attempts at reproducing it an affront to black people. Black people's "language" was inevitably tied to the seamier side of black working-class life—illicit sex, mindless violence, careless comedy, raucous behavior. Or so it must have seemed to Garvey.

In keeping with that belief, Garvey's *Negro World* scrupulously avoided publishing dialect verse (although its generally democratic Poetry of the People section was inclusive of all kinds of poetry).[14] Instead, it extolled the "decent" literature of black authors who eschewed dialect: "We must encourage our own Black authors who have character, who are loyal to their race, who feel proud to be Black, and in every way let them feel that we appreciate their efforts to advance our race through healthy and decent literature."[15] Garvey's antipathy to black cultural forms extended beyond the vernacular; he considered original black musical genres such as spirituals, blues, and jazz to be second-rate, reportedly declaring that "spiritual and jazz music are credited to the Negro...simply because we did not know any better music."[16] A cultural traditionalist, Garvey included in the politically radical 1929 manifesto of his People's Political Party a demand for a Jamaican national opera house.

However Garvey was not particularly consistent in his anti-dialect stance. He was, in fact, an enthusiastic supporter of the pioneering black Jamaican comedian E. M. Cupidon, whose signature comic characteristic was his dialect speeches on the Jamaican stage.[17] Said Garvey of Cupidon on the eve of his trip to England, "He is young and ambitious, he has a fairly liberal education and he has been trained to realize his responsibilities. We can therefore trust him as our Jamaican student exponent in England of his line of art."[18] On the other hand, Garvey derided the famous African-American actor Paul Robeson for his "slanderous" dialect-infused portrayals of black people.[19] All black performers were not equal, clearly, especially those who performed or wrote primarily for white patrons.

In particular, Garvey hated fellow immigrant McKay's *Home to Harlem*. The novel was shaped by political imperatives similar to those which drove Garvey himself. As Leah Rosenberg notes, *Home to Harlem* responded to Alain Locke's

---

[14] Tony Martin, *Literary Garveyism: Garvey, Black Arts, and the Harlem Renaissance* (Dover, MA: Majority Press, 1983), p. 110.

[15] Marcus Garvey, "'Home to Harlem,' Claude McKay's Damaging Book, Should Earn Wholesale Condemnation of Negroes," *Negro World* (September 29, 1928), pp. 1–2.

[16] Cecil Gutzmore, "The Image of Marcus Garvey in Reggae Orature," in *Storms of the Heart: An Anthology of Black Arts and Culture*, edited by Kwesi Owusu (London: Camden, 1988), p. 283. See also Tony Martin, *Literary Garveyism* (1983), p. 110; and Herbie Miller, "Marcus Garvey and the Radical Black Music Tradition," *76 King Street: Journal of Liberty Hall: The Legacy of Marcus Garvey*, vol. 1 (2009), p. 106.

[17] See Belinda Edmondson, *Caribbean Middlebrow* (2009), p. 90, for an extended discussion of E. M. Cupidon's legacy as a pioneering figure in the development of a Creole theatre tradition.

[18] Marcus Garvey, editorial, *The Blackman* (June 14, 1929), cited in Beverly Hamilton, "Marcus Garvey: Cultural Activist," pp. 21–31, *Jamaica Journal* 20 (3) (August–October 1987), p. 22.

[19] See Tony Martin, *Literary Garveyism* (1983), pp. 117–18.

aesthetic directive for "a primitivism in black arts" in *The New Negro*.[20] McKay's version of the primitivist aesthetic is similar to that of fellow Harlem Renaissance writer Zora Neale Hurston: it features plenty of sex, comedy, and violence. And, like Hurston's fiction, its use of African-American dialect is a central feature. Garvey himself favored classically Victorian meter ("Would I not like Macbeth's ghost / Walk the earth forever / For you?"[21]). Bad black authors like McKay got published by the mainstream press, Garvey complained, while good black authors did not: bad authors, he believed, pandered to whites by the strategic use of racist stereotypes. He condemned McKay's novel as a "damnable libel against the Negro:"

> The white people have these Negroes to write the kind of stuff that they desire to feed their public so that the Negro can still be regarded as a monkey or some imbecilic creature. Whenever authors of the Negro race write good literature for publication the white publishers refuse to publish it, but whenever the Negro is sufficiently known to attract attention he is advised to write in the way that the white man wants—that is just what has happened to Claude McKay. The time has come for us to boycott such Negro authors whom we may fairly designate as "literary prostitutes."[22]

Other designated "literary prostitutes" included fellow West Indian, Harlemite (and former Garveyite[23]) Eric Walrond for his dialect-infused novel *Tropic Death*, which Garvey called on black readers to boycott along with the "sappy poems from the rising poets," likely Countee Cullen and Langston Hughes.

If Garvey believed that white American publishers shaped the output of black vernacular literature, that was probably because they did. Dialect narratives were all the rage in the nineteenth and early twentieth centuries, part of what Gavin Jones calls "the cult of the vernacular" that swept the United States after the Civil War. All kinds of dialect narratives were being created and consumed, from stories in the Appalachian dialect to skits in "New Yorkese." But it was black dialect in particular that was in high demand.[24] Yet dialect writing in the early twentieth century

---

[20] Alain Locke, "Negro Youth Speaks" and "The Legacy of the Ancestral Arts," in *The New Negro* (New York: Albert and Charles Boni, 1925), pp. 51, 254–67, cited in Leah Rosenberg, *Nationalism and the Formation of Caribbean Literature* (New York: Palgrave Macmillan, 2007), p. 99 footnote 39.

[21] Tony Martin, *Literary Garveyism* (1983), p. 141.

[22] Marcus Garvey, "'Home to Harlem,' Claude McKay's Damaging Book, Should Earn Wholesale Condemnation of Negroes," *Negro World* (September 29, 1928), p. 1. Garvey was not alone in his charge that *Home to Harlem* pandered to whites: Dewey Jones complained in *The Chicago Defender*, "white people think we are buffoons, thugs, and rotters anyway. Why should we waste so much time trying to prove it? That's what Claude McKay has done." In Claude McKay, *Home to Harlem* (Lebanon, NH: Northeastern University Press, 1987), p. xviii (foreword by Wayne Cooper).

[23] See Tony Martin, *Literary Garveyism* (1983), p. 126.

[24] See Hamlin Garland, "Vernacular Poets and Novelists," in *Roadside Meetings* (New York: Macmillan, 1930), p. 104, quoted in Gavin Jones, *Strange Talk: The Politics of Dialect Literature in Gilded Age America* (Los Angeles: University of California Press, 1999), p. 1. Jones also describes the public hunger for the different kinds of dialects in the United States.

was still perceived by American readers and publishers as comic or sentimental, not as inherently political. African-American poet Langston Hughes fell out with his white patron when he stopped writing "primitive" dialect poetry in favor of a more overtly political style.[25] Publishers were interested in black authors who wrote "authentic" narratives of black life, and dialect was a marker of that authenticity.[26] Late-nineteenth-century African-American author Charles Chesnutt wrote to the specifications of his publisher, who had proposed that he write in dialect. When Chesnutt decided to write non-dialect fiction about mixed-race characters who were other than "blacks, full-blooded," he could not get any editors interested.[27]

Garvey was not the only black leader who hated *Home to Harlem*. W. E. B. DuBois, who had called for black writers to produce "romances" of African-American life, claimed that he felt unclean after reading it.[28] Garvey doubtless also found suspect the very fact that the novel was a bestseller in New York City.[29] For *Home to Harlem* was a sensation to the white sophisticates who flocked to Harlem seeking African-American culture. They praised it as "the real thing in rightness . . . the lowdown on Harlem, the dope from the inside."[30] (Garvey was also not alone in his charge that *Home to Harlem* pandered to whites: Dewey Jones complained in *The Chicago Defender*, "White people think we are buffoons, thugs, and rotters anyway. Why should we waste so much time trying to prove it? That's what Claude McKay has done."[31]) McKay himself was fully aware of the irony. "We must leave the appreciation of what we are doing to the emancipated Negro intelligentsia of the future, while we are sardonically aware now that only the intelligentsia of the

[25] The tension between Hughes and his patron Charlotte Mason reflects an odd correlation between "Africa" and "dialect" and the primitive on one hand, and an urban African-American sensibility on the other: "She wanted me to be primitive and feel the intuitions of the primitive. But. . . I was only an American Negro . . . I was not African. I was Chicago and Kansas City and Broadway and Harlem. And I was not what she wanted me to be." See Langston Hughes, *The Big Sea: An Autobiography* (New York: Hill and Wang, 1940/1993), p. 325.

[26] See Gavin Jones, Chapter 2 ("The Cult of the Vernacular") and Chapter 7 ("Paul Laurence Dunbar and the Authentic Black Voice"), in Gavin Jones, *Strange Talk* (1999).

[27] See Richard Brodhead, Introduction, in Charles Chesnutt, *The Conjure Woman and Other Tales*, edited by Richard Brodhead (Durham and London: Duke University Press, 1993), pp. 1–2; and Charles Chesnutt's letter to George Washington Cable (June 1890), cited in Helen M. Chesnutt, *Charles Waddell Chesnutt: Pioneer of the Color Line* (Durham and Chapel Hill: University of North Carolina Press, 1952), pp. 57–8.

[28] W. E. B. DuBois, "Criteria of Negro Art," *Crisis* (October 1926), p. 292, quoted in Leah Rosenberg, *Nationalism and the Formation of Caribbean Literature* (2007), p. 99, footnote 40.

[29] Wayne Cooper writes, "In April, 1928, McKay noted…with satisfaction that 'I see *Home to Harlem* like an impudent dog has [moved] right in among the best-sellers in New York.'" See Wayne Cooper, Forward, in Claude McKay, *Home to Harlem*, edited by Wayne Cooper (Boston: Northeastern University Press, 1928/1987), pp. xviii–xix.

[30] John R. Chamberlain, "When Spring Comes to Harlem; Claude McKay's Novel Gives a Glowing Picture of the Negro Quarter," *New York Times* (March 11, 1928), p. 59, quoted in Wayne F. Cooper, *Claude McKay: Rebel Sojourner in the Harlem Renaissance, A Life* (Baton Rouge: Louisiana State University Press, 1987), p. 247.

[31] Cited in Wayne Cooper, Forward, Claude McKay, *Home to Harlem*, ed. Wayne Cooper (Lebanon, NH: Northeastern UP, 1987), p. xviii.

superior race is developed enough to afford artistic truth," he mused.[32] McKay resented that the African-American intellectual elite saw his rendering of African Americans as a racial smear by an immigrant. He rebutted his critics by pointing out that he rendered both West Indians and African Americans in what he understood to be their authentic context as black peoples of the world, whether in rural Jamaica or urban Harlem:

> If my brethren had taken the trouble to look a little into my obscure life they would have discovered that years before I had recaptured the spirit of the Jamaican peasants in verse, rendering their primitive joys, their loves and hates, their work and play, their dialect. And what I did in prose for Harlem was very similar to what I had done for Jamaica in verse.[33]

Given his innovative use of black dialect in both his Jamaica and Harlem writings, McKay's rendering of black life in both the Caribbean and the United States is clearly linked. McKay connects both communities as not just nodal points in what Michelle Stephens calls the black empire of the black radical imagination, but claims black dialect in particular as a feature of that black empire. In other words, McKay defines the black vernacular as characteristic of what Elizabeth Dillon, following Immanuel Kant, calls the black Atlantic sensus communis.[34] In so doing he articulated a translocal black aesthetic, one that straddled local authenticity and cosmopolitan status. Still, the ambivalence of black intellectuals towards black vernacular literary forms was unsurprising at this juncture, given its birth as a form of racial ventriloquism for often racist or other political ends at the expense of black and non-white peoples. As I have discussed, it was largely white elite benefactors who sponsored and encouraged black dialect performers; it was elite Caribbean newspapers that published Creole writing of all kinds, and dispatched reporters to review local Creole performances. This was emphatically not true of the colored newspapers. Black nationalist leaders of an earlier era, such as Jamaica's Robert Love, echoed Garvey's disapproval in their condemnation of the use of dialect by black performers or writers. In Jamaica, in particular, innovators such as McKay and Thomas MacDermot ("Tom Redcam")[35] experimented

---

[32] Cited in Wayne F. Cooper, *Claude McKay: Rebel Sojourner in the Harlem Renaissance, A Life* (Baton Rouge: Louisiana State University Press, 1987), pp. 245, 247; and in Wayne Cooper, Forward, in *Home to Harlem* by Claude McKay, edited by Wayne Cooper (1987), p. xix.

[33] See Claude McKay, "A Negro Writer to His Critics," *New York Herald-Tribune Books* (March 6, 1932), cited in Claude McKay, *The Passion of Claude McKay: Selected Poetry and Prose, 1912–1948*, edited by Wayne Cooper (New York: Schocken Books, 1973), p. 135.

[34] See Michelle Stephens, *Black Empire: The Masculine Global Imaginary of Caribbean Intellectuals in the United States 1914–1962* (Durham and London: Duke University Press, 2005); Elizabeth Dillon, *New World Drama: The Performative Commons in the Atlantic World* (Durham and London: Duke University Press, 2014), p. 18.

[35] Thomas MacDermot has been variously referred to as a white or brown Jamaican. He appears to have functioned as a white Jamaican, but was of mixed race ancestry.

with Creole and the literary genres of the ballad and the novel form. Dialect literature began to crystallize as a more authentic genre to carry the full weight of black desires for full equality. As literary dialect genres became increasingly associated with the articulation of black political freedom, black leadership became increasingly vocal about its objections to the use of black dialect in the wider public sphere.

In the United States a parallel development was taking place in the evolution of African-American vernacular as a major vehicle for black speech. Alain Locke's concept of the New Negro became a pivotal concept in the promotion of the black vernacular.[36] Eagerly promoted by African-American intellectuals, the New Negro was a symbolic black citizen, often urban in orientation, who challenged the segregationist status quo and stood up for his rights even as he unashamedly embraced a black cultural identity. It was in Harlem, the home of the New Negro movement, that the black vernacular literature was most explicitly connected to radical black nationalist politics. Despite Locke's qualifier that the New Negro movement was "radical in tone, but not in purpose," the cultural expressions of the movement were linked, implicitly or explicitly, to its political ones.[37] As the twentieth century commenced the sound of the black voice became indissociable from black freedom. That voice may have been born in the country, but it was now the sound of the city—a voice associated with the modern, the urban, the oppositional. The struggle for black rights in the Caribbean and the United States was, increasingly, an urban struggle, one of policy, enfranchisement, legal issues, fought closest to the corridors of power. The voice of black cultural expression was in direct contrast to the formal prose of black political leadership, and yet that voice was essential to make the case for the new dispensation. In the francophone Caribbean, this New Negro voice found expression in African diaspora intellectual and artistic movements such as Négritude and Indigenisme, especially in locales such as Paris. But for many of the anglophone Caribbean writers and performers of the early twentieth century, that voice crystallized in Harlem, first home to black internationalism in the New World.[38]

Marcus Garvey may have hated the kind of fiction that, he felt, mocked and stereotyped black people, but in Harlem it was all around him. Closer than he might have liked, too. While Garvey was engaged in militant organizing, his former wife was writing and producing plays that relied heavily on the very black vernacular of the Caribbean and the United States which Garvey found so contemptible. Marcus Garvey's emphasis on diasporic artistic practice as an upliftment

---

[36] See Alain Locke, Forward, *The New Negro* (1925), p. ix.

[37] For a useful discussion of the radical politics of the New Negro Movement and the various attempts to suppress or co-opt them, see Barbara Foley, Chapter 1, *Spectres of 1919: Class and Nation in the Making of the New Negro* (Urbana: University of Illinois Press, 2008).

[38] For the most sustained and influential discussion of the evolution black internationalist expression in Paris see Brent Edwards, *The Practice of Diaspora* (Cambridge: Harvard University Press, 2003).

strategy ironically provided a political justification for the diffusion of black vernaculars from the Caribbean and the United States. His version of the New Negro philosophy animates that of the Caribbean immigrant artists in early twentieth century Harlem. Garvey's Creole contradictions were in essence a Caribbean version of the New Negro. The other Caribbean actors in the vernacular axis worked within and against this conception of the twentieth-century Caribbean blackness. Their careers are a magnified version of the many early writers and performers who sought audiences in both locales. In so striving they continued the work of delineating the black Atlantic sensus communis begun by Henry Murray and the Jubilee Singers decades earlier.

Claude McKay's Creole Migrations

As a pioneering dialect poet and canonical author claimed by both the United States and the Caribbean, McKay's career exemplifies the influence of black internationalism on Caribbean Creole traditions in literature and performance. McKay the intellectual writer joined the throng of Trinidadian and British Guianese calypsonians who shaped, and were shaped by, New York in the decades of the early twentieth century. New York was home to half the foreign-born blacks residing in the United States in the 1920s. Most of these were from the anglophone Caribbean, most of them concentrated in Harlem.[39] Beyond New York's obvious appeal as a hub of commercial enterprise for economic immigrants, black artists, and creative types from throughout the African diaspora were also attracted to Harlem's "penchant for grandiose performativity," as Louis Chude Sokei has noted.[40] This love of the large theatrical gesture was not confined to artists. Radical political activists from the Caribbean flourished in Harlem and attracted African-American as well as Caribbean and Latin American audiences. Indeed, several observers suggested that the political radicalism of New York blacks was largely due to the presence of West Indians.[41] This view was affirmed by the presence of activists like Garvey and the aforementioned Wilfred Adolphus

---

[39] W.A. Domingo, editor of U.N.I.A.'s *Negro World,* provides numerical estimates of foreign-born blacks from the U.S. census of 1920 in his essay, "The Tropics in New York," in Alain Locke, ed., *The NewNegro* (1925), p. 648, accessed January 5, 2021, https://docs.google.com/viewer?url=http://64.62.200.70/PERIODICAL/PDF/TheSurvey-1925mar01/30-33/.

[40] Louis Chude-Sokei, *The Last Darky* (2006), p. 207.

[41] Winston James summarizes a number of these views of the radicalism of West Indians in 1920s Harlem by African-American intellectuals, and reproduces the report of an FBI agent assigned to keep black political activists under surveillance in Harlem in 1921. The report reads in part, "I beg to state that nearly all these Negro radicals carry the *Bolshevic [sic] red card* and pay their monthly dues. . .It might be interesting to learn that nearly all of them are West Indian men who have not been naturalized or even in possession of their first papers." See Winston James, *Holding Aloft the Banner of Ethiopia: Caribbean Radicalism in Early Twentieth Century America* (New York: Verso, 1999), pp. 2–3.

(W. A.) Domingo, the latter an early advocate for Jamaican independence who, like Garvey, was jailed for his political views.

Along with the other black and brown immigrants to Harlem were Caribbean artists: writers like McKay and Walrond, calypso and vaudeville performers like Sam Manning and Sir Lancelot. They brought with them their skills, their ambition, and their finely honed use of dialect as a genre of artistic interpretation. These immigrants-cum-artists found Harlem a congenial home for their work, where it acquired new dimensions. As a black space where Caribbean immigrants mingled with African Americans and Afro-Latinxs, Harlem proved a singular spot for both pan-African political organizing and cultural commingling.[42] Domingo saw Harlem as the place where West Indians came to breathe new life into African-American culture. "The Tropics in New York," his well-known contribution to Locke's *The New Negro*, takes its title from a Claude McKay poem and features McKay's—non-dialect—poetry throughout. In "The Tropics in New York" Domingo outlines what he sees as the Caribbean contribution to the New Negro movement. With perhaps more than a touch of immigrant hubris, he describes West Indians as a sober lot, not given to the "hysteria" of African Americans, providing a kind of manliness to the African-American struggle for self- determination:

The outstanding contribution of West Indians to American Negro life is *the insistent assertion of their manhood in an environment that demands too much servility and unprotesting acquiescence from men of African blood.* This unwillingness to conform and be standardized, to accept tamely an inferior status and abdicate their humanity, finds an open expression in the activities of the foreign-born Negro in America.[43]   [emphasis mine]

Domingo was not the only West Indian to use an unflattering comparison with African Americans as a way to mark West Indian political assertiveness. Wrote McKay by way of comparison, "Our Negroes even though they were very poor would not sing clowning songs for white men and allow themselves to be kicked around by them."[44] Domingo, like others of his era, used masculinity as a way to talk about assertive political concepts, like civil rights advocacy. In this sense, his romantic view of West Indian self-determination was also a way to note a burgeoning political consciousness on the part of West Indian immigrants. It is all

---

[42] See Winston James, *Holding Aloft the Banner of Ethiopia: Caribbean Radicalism in Early Twentieth Century America* (1999).

[43] W. A. Domingo, "The Tropics in New York," in *The New Negro*, edited by Alain Locke (1925), p. 650, accessed January 5, 2021, https://docs.google.com/viewer?url=http://64.62.200.70/PERIODICAL/PDF/TheSurvey-1925mar01/30-33/.

[44] Claude McKay, *My Green Hills of Jamaica*, unpublished manuscript, Schomburg Center for Research in Black Culture (New York: New York Public Library), p. 80, cited in Chude-Sokei, *The Last Darky* (2006), p. 212.

the more ironic, therefore, that his invocation of the "quiet, halting speech" of West Indians indicates in the American imagination precisely the opposite traits: those associated with docility. This suggests a larger conceptual problem for politically aware writers and performers: What should a confident, educated black man *sound* like? The question of the assertive black man's authentic voice was one that would frame discussions of black performers such as Sidney Poitier well into the twentieth century.[45]

Notwithstanding Domingo's masculinist view, it is clear that the artistic and performative traditions of the Caribbean were indeed, themselves, given a new life in Harlem. It was there that African diasporic traditions merged and emerged. Not that Harlem invented Caribbean dialect art forms in literature and music. Quite the contrary. But it was through Harlem that dialect in all of its manifestations—literature, performance, theater—gained a pan-Caribbean audience and, sometimes, sometimes an internationalist perspective. Dialect was more easily produced and consumed as a mass market product. The back and forth of immigrants between metropole and "home" widened the scope of dialect art forms. Harlem's vernacular axis connected the political imperatives of the New Negro movement to the economic incentives of the immigrant community, which saw in these old cultural practices the promise of economic and political mobility.

If W. A. Domingo believed West Indians were a vigorously masculine lot, refusing to back down in the face of white American prejudice, it seems clear that their vernacular speech was not seen as reflective of this innate assertiveness—certainly not by nationalist blacks like Garvey, and not by the whites who championed black writers of dialect fiction. In the United States, popular images of African-American dialect were blackface performers singing "mammy songs," in what one called the "production of effeminacy" of the "cultured pansy-like negro."[46] These images were part of a performance vocabulary that, as we have seen, was transmitted to the Caribbean. A decade earlier, in his preface to Claude McKay's seminal book of dialect poetry, *Songs of Jamaica* (1912), McKay's expatriate English mentor Walter Jekyll identifies the charms of "negro English" as providing a softening effect on standard grammar. It is, he asserts, a "feminine version of masculine English:"

What Italian is to Latin, that in regard to English is the negro variant thereof. It shortens, softens, rejects the harder sounds alike of consonants and vowels; I

[45] See my discussion of both white and black audience perceptions of Sidney Poitier's "well spoken" onscreen persona in Belinda Edmondson, "Caribbean All-Stars: Sidney Poitier, Harry Belafonte, and the Rise of the African-American Leading Man," in *Poitier Revisited: Reconsidering a Black Icon in the Obama Age*, edited by Ian Strachan and Mia Mask (New York: Bloomsbury, 2014), pp. 61–72.

[46] Singer and performer Eddie Cantor, cited in Jeffrey Melnick, "Some Notes on the Erotics of 'Black-Jewish Relations," *Shofar: An Interdisciplinary Journal of Jewish Studies* 23 (4) (summer 2005), p. 12; cited in Tony Martin, *Literary Garveyism* (1983), p. 117.

might almost say, refines. In its soft tones we have an expression of the langorous sweetness of the South: it is a feminine version of masculine English; pre-eminently a language of love, as all will feel who setting prejudice aside, will allow the charmingly naïve love-songs of this volume to make their due impression upon them.[47]

Jekyll was a folklorist in his own right, the well-known author of *Jamaican Song and Story* (1907). It was he who (along with the progressive governor of Jamaica, Sydney Olivier) first encouraged McKay to write in dialect; it is to him that the classic, dialect-infused Jamaican novel *Banana Bottom* is dedicated; and it is Jekyll who appears within it as the character Squire Gensir. Yet, despite his interest and expertise in Jamaican folklore, Jekyll still believed that Jamaican dialect was merely an early stage of development toward Standard English.[48] Despite his affection for Jamaican Creole, in *Jamaican Song and Story* he still collapses all "negro" dialects together. He suggests that, from the United States to the Caribbean, they all reflect the "naïve," "langorous sweetness of the South." This remarkable comment is not merely a reflection of Jekyll's own racism and ignorance, but a common conception across the Atlantic, that there was little difference between the vernacular traditions of black people from the United States and the Caribbean. (Tellingly, George Bernard Shaw wrote, "Dis chile gwine ter Jamaica," in a stereotypical—and feminized—approximation of African-American dialect.[49])

Despite its varieties across the world, the black vernacular was just that for Jekyll: one tradition, its variants united by its overarching "sweetness," naïvete, its "feminine" sensibilities. Jekyll's views about black peoples themselves are revealed through these displacements onto black language. They are indeed the other side of the same racist coin of an earlier era: that black language signals irrationality, sensuousness, a lack of intelligence. These assumptions—that the black vernacular was a feminized, irrational language, reflective of a feminized, irrational people—are what Garvey, W. A. Domingo, McKay, and other black artists and activists were up against in their efforts to articulate the black experience. Their responses, as we shall see, were various. American "plantation" songs influenced both white interlocutors like Jekyll and others who studied Caribbean music and literature, as well as black Caribbean performers and singers who also saw themselves as "race men." In the white imagination, if not entirely in the black, these were the songs of black pacification and contentment. It surely is not coincidental that Jekyll held conservative political views of black self-determination: he was

---

[47] Walter Jekyll, preface, *Songs of Jamaica* (Kingston: Aston W. Gardner & Co., 1912), p. 5.

[48] See Walter Jekyll, *Gleaner* (April 21, 1913), p. 13, quoted in Leah Rosenberg, *Nationalism and the Formation of Caribbean Literature* (2007), p. 95, footnote 18.

[49] George Bernard Shaw, Letter to Sylvia Brooke (December 22, 1910), quoted in Stanley Weintraub, vol. 5, *Shaw Abroad* (1985), p. 37.

critical of the black rebels of the Morant Bay Rebellion.[50] Beyond Jekyll and other folklorists, black dialect across the diaspora was associated with "feminine" attributes. Until the twentieth century literary dialect was the preserve of laughter, emotion, "langorous sweetness"—not of anger, intellect, or opposition. It was not, in a word, associated with manliness. Domingo, an editor of United Negro Improvement Association's *Negro World* magazine, was as invested as Garvey in challenging the racism of the status quo. Yet when Domingo articulated a masculinist agency for West Indian immigrants to New York, the active voice of those immigrants, as conceived by Garvey and others, was at odds with the very agency he espoused. It is not hard to link Garvey's repudiation of dialect in some measure to these supposedly feminized overtones of dialect. One wonders if McKay's avoidance of the dialect poetry that had made his reputation in the Caribbean had something to do with its association with the feminized subaltern status when in Harlem he penned his anti-racist classic poem, "If We Must Die" in standard English, as well as his other pointedly non-dialect poems associated with the political radicalism of his Harlem years.

Negotiating a compromise between political convictions and personal necessities was a hard business in the early twentieth century, from Jamaica to Harlem. McKay was a free thinker with a conservative white mentor; a political radical who depended on the charity of well-off patrons; and a poet who wanted to express his "fierce hatred of injustice"[51] in ways in which it could be taken seriously. Accordingly he used dialect in prose, but no longer in the poetry of his Jamaica years. Other writers who benefited from the patronage system also used dialect, with the encouragement of their patrons (Zora Neale Hurston, Langston Hughes, and H.G. de Lisser come to mind). McKay's novels shift between dialect and standard grammar to create a radical political commentary. In this he continued a blending of standard and dialect grammar that we have seen from Henry Garland Murray. Contemporary Barbadian critic Kamau Brathwaite acknowledges the importance of McKay's volumes of Creole poetry in the development of nation language, but argues that his poetry is not, itself nation language, merely "dialect" because McKay "allowed himself to be imprisoned in the [iambic] pentameter."[52] Brathwaite concludes that, once he left Jamaica, McKay "forsook his nation language . . . and went to the sonnet." Implying a compromised authenticity on McKay's part, Brathwaite excludes McKay from the pantheon of nation language writers in his history of the Caribbean voice.[53]

---

[50] See Rhonda Cobham, "Fictions of Gender, Fictions of Race: Retelling Morant Bay in Jamaican Literature," *Small Axe* 8 (September 2000): 1–30.

[51] "...in my particular case, a peculiar sensitiveness which made certain forms of discipline irksome, and a fierce hatred of injustice." See Claude McKay, *Songs of Jamaica* (1912), cited in Winston James, *"A Fierce Hatred of Injustice:" Claude McKay's Jamaica and His Poetry of Rebellion* (New York: Verso, 2000), p. xi.

[52] Edward Kamau Brathwaite, *History of the Voice* (1984), p. 7.

[53] Edward Kamau Brathwaite, *History of the Voice* (1984), p. 20, footnote 21.

Taken together, Garvey's and Brathwaite's critiques, as well as Jekyll's and Domingo's praise, illustrates the difficult terrain in which McKay and artists of his era navigated as they sought an original voice, a nation language, that was cosmopolitan, local, wide-ranging and yet authentic, true to their communities. Despite Brathwaite's dismissal, Claude McKay remains one of the most famous Caribbean writers in the world. His reputation rests both on his dialect novels and his standard English poetry. Yet (and perhaps this speaks to Brathwaite's concern) it emphatically does not rest on his dialect poetry, despite the fact that this is how he originally came to prominence in Jamaica and England. McKay, like Garvey, represents the generation that straddles both the nineteenth and twentieth centuries, the heritage of Britain even in its anti-colonial discourse, and the influence of African-American expression. McKay's oeuvre reflects the tensions inherent between the two models for black Caribbean expression.

Born into a land-owning black peasant family in 1889, McKay had a habit of radical philosophical inquiry early on, encouraged by his older schoolmaster brother. It would be a mistake, therefore, to associate McKay's later political radicalism entirely with Harlem, given its roots in rural, peasant Jamaica.[54] McKay's family very much resembled that of the rural peasant heroine Bita Plant in 1933's *Banana Bottom*. In the cultural attitudes and spoken expression of the African-identified rural Jamaican peasantry the young McKay recognized a valuable inchoate model of independent expression. Yet he was also a product of the patronage system that prevailed among black and non-white writers in both Jamaica and the United States in the early decades of the twentieth century. McKay's literary voice was, like Murray's before him, both dependent on white largesse and yet independent: an original, modern voice, both radical and tied to the status quo.

With the movement towards, and circulation within, Harlem, in the early twentieth century the Creole artistic tradition appeared as parallel strands, one a local Caribbean tradition and the other a part of an evolving pan-Caribbean, even pan-African tradition. The two were more closely related than they might appear at first glance. The vernacular axis, the Caribbean–Harlem continuum around which so much twentieth-century Creole literature and performance was created, forces us to consider that these traditions might be really one, multidimensional transatlantic tradition. With a couple of notable exceptions critics have downplayed the formative influence of his Jamaican dialect writing.[55] Yet McKay, like other twentieth-century Caribbean writers, reaped the benefit of a consistent stream of dialect narrative forms from the many newspapers available to him in

---

[54] Winston James discusses McKay's early upbringing as the source of his political radicalism in Winston James, *A Fierce Hatred of Injustice* (2000), pp. 3–51.

[55] Winston James makes the strongest case for close scholarly analysis of McKay's Jamaican poems as a foundation for his later efforts in Winston James, *A Fierce Hatred of Injustice* (2000). See also Belinda Edmondson, Chapter 3, *Caribbean Middlebrow* (2009).

Jamaica. Caribbean newspapers in Jamaica, British Guiana, Trinidad, and Barbados were already filled with various kinds of Creole and non-Caribbean literary dialect, as I have discussed. McKay's early career as a local dialect poet to a large extent exemplifies the circulation of dialect narratives in the trans-Atlantic community *before* he migrated to Harlem. It is likely that he, like other educated black Jamaicans of his generation, was familiar with the dialect poems of African-American Paul Lawrence Dunbar, popular in Jamaica at the time.[56]

McKay's first dialect poem, "a little thing called 'Hard Times,'"[57] describes the brutal conditions of rural laborers. Thereafter he wrote regular dialect verse and comic sketches for Jamaican newspapers and published two collections of poetry in 1912; the first, *Songs of Jamaica* in Kingston, and the second, *Constab Ballads*, in London.[58] His work would earn him the prestigious Musgrave Medal from the Institute of Jamaica, reportedly the first black to get one. Later that year he left for the United States. Eventually, like so many other Caribbean immigrants, he would end up in Harlem. Although it would not be the last stop in his peripatetic life, Harlem was the place where McKay's innovations in the Creole form would expand. It gives short-shrift to the influence of Caribbean vernacular literature if McKay's Jamaican poetry is overlooked in favor of his more famous creations during the Harlem Renaissance. Yet, we must also account for influence of movement and place on the development of this pivotal Caribbean Creole writer. McKay's life and work provides a model template to explore the dynamic axis of the vernacular that operated between the Caribbean and Harlem in the early twentieth century (Figure 5.1).

It is in these early dialect poems that we see McKay experiment with intermingling the use of dialect and standard English as a medium of political protest. It was an awkward first meeting. Although McKay felt impelled to give voice to the black majority in his popular dialect poetry he was still the product of a Victorian education. Dialect and classic Victorian narrative traditions co-existed uneasily within him. Most of his poems were in standard English until Jekyll urged him to write and publish more of his dialect poems:

> He read my poetry one day. Then he laughed a lot . . . All these poems that I gave him to read had been done in straight English, but there was one short one in the Jamaican dialect. That was the poem he was laughing about. He told me then that he did not like my poems in straight English—they were repetitious. "But

---

[56] See U. Theo McKay, "The Use of Dialect," *Daily Gleaner* (January 28, 1915), p. 4. Amy Ashwood also recited Dunbar's poetry as a young woman in Kingston. See *Daily Gleaner* (October 29, 1914, p. 14), cited in Tony Martin, *Amy Ashwood Garvey: Pan-Africanist, Feminist, and Wife No. 1*(Dover MA: Majority Press, 2007), p. 24.

[57] See A.W. Stephenson, "The Work of a Gifted Jamaican," *Daily Gleaner* (October 7, 1911), cited in Winston James, *A Fierce Hatred of Injustice* (2000), p. 167.

[58] See Claude McKay, *Songs of Jamaica* (Kingston: Aston. W. Gardner, 1912); and *Constab Ballads* (London: Watts and Co., 1912).

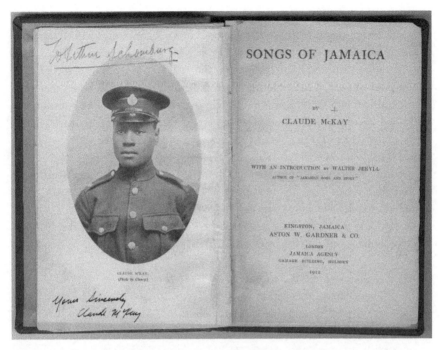

Figure 5.1 Portrait of Claude McKay in *Songs of Jamaica* (1912), courtesy of the Schomburg Center for Research in Black Culture.

this," he said, "is the real thing. . . Now is your chance *as a native boy* to put the Jamaican dialect into literary language. I am sure your poems will sell well."[59]

[emphasis added]

Jekyll's condescension ("your chance as a *native boy*") coupled with his commingling of the aesthetic and the commercial is an essential part of the story of dialect literature. As Marcus Garvey distastefully noted, whites had a passion for consuming "primitive" verse by black writers. There was the rendering of dialect as an uplift strategy; and then there was the rendering of dialect as a commercial one. Commercial success for a writer was, inevitably, success with white audiences. The two strategies were not, on the face of it, compatible. Perhaps for this reason, McKay was sensitive that even his "authentic" Jamaican dialect poetry had distinctly British influences. Popularly referred to as "the Jamaican Bobby Burns," McKay acknowledged that his poems did indeed give "thoughts of Burns—with

---

[59] See Claude McKay, *My Green Hills of Jamaica* (1979), pp. 66–7; for more on Jekyll's influence see Edward Baugh, "A History of Poetry," in *A History of Literature in the Caribbean,* edited by James A. Arnold, vol. 2 (Amsterdam: John Benjamins, 1995), p. 234; also Claude McKay, *The Passion of Claude McKay,* edited by Wayne Cooper (1973), pp. 58–9.

apologies to his immortal spirit for making him speak in Jamaican dialect."[60] (Popular reception aside, critics have more or less felt the same. In 1971, Jamaican critic Edward Baugh dismissed McKay's poems as "weakly derivative, Burns without the tang of wit and humour, without the acuity and depth of perception."[61]) McKay was interested in rendering a heroic Jamaican narrative, when that voice was identified with manliness—and standard grammar syntax. The question that bedeviled McKay anticipates that which vexed Garvey and others in Harlem a decade later. How to meld a black Jamaican working class voice with the English ballad form in a way that was not satirical?

"George William Gordon to the Oppressed Natives," McKay's ode to the Morant Bay rebels, was his attempt at just such a hybrid form. But the result sounded forced, a voice that was not altogether his. The narrative voice is meant to be that of Gordon, the brown hero of the Rebellion (and present-day National Hero of Jamaica), urging the black rebels to fight:

> O, you sons of Afric's soil,
> Dyin' in a foreign land,
> Crushed beneat' de moil and toil,
> Break, break de oppressor's hand!
>
> Wake de lion in your veins,
> De gorilla in your blood;
> Show dem dat you ha' some brains,
> Though you may be coarse an' rude.
>
> Wil'erforce [Wilberforce] has set you free,
> Sharpe an' Buxton worked for you;
> Trample on de tyranny
> Still continued by a few!
>
> Keep before you Clarkson's name!
> Ef your groans caan' win de fight,
> Jes' to put do'n dis great shame
> Lawful 'tis to use our might.
>
> England paid you' ransom down!
> Meant to save you from the pain;
> Now, freed men o' England's crown,
> Burst de cruel tyrant's chain!

---

[60] See J. E. Clare McFarlane, "Claude McKay" (1956), pp. 97–8, in *The Routledge Reader in Caribbean Literature*, edited by Alison Donnell and Sarah Lawson Welsh (London and New York: Routledge, 1996), p. 97; also Claude McKay, *My Green Hills of Jamaica* (1979).

[61] Edward Baugh, "West Indian Poetry 1900–1970: A Study in Cultural Decolonisation" (1971), reprinted in *The Routledge Reader in Caribbean Literature*, edited byAlison Donnell and Sarah Lawson Welsh (1996), p. 103.

Never would an English mind
Bow beneat' such tyranny;
Rise, O people of my kind!
Struggle, struggle to be free!

Shake de burden off your backs,
Show de tyrants dat you're strong;
Fight for freedom's rights, you blacks,
Ring de slaves' old battle-song!

Gordon's heart here bleeds for you,
He will lead to victory;
We will conquer every foe,
Or togeder gladly die.[62]

Evident in these verses is McKay's struggle to find a form that could capture what a heroic Jamaican Creole voice should actually *sound* like. Searching for a hybrid voice, the poem shifts uneasily back and forth between Africa and England, obscuring the event's Caribbean origins altogether. It reads like an overwrought nineteenth century anti-slavery manifesto, full of heroic images of English abolitionists and *noble sauvage* stereotypes about Africans ("Wake de lion in your veins, de gorilla in your blood.") The hybrid genre of dialect and standard English was clearly one that McKay felt was suitable to the occasion, but as he continued to write protest poetry the use of dialect would recede further and further. According to McKay, this was so that he would be taken seriously by literary critics.[63] How ironic it was, then, that McKay received the most critical regard for his novels, in which the vernacular voice of his characters is essential to the story.

From these early dialect poems we can already see the evolution of McKay's thinking on how to frame the black working class Jamaican voice in ways that combine a forceful ideological vision with the everyday sound of Creole. By 1919 he had moved in the opposite direction. The didactic, direct nature of the Creole poetic voice was rejected altogether as McKay penned his most famous poem, "If We Must Die." A response to the race riots roiling the United States at the time, the poem, a classic standard grammar sonnet, and was immediately embraced by black intellectuals and leftists as a representative voice of the people.[64] Its conclusion tellingly echoes the forceful working-class voice of "Passive Resistance" and, more particularly, the willingness to die for the cause of freedom that concludes "George William Gordon." It could be that the essentially Jamaican voice of his

---

[62] Claude McKay, "William Gordon to the Oppressed Natives," *T.P.'s Weekly* (April 1912), cited in Winston James, *A Fierce Hatred of Injustice* (2000), pp. 208–9.

[63] See Claude McKay, *My Green Hills of Jamaica* (1979), p. 117.

[64] See William Maxwell, *New Negro, Old Left* (New York: Columbia University Press, 1999), accessed June 11, 2014, http://www.english.illinois.edu/maps/poets/m_r/mckay/mustdie.htm.

dialect poems was unsuitable for the American context—especially if, like Jekyll, Americans associated dialect with the feminine or feminized, and the masculine with the overtly didactic, authoritative or political. But if McKay abandoned the Creole voice in poetry he found a home for it in the novel form.

Both *Home to Harlem* and *Banana Bottom* allow McKay to identify an essential black cultural identity that transcends cultural and class differences. *Home to Harlem* showcases African-American urban life and its demi-monde in all its jaded glory, while *Banana Bottom* is, at first glance, its antithesis. Where they are similar is in their primitivist attributes: the emphasis on the supposed "feminine" attributes of working class, African-descended people as instinctive, sexual, and sensuous; their use of the black vernacular, whether African-American or Jamaican, to denote a range of black expression.

McKay provided the axis that connected the local Caribbean's literary dialect tradition to the parallel African-American tradition. As noted earlier, even in Jamaica McKay appears to have been familiar with African-American innovations in dialect through the poetry of Paul Lawrence Dunbar. Just as importantly, he appears to have been acquainted with African-American intellectual discourse. McKay's older brother, Uriah Theo, who exerted great intellectual influence on the younger brother, argued that "Those who are acquainted with the dialect poetry of [the African-American author] Paul Lawrence Dunbar, must but admit that the melody of his lines is among the sweetest found in literature" and that the presence of dialect poetry featuring African-American voices "did not prevent the existence of a Booker T. Washington or a DuBois."[65]

McKay's work reminds us that vernacular traditions move around, that they are not just local curios but rather the result of syncretic processes of migration and adaptation. This is particularly true of the vernacular's written forms. McKay's use of Creole and African-American vernacular in his novels was groundbreaking for its time not because it was a "first," which it was not; but because it promoted the idea, still with us, that there is such a thing as black vernacular speech; and that speech, whether Caribbean or African American, is an essential characteristic of blackness. In this way McKay's use of dialect in his fiction moved beyond its limited use in his early poetry to cement a view of Caribbean Creole as an African diasporic characteristic. He was not alone in this effort. Theories celebrating an essentialized black culture could be found in a swath stretching from Harlem to the Caribbean, from the primitivist narratives of McKay and Hurston in Harlem to the literature of Indigenisme and Négritude in the francophone Caribbean, and in Afro-Cubanísmo in Cuba. Many of McKay's American contemporaries were ardent students of Afro-Caribbean cultural mores. Langston

---

[65] U. Theo McKay, "The Use of Dialect," *Daily Gleaner* (January 28, 1915), p. 4. For a detailed discussion of McKay's relationship with his brother see Winston James, *A Fierce Hatred of Injustice* (2000), pp. 36–41.

Hughes translated into English *Masters of the Dew*, Haitian writer Jacques Roumain's Indigenist classic about black, Kreyol-speaking peasants. Zora Neale Hurston visited the Caribbean several times and incorporated Caribbean culture into her vision of African-American rural life in *Their Eyes Were Watching God*. She wrote a book on her travels, and even choreographed Bahamian dances.[66] For Zora Neale Hurston and other African American authors, the Caribbean represented a kind of substitute Africa, a black space in the West through which to gaze on a more intense, less mediated, version of blackness. The language of black people was a particularly potent way to symbolize that sense of black difference. Emphasizing Creole's culturally and racially mixed genealogy detracted from that mission. That the Gullah peoples of the South Carolina sea islands, for example, spoke a form of Creole like West Indians would not, in these circumstances, confirm the syncretic or adaptive modes of Creole language but rather its opposite; the unchanging nature of black identity across both rural and urban landscapes, from the United States throughout the Caribbean, as represented by its language. That McKay's vernacular oeuvre flourished in Harlem, a space that produced the idea of an essential blackness, is in line with this vision of the Caribbean as part of an Africanesque continuum. Novels like *Home to Harlem* and *Banana Bottom* balance two cultural models. They both function as counter-narratives to European canonical norms as well as original genres that present the black vernacular as an indigenous, autonomous product of black life across the Atlantic. Both models played a key role in the development of the Creole literary tradition.

Harlem's Caribbean Vernaculars: The Transnational Career of Sam Manning

Aided by the advent of records and radio, by the 1920s Caribbean cultural influence was established throughout New York City.[67] As we have seen, by the mid-nineteenth century New York and Caribbean performers, both theatrical and musical, were part of a well-established circuit between the two regions. By the late nineteenth century the *New York Herald* had published weekly Anancy stories from the Caribbean in its Sunday edition.[68] In the early twentieth century, publications like *The West Indian-American* and *The West Indian Times and American Review* were launched to "place the ideals of the West Indian before the American

---

[66] See Anthea Kraut, *Choreographing the Folk: The Dance Stagings of Zora Neale Hurston* (Minneapolis: University of Minnesota Press, 2008).

[67] See Donald Hill, *Calypso Callaloo: Early Carnival Music in Trinidad* (1993). p. 159.

[68] See Izett Anderson and Frank Cundall, *Jamaica Negro Proverbs and Sayings,* 2nd edition (Kingston: Institute of Jamaica, 1927), and *Daily Gleaner* (February 4, 1899), quoted in Errol Hill, *The Jamaican Stage* (1992), p. 214.

public" and to bring "West Indians abroad in closer contact with those at home."[69] The *West Indian Times and American Review* circulated within the Caribbean and had correspondents who reported from there. Even Jamaica's *Daily Gleaner* reproduced one of the *West Indian Times* and *American Review* stories.[70] Caribbean writers and performers were well-known members of the New York arts scene. The calypso circuit running between New York and Trinidad was leaving its mark on both places. While in the city Trinidadian calypsonians would cut calypso records in preparation for the carnival season back home in Trinidad and sing in Harlem nightclubs before black and white patrons. Some of them further honed their skills at Harlem "rent parties" and outdoor musical events, where African-American musical traditions reigned. Some went further: Trinidadian musician Donald Heywood became a prominent bandleader and playwright in Harlem who composed music for several African-American musical revues during the 1920s.[71]

The distinctive sound of anglophone Caribbean voices started to permeate what was understood as African-American music, and eventually Caribbean music was included as part of the "race" recordings of music companies.[72] Among these "race" recordings were ribald, vernacular-laced calypsos with titles like "Touch Me All About, But Don't Touch Me Dey," "Mongoose Hop," and "Goin' Back to Jamaica." As John Cowley notes in "West Indies Blues," these songs are a hybrid of anglophone Caribbean and African-American music, both in form and lyrical content. For example, "Mister Joseph Strut Your Stuff," the song recorded on the other side of "Touch Me All About," is "pure black North American vaudeville in execution, though its subject is the Trinidadian West Indian in New York and it is sung to an island melody." Many of these hybridized blues/calypsos had as their theme romantic relationships between Caribbean men and African-American women; "Goin' Back to Jamaica," for example, interpolates the voice of an African-American woman with that of Sam Manning, who sings the part of the wronged Jamaican lover ("Woman, I see what you is going to do, you is going to get me 'cacerated [sic]....That's the way with you 'Merican women.")[73]

The most prominent of these hybrid calypsonians/vaudevillians was Trinidadian Sam Manning, one of the pivotal figures in the vernacular axis that I have identified above. Although Claude McKay and the two Garveys are far better known, Sam Manning is a pioneering figure in his own right. A Trinidadian calypsonian who left Trinidad to perform for British troops in North Africa during World War 1, Manning eventually settled in Harlem and became a

---

[69] Amy Ashwood Garvey, quoted in *Trinidad Guardian* (July 3, 1929), p. 1, cited in Tony Martin, *Amy Ashwood Garvey* (2007), p. 106.

[70] See Tony Martin, *Amy Ashwood Garvey* (2007), p. 106.

[71] See Errol G. Hill, "The Caribbean Connection," in *A History of African-American Theatre*, edited by Errol Hill and Henry V. Swatch (Cambridge: Cambridge University Press, 2003), p. 276.

[72] John Cowley discusses the Caribbean "race" recordings of OKeh Records in John Cowley, "West Indies Blues" (2006), p. 217.

[73] John Cowley, "West Indies Blues (2006), pp. 217, 221–5, 230–2.

vaudeville performer at the Alhambra Theatre there.[74] It was in Harlem that he met Marcus Garvey's ex-wife Amy Ashwood. Ashwood Garvey and Manning would become a creative and romantic couple, working and travelling together. With Ashwood Garvey as his agent, Manning would go on to form one half of a blackface comedy duo with African-American comedian Syd Perrin. Manning and Perrin would travel around the Caribbean before returning to New York in the 1940s to join a pan-Caribbean musical production called *Caribbean Carnival,* which included Trinidadian choreographer Pearl Primus and Jamaican band-leader Adolphus Thenstead.[75] Manning's blackface routine was popular, but not without its critics. Opined one Trinidadian reviewer, not altogether approvingly, "To see [Manning] before the footlights with his face blackened and with big white glares, is to recall Al Jolson. . . , In his 'mammy' songs Sam Manning clearly shows Al Jolson's influence, but this is not to his discredit, for no coloured singer on Broadway has not fallen under Jolson's spell."[76]

Sam Manning's career as a vaudevillian coincided with his time was as a Garveyite, a disciple of Garvey's Back to Africa Movement, although he later dissociated from the movement.[77] Although Manning eventually sued Marcus Garvey and his newspaper *The Blackman* for libel, he remained, along with Ashwood Garvey, a committed Pan-Africanist. For Manning and doubtless other vaudeville performers, the ideology of Garveyism and the practice of vaudevillian entertainments were not incompatible. The Harlem of radical black uplift politics and the Harlem of vaudeville and blackface comedy were not, as modern readers might suppose, mutually exclusive worlds. Manning's publicity photos are similar to that of the Native Jamaica Choir in both "native" and formal evening dress. One photo of Manning shows him in a straw hat, the other in a suite and tie. The combination of "primitive" and "modern" images evoke a modern blackness, a New Negro-ness that was also Caribbean. Herbie Miller argues that Manning, as the most popular West Indian performer in New York in the 1920s, used his popularity to promote the United Negro Improvement Association (U.N.I.A.), combining popular entertainments and radical politics. Manning performed at U.N.I.A. rallies and composed popular music such as "African Blues" (1924), a song about black repatriation to Africa with a distinctly Garveyite perspective: "Let me go, where there ain't no ice and there ain't no snow, / When you. . . miss my familiar face I'm gone, / To the land where I belong, / Africa, that land of the

---

[74] Errol Hill, "The Caribbean Connection" (2003), p. 278. Hill notes that Manning played the character of "Rastus" in the Dadaist-inspired vaudeville play *Processional.* According to Jonathan Chambers the playwright John Howard Lawson sketched Rastus as a "stereotypical vaudeville Negro" who "plays banjo and sings most of the time." See Jonathan Chambers, *Messiah of the New Technique: John Howard Lawson, Communism, and American Theatre 1923-1937* (Carbondale: Southern Illinois University Press, 2006), p. 61.

[75] See Errol Hill, "The Caribbean Connection" (2003), p. 278.

[76] *Trinidad Guardian* (June 28, 1929), p. 1, cited in Tony Martin, *Amy Ashwood Garvey* (2007), p. 118.

[77] Tony Martin, *Amy Ashwood Garvey* (2007), p. 112.

blazing sun."[78] Another song about the Bahamas, "Englerston Blues" (1925), echoes the same view:

> I'm going home and it won't be long
> When I get to Englerston
> You better watch me Harvey
> Cos I'm gonna be a big, big man
> Like my friend Marcus Garvey.[79]

The cross-pollination of Caribbean and African-American music is also evident in "Englerston Blues:" it appears that Manning used as his template for "Englerston Blues" the song "West Indian Blues" by the African-American legendary pianist Fats Waller and his group the Jamaican Jazzers recorded four years earlier.[80] Even more than Manning's Garvey-centered songs were his wider corpus that reflected a diasporic consciousness and featured a combination of Caribbean and African-American musical theme, such as "Barbados Blues" and "Jamaica Blues." Manning's Garveyite politics arguably made visible the diasporic consciousness already in evidence among the Caribbean-to-Harlem artists of his generation.

Among the many Trinidadian calypsonians/vaudevillians who moved between Trinidad and Harlem, Sam Manning stood out. A famous Caribbean performer who "did not hide his nationality" from American producers at a time when West Indians were frequently derided as "monkey chasers" by African Americans, Manning was a source of regional pride.[81] He toured the wider anglophone Caribbean, particularly Jamaica. Many of his hybridized calypsos were versions of well-known Jamaican folk songs such as "Sly Mongoose" and "Lignum Vitae."[82] Manning visited Jamaica with Syd Perrin in 1929, as part of a triumphant regional tour arranged by Ashwood Garvey. The Jamaican press was enthusiastic. Noting his spectacular salary of $500 a week "plus royalties," one reviewer gushes that Sam Manning is "admittedly the most famous and popular artiste in America and to get him down to Jamaica is an achievement. . . . We have heard his voice on the gramophone. We have jazzed and sang to his music. . . .He will always be remembered not only as a notable actor and producer of coloured musical entertainment but as the originator of the West Indian character on the stage in New York."[83]

---

[78] Sam Manning, "African Blues," OKeh Recordings (1924), cited in John Cowley, "West Indies Blues" (2006), pp. 204–5.

[79] See Herbie Miller, "Marcus Garvey and the Radical Black Music Tradition," *76 King Street: Journal of Liberty Hall*, vol. 1 (2009), p. 111.

[80] See Herbie Miller "Marcus Garvey and the Radical Black Music Tradition" (2009), p. 111.

[81] See "Trinidad Comedian Returns Home," *Trinidad Guardian* (June 22, 1929), p. 1; also, "Sam Manning and Syd Perrin Are Now with Us," *Daily Gleaner* (May 1, 1929), p. 10.

[82] See John Cowley, "West Indies Blues" (2006), p. 240.

[83] "Sam Manning and Syd Perrin Are Now with Us," *Daily Gleaner* (May 1, 1929), p. 10.

Amidst the effusive praise there was a touch of inter-island competition: Manning was expected to attend the concert of E. M. Cupidon, the timing of which closely coincided with his own.[84] It was in Harlem, however, that Manning and Ashwood Garvey met and wrote their groundbreaking musical play that featured both Caribbean and African-American dialect.

Amy Ashwood Garvey is best known as Marcus Garvey's first wife, but had a long history of engagement with Pan-Africanist politics in her own right. They met while they both still lived in Jamaica. Young Amy Ashwood was passionately involved in the early years of the U.N.I.A. in Kingston. She eventually became, in the words of an F.B.I. agent, Garvey's "chief assistant, a kind of managing boss."[85] The couple left Jamaica, where Amy's middle class parents disapproved of the relationship and in any event Garvey was persona non grata because of his seditious political activism. They settled in Harlem, where they were married. The marriage did not last long, and the Garveys endured a bitter divorce. Despite the split from Garvey, she maintained her connection to black nationalist political circles, travelling extensively throughout the African diaspora lecturing on Pan-Africanism and the international women's movement.[86] Amy Ashwood joined African activists calling for African independence and founded the Nigerian Progress Union. She was active in the West Indies National Council in New York, and in later years campaigned for African-American politician Adam Clayton Powell.[87]

Ashwood Garvey's and Manning's commitment to Pan-Africanism is relevant to their efforts to create an African diasporic artistic practice. Scholars, even those who finally see Ashwood Garvey's relevance beyond Garvey himself, treat Ashwood Garvey's playwriting as a sideline, a footnote to her larger Pan-Africanist politics and political organizing, much as Manning's work in entertainment is mostly separated from his politics. However, just as Harlem's artistic and political movements were intertwined, so too were Ashwood Garvey's artistic efforts linked with her diasporic politics, formed in Jamaica and given full flower in Harlem (Figures 5.2 to 5.4).

---

[84] "The Cupidon Concert on Saturday," *Daily Gleaner* (May 2, 1929), p. 8: "Coinciding rather appropriately with this happy idea is the opportunity for us to bring gifts of approval of our Cupidon . . . I have no doubt that Sam Manning and Syd Perrin will be present on Saturday evening if for a part of the show. A performance of the kind cannot fail to have their sympathy."

[85] See "People and Events: Amy Ashwood 1897–1969," PBS online, accessed August 6, 2014, http://www.pbs.org/wgbh/amex/garvey/peopleevents/p_ashwood.html. See also Louis J. Parascandola, *"Look for Me All Around You: Anglophone Caribbean Immigrants in the Harlem Renaissance* (Detroit: Wayne State University Press, 2005), p. 197.

[86] See Nydia Swaby, "Amy Ashwood-Garvey: A Revolutionary Pan-Africanist Feminist," posted April 1, 2010, accessed August 6, 2014, http://revisionistslc.com/2010/04/01/amy-ashwood-garvey-a-revolutionary-pan-african-feminist/.

[87] See the entry for Garvey, Amy Ashwood (1897–1969) in *The Black Past*, accessed August 6, 2014, http://www.blackpast.org/aah/garvey-amy-ashwood-1897-1969; and Tony Martin, *Amy Ashwood Garvey* (2007).

Figure 5.2   Sam Manning, publicity photo, 1936
[suit and tie]. From the collection of John Cowley.

In Jamaica Amy Ashwood Garvey had already been exposed to both Jamaican and African-American vernacular literatures. The nineteenth century African-American dialect poet Paul Laurence Dunbar was a particular favorite of hers: she even recited one of his poems—albeit a non-dialect one—for a U.N.I.A. elocution contest in 1914.[88] By the time Ashwood Garvey turned to playwriting, the success of Heywood and other West Indians in popular entertainments was a familiar feature of Harlem.

It was in this heady atmosphere of artistic and political energy in 1925 that Ashwood Garvey and Manning collaborated to produce their hit musical theater play, *Hey, Hey!* in which Manning also starred. Coming on the heels of the watershed African-American musical *Shuffle Along* four years earlier, *Hey, Hey!* was so successful it went on tour to Pittsburgh, New Orleans, Chicago and other major cities around the U.S., drawing large crowds of African-American and West Indians.[89] With a title that was a popular catchphrase of 1920s Harlem, *Hey, Hey!* conjoined Caribbean and African-American musical and cultural forms of dance and music through calypso and the blues. Further, the show featured Caribbean and African-American characters who pioneered the use of both Caribbean Creole and African-American vernacular speech in the same narrative.[90] Noting the play's Pan-Africanist significance in later decades, African-American historian

---

[88] See *Daily Gleaner* (October 29, 1914), p. 14, cited in Tony Martin, *Amy Ashwood Garvey* (2007), p. 24.
[89] See Tony Martin, *Amy Ashwood Garvey* (2007), p. 100.
[90] "'Hey, Hey' Off to Splendid Start at Lafayette," *Amsterdam News* (November 10, 1926), p. 11.

Samuel L. Manning. Calypsonian, lyricist, musician and playwright.

Figure 5.3 Sam Manning, publicity photo, 1936 [straw hat]. From the collection of John Cowley.

Figure 5.4 Amy Ashwood Garvey, circa 1920s.

Harold Cruse asserted that it was "composed of African, West Indian and American negro folk elements, blended together in aesthetics, as well as historical, unity."[91]

The plot involved two African-American men kicked out of their homes by their wives. The men go to Africa in search of their soul mates, only to realize that their true soul mates were the wives they left behind in America.[92] Many critics remarked on the play's not-so-subtle satire of Marcus Garvey, who had recently

[91] See Harold Cruse, *The Crisis of the Negro Intellectual* (New York: New York Review, 1967/2005), p. 82.
[92] Errol Hill, "The Caribbean Connection" (2003), p. 278.

been imprisoned for mail fraud. The main character "Morco Garbo"—played by Manning—is a philandering trickster whose hustling lands him "in the jailhouse now." (After his divorce Marcus Garvey had married Ashwood Garvey's former friend Amy Jacques, and there was some speculation as to whether they had had an affair while he was still married to Ashwood Garvey.) To accentuate the connection, the title was expanded to *Hey, Hey! We're in the Jail House Now* when the play went on the road. A review in the African-American newspaper the *Pittsburgh Courier* was subtitled, "Amy Ashwood, Consumed by Fires of Vengeance, Tells of Lack of Sex Appeal of U.N.I.A Leader in Sensational Interview with Courier Reporter—'Hey, Hey', Her Play, a Burlesque of His Life."[93] Another review noted: "Garvey's rise and fall are clearly shown, and his various ideas relative to such things as a kingdom in Africa, sailing vessels, etc. [are] used as opportunities to present dances, songs, and the like, as for instance, in the court room scene in one of two acts."[94]

Ashwood Garvey and Manning had hit upon a winning combination for black audiences: African diasporic subject matter with comedic, vernacular musical and expressive features. The following year they collaborated on two more Caribbean/African diaspora-themed plays: *Brown Sugar*, about a black heroine courted by an Indian prince and an African-American mechanic, as well as a third titled *Black Magic*, featuring calypsos.[95] Although these musicals are now lost to history—no known copy of them remains—like *Shuffle Along* they suggest that 1920s Harlem was not just a starting point for a flowering of the arts for African Americans, it was also a catalyst for Creole popular cultures in the anglophone Caribbean. In the early twentieth century the trajectory of Creole literature and performance might have appeared bifurcated, as two separate, unrelated traditions: one a "local" Caribbean tradition, confined to regional newspapers, the other part of a more cosmopolitan circulation. Yet both are closer than they appear. At a time when African-American racial uplift publications were banned by colonial Caribbean governments, these expressions of popular culture performed a kind of uplift, political in its implications.[96] They showed black artists as creators, Creole voices as principal actors, not just background; they drew black audiences in as participants in a performative commons of the black Atlantic. The dissemination of calypso as a pan-Caribbean cultural feature owes much to these

---

[93] See Delos Johnson, review of "Hey! Hey!," *Pittsburgh Courier* (December 11, 1926), section 2, p. 2, quoted in Tony Martin, *Amy Ashwood Garvey* (2007), pp. 100–1.

[94] Review, "Hey! Hey!," *Pittsburgh Courier* (January 8, 1927, section 2, p. 1), cited in Tony Martin, *Amy Ashwood Garvey* (2007), pp. 100–10.

[95] See Herbie Miller, "Marcus Garvey and the Radical Black Music Tradition" (2009), p. 111.

[96] Office Administering the Government, C. Clementi to Rt. Hon. Viscount Milner, PC, etc. etc. (September 2 1919), CO 111/624, Public Record Office, London, cited in Tony Martin, "African and Indian Consciousness," p. 279 footnote 250, in *General History of the Caribbean: The Caribbean in the Twentieth Century*, edited by P. C. Emmer, Bridget Brereton, B. V. Higman, vol. 6 (London: UNESCO, 2004).

early calypsonians, moving between New York and the Caribbean, establishing Caribbean culture as a force in both. The success of Afro-Caribbean star Harry Belafonte in the US the succeeding decades of the twentieth century is built on the legacy of these early progenitors: like Sam Manning, Belafonte is famous both as a crooner of Creole-inflected folk tunes like "Day-O" and as a vocal civil rights activist. The rise of the vernacular axis between the Caribbean and Harlem also signaled the advent of vernacular expression as an attribute of a masculinized New Negro-ness. Despite the hostility of Garvey and other "race men" to dialect, the vernacular axis established by McKay, Manning, Ashwood Garvey along pathways established by Garvey himself, would expand the contours of Creole into an expressive feature of the black Atlantic.

Epilogue

Global Creole

In 2014 Jamaican writer Marlon James' published his third novel, *A Brief History of Seven Killings*. It made a sensation. A panoramic story of 1970s Jamaica told by a range of mostly Creole-speaking black characters, the book was an immediate, sprawling, 700-page international success. "Compulsive ventriloquism," one reviewer called it.[1] "It's like a Tarantino remake of `The Harder They Come' but with a soundtrack by Bob Marley and a script by Oliver Stone and William Faulkner, with maybe a little creative boost from some primo ganja," enthused another.[2] Ganja-boosting aside, the book won a slew of prestigious international prizes, including Britain's Man Booker prize. Most striking of all, it is being adapted for film by an acclaimed young American director.[3]

But the most extraordinary thing about *A Brief History of Seven Killings* is that a book written mostly in Jamaican Creole found not just an international audience but a *popular* one. Jamaican Creole, one of the baddest of the bad grammars, is now part of a global lexicon of, not English, but *Englishes*. As Jamaican cultural critic Carolyn Cooper puts it, "[Jamaican] people like to talk about how Jamaican is a lickle local language and nobody else nah go understan' it, an' we have to big up English; and here is this book, whole swaths of it are in Jamaican, and that hasn't been a problem for the readers to decide that this is an important work, so I think we need to stop undermining ourselves, recognize that Jamaica is a global culture, our language is global and just go t'rough!"[4]

What happened?

[1] Zachary Lazar, "A Brief History of Seven Killings by Marlon James," *New York Times* (October 23, 2014), accessed October 9, 2015, http://www.nytimes.com/2014/10/26/books/review/a-brief-history-of-seven-killings-by-marlon-james-review.htm.

[2] Michiko Kakutani, "Jamaica via a Sea of Voices," Books of the Times, *New York Times* (September 21, 2014), accessed October 9, 2015, http://www.nytimes.com/2014/09/22/books/marlon-jamess-a-brief-history-of-seven-killings.html.

[3] Borys Kit, "'Insecure' Director to Adapt Man Booker Prize-Winning Novel for Amazon Studios (Exclusive)," *The Hollywood Reporter* (September 25, 2017), accessed January 8, 2021, https://www.hollywoodreporter.com/news/insecure-director-adapt-man-booker-prize-winning-novel-amazon-studios-1042835.

[4] Carolyn Cooper, "Celebrating the Success of Marlon James," "Celebrating the Success of Marlon James", Cliff Hughes and Dennis Brooks, *Nationwide News Network* (October 13, 2015), https://soundcloud.com/nationwide-newsnet/celebrating-the-success-of-marlon-james-oct13-2015.

Creole Noise: Early Caribbean Dialect Literature and Performance. Belinda Edmondson, Oxford University Press.
© Belinda Edmondson 2022. DOI: 10.1093/oso/ 9780192856838.003.0007

When Claude McKay wrote the primitivist classic *Banana Bottom* in 1933 he included a glossary of Jamaican Creole words, presumably for metropolitan audiences who would need help decoding "backra" and "busha." The glossing tradition for Creole literature continued through the 1980s, from school-oriented anthologies like *The Penguin Book of Caribbean Verse in English* to contemporary feminist novels like Michelle Cliff's *Abeng*.[5] In the meantime, Caribbean immigrant fiction was transforming the American and British landscapes. Dialect words, Creole phrases, started appearing in influential British and American novels like *The Satanic Verses, White Teeth, Continental Drift*, and *Netherland*.[6] Then Caribbean immigrant Junot Diaz dropped a linguistic bomb on the entire Caribbean glossing tradition with his 2007 novel, *The Short Wondrous Life of Oscar Wao*, a novel so steeped in the New Jersey Dominican vernacular—shall we call it a Creole?—that it spawned amateur glossaries and annotations *after* publication; authored, notably, not by the writer himself but by his admiring readers.[7]

Junot Diaz upended the glossing tradition because he simply refused the idea that unfamiliar phrases and difficult cultural concepts needed to be explained to non-Dominican—better yet, non-Dominican-American—readers. Just as generations of English majors had to wend their way through the endless allusions of T. S. Eliot's *The Wasteland*, or the thicket of Scottish dialect in Robert Burns' "Tam O'Shanter," contemporary readers must sink or swim in this newest of American dialects. The reader is expected to do the difficult work; the reader comes to the text, not the other way around. The Caribbean author is no longer a supplicant for the attentions of the non-local reader.

Like Diaz, Marlon James refuses the idea that the Jamaican text must always be explaining itself. James' novels are fundamentally grounded in Creole, unlike precursors like *Banana Bottom* or *Tropic Death*, which are Creole-inflected. To experience *A Brief History* the reader must enter the world of the text in all of its multi-vocal, multi-allusory glory or be lost altogether. It isn't just the Creole that is difficult; it is the Kingston slang of the 1970s, the allusions to cultural moments earlier decades on an island not so far-far away. The characters include white Americans along with black Jamaican gangsters, politicians, and icons (the ubiquitous Bob Marley, although this time as victim, not celebrity). Their inclusion reflects the trans-Atlantic origins of Jamaican Creole as much as its local ones.

This is not to say American marketing concerns played no part in this decision: marketing is a trans-Atlantic influence, too. James himself notes wryly that it was

---

[5] Paula Burnett, ed., *The Penguin Book of Caribbean Verse in English* (1986); Michelle Cliff, *Abeng* (New York: The Crossing Press, 1984), p. 167.

[6] Salman Rushdie, *Satanic Verses*, (1988); Zadie Smith *White Teeth* (2000); Russell Banks, *Continental Drift* (1985); Joseph O'Neill, *Netherland* (2008).

[7] See Erin Judge, "The Annotated Oscar Wao," accessed November 9, 2015, http://www.annotated-oscar-wao.com/. Judge says she first began "The Annotated Oscar Wao" for her mother, who was struggling with all of the non-English words and Caribbean allusions.

not his idea but his American editor's to take out the glossary he had constructed for his first novel *John Crow's Devil*. The editor argued that the glossary implied that the novel was "different."[8] James also notes that he had to create a dictionary of Jamaican Creole *for himself* before writing *A Brief History of Seven Killings*.[9] It is, after all, a language that even the native speaker has to annotate.

It is a new world. A Creole novel for a creolized New World. And yet not so new after all. The loudest objections to James' use of Creole came, not from white Americans, but from Jamaicans who told him he was "ruining" his novels and his chance to "break through."[10] This was more or less the same objection leveled by his fellow Jamaicans that Henry Garland Murray faced 150 years earlier. It did not matter that Creole is the favored voice for local writing and the famous Jamaican music industry: the very familiarity of Creole might be the problem for these local critics. As V. S. Naipaul famously noted, historically Caribbean readers have had an ambivalent, if not schizophrenic, relationship to the use of dialect in "serious" literature: "They do not object to its use locally…[b]ut they object to its use in books which are read abroad.…The Trinidadian expects his novels…to have a detergent purpose."[11]

The objections of local Caribbean audiences to the use of Creole for "outside" audiences is complicated by their sense that Caribbean writers who write from outside the region are validating a proposition, promoted by a historical statements by famous "exiled" Caribbean writers such as C. L. R. James and Naipaul all the way to James himself, that writers, in order to fulfill themselves as writers, have to leave the Caribbean. More than mere fulfillment, James presents exile as the *only* condition that can give him life as a writer. In earlier years he bemoaned the lack of a literary community in Jamaica; later he declared his exile status in a *New York Times* magazine essay with the provocative subtitle, "I knew I had to leave my home country—whether in a coffin or on a plane."[12]

James' exile story in the US is entwined with his life as a closeted gay man in Jamaica—he reveals that he is gay at the same moment that he "outs" himself as an exiled writer. James' identity as an international author in exile, therefore, is inseparable from his identity as a gay black Jamaican man. James' declaration

[8] See Annie Paul, "reading, writing, religion: Mark McWatt and Marlon James talk with Annie Paul," *Caribbean Review of Books* (November 10, 2006), accessed February 5, 2016, http://caribbeanreviewofbooks.com/crb-archive/10-november-2006/reading-writing-religion/.

[9] See "Marlon James on his Booker-winning novel *A Brief History of Seven Killings*," *The Guardian* (October 16, 2015), accessed February 3, 2021, http://www.theguardian.com/books/audio/2015/oct/16/marlon-james-brief-history-seven-killings-booker-prize-podcast.

[10] See Annie Paul, "Reading, Writing, Religion: Mark McWatt and Marlon James Talk with Annie Paul," *Caribbean Review of Books* (2006).

[11] See V.S. Naipaul, *The Middle Passage* (New York: Vintage, 1981/1962), p. 69.

[12] See Nazma Muller, "The Mis-Education of Marlon James," in *Jamaica Observer* (July 23, 2006); andMarlon James, "From Jamaica to Minnesota to Myself," *New York Times* (March 10, 2015), accessed February 5, 2016, http://www.nytimes.com/2015/03/15/magazine/from-jamaica-to-minnesota-to-myself.html?_r=0.

took place in 2015, at a watershed moment in U.S. history when the U.S. Supreme Court put the nail in the coffin of legalized homophobia by affirming, albeit belatedly, the right to same-sex marriage.[13] Given the inextricable nature of commercial aims from artistic ones, it is tempting to consider whether the rise of LGBT rights in the U.S. as the *cause celebré* of this generation is linked to the timing of James' declaration of his twinned exile and sexual status. Certainly American readers have become more interested in black or non-Western LGBT experiences as a result of the country's shift in attitudes towards LGBT populations. Yet African LGBT activists have complained that American zeal to proselytize its new-found embrace of LGBT rights has, paradoxically, done more to endanger their lives by strong-arming African governments into compliance than if the United States had simply left these communities alone.[14] Likewise, many Jamaicans have complained that the United States' criticism of Jamaica's openly violent expressions of homophobia, and the banning from U.S. and U.K. commercial venues of popular Jamaican dancehall artists whose songs advocate a violent homophobic response to LGBT populations, is a form of Western imperialism. In this context, James' declaration might be read as a validation of the popular American view of non-Western, non-white countries as violent and repressive, and a corresponding validation of the U.S. view of itself as a tolerant haven for dissident "sexiles."[15] Even some Caribbean LGBT advocates were wary of what one called James' "reductionism of the exile narrative" ("I'm sorry, but we need other narratives of the queer Caribbean than die or leave. What about those who stayed and struggled?"[16])

The question of who gets to use Creole for international audiences, therefore, may be just as much a question of allegiances, national and otherwise. For authors like James, that may be a non-question. Rules of engagement in art are odious, is the usual answer; an artist's commitment is not to a constituency but to the truth of their craft. For Caribbean readers, already sensitive to a history of appropriation, that question might be central to the book's reception. Accordingly the question might be framed as a series of questions: Are you one of us? Are you promoting us, or betraying us? Is your use of Creole a badge of authenticity, not for us, the

---

[13] Timothy Stewart-Winter notes that the U.S. was the 20th country to legalize gay marriage, not the first. See Timothy Stewart-Winter, "The Price of Gay Marriage," *New York Times* (June 26, 2015), accessed February 5, 2016, http://www.nytimes.com/2015/06/28/opinion/sunday/the-price-of-gay-marriage.html.

[14] See Norimitsu Onishi, "U.S. Support of Gay Rights May Have Done More Harm Than Good," *New York Times* (December 20, 2015), accessed February 5, 2016, http://www.nytimes.com/2015/12/21/world/africa/us-support-of-gay-rights-in-africa-may-have-done-more-harm-than-good.html?smid=nytcore-iphone-share&smprod=nytcore-iphone.

[15] I borrow the term "sexiles," a conflation of sexual exile, from Yolanda Martinéz-San Miguel. See Yolanda Martinéz-San Miguel, *Coloniality of Diasporas*(New York: Palgrave Macmillan, 2014).

[16] Trinidadian LGBT activist Colin Robinson's Facebook comments, quoted in Annie Paul, "Bloodcloth! Marlon James and the #ManBooker2015," *Active Voice* (October 28, 2015), accessed February 5, 2016, http://anniepaul.net/2015/10/28/bloodcloth-marlon-james-and-the-manbooker2015/.

local audience, but for *them*, the Americans and the British, black or otherwise, whose approval will yield book contracts and movie deals? Are you serving up Creole for the metropolitan society that requires "the real thing" to showcase its commitment to diversity even as your portraits of us confirm old stereotypes of our violence, hedonism, thievery?

Or, the question could simply be about money: Will this book sell? Will it help tourism? What's in it for us? If we benefit, go right ahead. Like authors everywhere, readers are also aware that culture has a price tag.

This division of national constituencies is muddied by continuing debates over what, exactly, constitutes "home" and "away," "them" and "us." The flight from Kingston to Miami is popularly referred to as a local bus, while Brooklyn is understood to be a district of Kingston. Jamaican Creole as a global language is embedded in the evolving idea of Creole as a global culture. Arguably Caribbean Creoles are forming the basis of a transnational lingua franca, peppering the music, idioms and, yes, literatures of the Atlantic world, sampled by writers like Salman Rushdie, entered into the sage Third International Oxford Dictionary as part of that global language we call English. Marlon James and his compatriot poet Kwame Dawes are part of a new cohort of Jamaican writers who believe that the rise of reggae—Bob Marley in particular—plays a pivotal part in the acceptance of Creole by Caribbean writers as a "legitimate" language of serious writing. A decade earlier Kwame Dawes penned a manifesto for a "new reggae aesthetic" that defined not just Jamaican but, he argues, Caribbean writing; and, as part of his acceptance speech for the Man Booker Prize, James credits reggae singers Bob Marley and Peter Tosh for allowing Jamaicans to "realize that the voice coming out of our mouths was a legitimate voice for fiction."[17]

The emphasis on the reggae-fication—or calypso-fication—of Caribbean literature may imply, to some, that the ultimate authentication process for Caribbean literature is through local culture. Given the global processes that shape, and have always shaped, Caribbean music, however, it also suggests the opposite. Bob Marley as an international figure, calypso as global music, has lubricated the entrance of Creole into the worlds of the trans-Atlantic. This is not to overlook the fact that James has lauded the American popular tradition as the primary formative influence for both himself and his generation, growing up in the Caribbean: "The Samuel Selvon narrative is foreign to us," he asserted in 2006.[18] More importantly, James has pointed out a phenomenon that few if any

[17] See Kwame Dawes, *Natural Mysticism: Towards a New Reggae Aesthetic in Caribbean Writing* (London: Peepal, 1999); also Alex Shephard, "Marlon James Wins 2015 Man Booker Prize," *New Republic* (October 13, 2015), accessed November 9, 2015, http://www.newrepublic.com/article/123111/marlon-james-wins-2015-man-booker-prize.

[18] See Annie Paul, "Plotting a Brief History of Seven Killings: An Exclusive Interview with Marlon James," *Active Voice* (October 6, 2014, original publication date September 30, 2014), accessed November 10, 2015, http://anniepaul.net/2014/10/06/plotting-a-brief-history-of-seven-killings-an-exclusive-interview-with-marlon-james/.

anglophone Caribbean writers have: the congruence of American and Caribbean dialect traditions. Alluding to over a century of literary dialect, James told a Jamaican interviewer, "I'm not convinced that there is much difference in intent between, say, Jamaican dialect and the dialect in *The Color Purple*—or the dialect in *As I Lay Dying* or in *Huckleberry Finn*."[19]

Lest one think that my use of "global" and "trans-Atlantic" are mere code words for "American" (which they often are), let me note that the old British tradition—as well as the new—still informs the story of Creole's evolution into a literary language. James refers to himself as a "Dickensian:" indeed, in his Booker speech he fondly recalls as a formative influence "dueling" Shakespeare soliloquies with his father in Jamaican rum shops.[20] It is, perhaps, no accident that the very British Man Booker prize is, thus far, considered James' greatest achievement. Perhaps not coincidence as well is the fact that the only other Booker winner from the Caribbean was also an innovator in the use of Anglo-Caribbean vernacular for a metropolitan audience. V. S. Naipaul, "England's favourite nineteenth-century Englishman" in the words of one critic, is, perhaps, James' antithesis in every other way except this one (the author biographies in Naipaul novels inevitably list both his knighthood and his Booker prize).[21]

So why, in this age of American cultural saturation, an age which has witnessed the rise of the Caribbean vernacular tradition to new trans-Atlantic significance; should we mention the Booker prize, Englishness, and the rest of the supposedly hoary colonial influences that kept the Caribbean in thrall to a British canonical tradition that no longer obtains? James' fellow Jamaican writer Colin Channer presumably spoke for the contemporary generation of Caribbean writers when, using Creole-inflected language for emphasis, he complained that "respectable" Caribbean writers, steeped in the colonial tradition, had failed to write about the very different realities of the postcolonial moment, divorced from the colonial tradition, that were occurring right under their noses:

> ...I was there in Jamaica in the seventies...Where were all our novelists then, the big men, with the big names, and the big positions when the gunmen...bun up the old lady them? Where were they when the army murdered some ghetto yout'...?...where were they when dem shoot Bob Marley?[22]

[19]   Annie Paul, "Reading, Writing, Religion: Mark McWatt and Marlon James Talk with Annie Paul," *Caribbean Review of Books* (2006).

[20]   See "Marlon James Wins the Man Booker Prize 2015," *The Guardian* (October 13, 2015), accessed November 10, 2015, *http://www.theguardian.com/books/2015/oct/13/marlon-james-wins-the-man-booker-prize-2015*. James lists American fiction influences in his interview with Annie Paul, "Reading, Writing, Religion: Mark McWatt and Marlon James Talk with Annie Paul," *Caribbean Review of Books* (2006).

[21]   Scott Winokur quotes C. J. Wallia in Scott Winokur, "The Unsparing Vision of V.S. Naipaul," in *Conversations with V.S. Naipaul*, edited by Feroza Jussawalla (Jackson: University of Mississippi Press, 1997), p. 122.

[22]   See Annie Paul, "Bloodcloth! Marlon James and the #ManBooker2015," *Active Voice* (October 28, 2015), accessed November 23, 2015, http://anniepaul.net/2015/10/28/bloodcloth-marlon-james-and-the-manbooker2015/.

This is a deceptive comment. Contemporary Caribbean writers' fidelity to grim "reality" is implied in Channer's comment, as if canonical writers were too genteel to address the hard realities of modern life that Creole narrates. Yet James' most celebrated Creole novels have not been about the present at all. They look *backwards* to formative historical moments. *A Brief History of Seven Killings* goes back over 40 years ago to tell a story that resonates in the present moment. Bob Marley is now a legendary figure, not a contemporary one. *The Book of Night Women* goes back even further: it rehearses in no small measure the colonial archive of those earlier Creole practitioners, Samuel Augustus Mathews and even H.G. de Lisser, whose historical novel *Psyche*, about a black slave mistress of the white planter who ignites a slave rebellion against him, seems like a pulp precursor of James' celebrated book.

The truth about the Creole literary tradition is that it was always engaged in the present, and from many ethnic perspectives. This is not a plea for a mushy multi-culturalist approach to the Creole tradition—nothing has obscured the levers of power more than the political deployment of Caribbean hybridity as an egalitarian, apolitical construct, as Shalini Puri has shown us.[23] Nor is it coöptation, a move to de-emphasize its Caribbean origins at the moment its global power is being recognized for what it is and has been. And that is a contest, a struggle, a collaboration. One-upsmanship. A mutual admiration society. The Creole creations of Samuel Augustus Mathews, Henry Garland Murray, the Jamaica Choir, "Quow," Claude McKay, Sam Manning, and any number of anonymous authors whose poems and skits lie forgotten in the pages of now-defunct newspapers, were the product of a dynamic and omnivorous literary dialect tradition that ricocheted from Kingston, Georgetown or Port of Spain to New York, from New York to London, and from London back to Kingston, Georgetown, and Port of Spain. Or the genre took a pan-Caribbean turn, from British Guiana to Trinidad to Barbados, and back again. To speak of the origins of Caribbean Creoles is to speak of Scottish dialects and Harlem vernaculars. It is to speak of the American blackface minstrels on tour in Kingston in the 1860s, and Bim and Bam, the popular blackface Jamaican comedy duo of the mid-twentieth century who toured New York and London.[24] It is to speak of the Caribbean tours of the Fisk Jubilee Singers and the English tours of the Kingston Choral Union, transformed into the Native Jamaica Choir. It is also to speak of sounds rooted specifically and irrevocably in the actual geographies of the Caribbean, itself. Like reggae, like calypso, the Creole literary tradition is a permanent contradiction, defined by its movement as much as its stasis.

---

[23] See Shalini Puri, "Canonized Hybridities, Resistant Hybridities," pp. 12–38, in *Caribbean Romances: The Politics of Regional Representation*, edited by Belinda Edmondson (Charlottesville and London: University of Virginia Press, 1999).

[24] Martin Banham, Errol Hill, and George Woodyard, eds, *The Cambridge Guide to African & Caribbean Theatre* (Cambridge: Cambridge University Press, 1994), p. 204; also, *Laugh with Bim and Bam*, re-issued CD (London: Jet Star, 2003).

Louise Bennett, that most iconic of Jamaican Creole poets, was for most of her career not regarded as an important poet by the literary establishment. She wrote in the island "patois" about subjects too familiar, too comic, too female-centric to merit serious consideration. Bennett was dismissed as a local sensation, at most a regional, not an international, presence. As it turns out, even our understanding of Bennett as a local presence is not entirely accurate. For, even as she became a familiar presence in Jamaican theatre and on the radio Louise Bennett, like the Trinidadian calypsonians and her compatriot Claude McKay, travelled to New York, where she was a hit on television and radio *there* as well, and where she enjoyed a two-decade friendship with African-American vernacular poet Langston Hughes, who admired her poetry and threw a party in her honor.[25] The divide between the local and trans-local was never that clear, even for Bennett. This local Creole poet influenced both "serious" Caribbean authors like Derek Walcott and the game-changing Jamaican "dub" performance poets of the 1970s like Mutabaruka and Linton Kwesi Johnson, whose London presence ensured the rise of the Creole poetic tradition there. As this study illustrates, Louise Bennett was, far from an anomaly, but one of a long line of Creole writers. She herself was influenced, just as she influenced: her first exposure to the written form of Creole was Claude McKay's *Constab Ballads*, given to her by her school teacher, poems which she memorized and recited to friends and relatives.[26] Yet McKay's legacy as an important influencer in the development of Creole literature has been questioned by critics.[27]

Still with us, then, is the question of cultural purity, still the question of how to create an authentic Caribbean literature uncontaminated by "universal"—or global, or non-Caribbean, or non-black—influences. In some ways, even as Creole ascends to ever higher artistic stature, Creole literature has not shaken off the anxieties of black nationalists like Marcus Garvey who rejected Creole literature based on who was producing it, and for whom. Garvey was offended by McKay's depiction of a dialect-speaking black world of violence and promiscuity, believing it to be fodder for white audiences eager to reinforce their racist suppositions about blacks. Jamaican-born journalist Christopher Farley trod this familiar terrain when, alluding to the endemic violence portrayed in *A Brief History of Seven Killings*, he asked Marlon James, "Do you think this book is going

---

[25] See Sam Vásquez, *Humor in the Caribbean Literary Canon* (New York: Palgrave Macmillan, 2012), p. 55; and Langston Hughes, Letter to Louise Bennett (August 13, 1953), MS, The William Ready Division of Archives and Research Collections, McMaster University, Hamilton Ontario; both cited in Bernard Lombardi, "On Reading Louise Bennett Glocally: Langston Hughes, Diasporic Politics, and Nationalist Poetry" (unpublished manuscript, 2015), pp. 5, 7. I thank Bernard Lombardi for sharing his research with me.

[26] See Mary Jane Hewitt, "A Comparative Study of the Careers of Zora Neale Hurston and Louise Bennett as Cultural Conservators" (Ph.D. dissertation, University of the West Indies, 1986), pp. 26–7, quoted in Winston James, *A Fierce Hatred of Injustice* (2000), p. 140.

[27] Edward Kamau Brathwaite, *History of the Voice* (1984), p. 20.

to boost tourism in Jamaica or hurt it?"[28] Thus do the concerns over cultural purity inhabit the same critical space as the culture of commodification, where Creole literature is worthy of international consumption only when it presents an accommodationist vision of Caribbean culture for the global tourist market. This is not to say there is no commercial aspect to publication of "violent" Creole fiction, which now can be marketed for popular international or transnational Caribbean audiences as either "serious" writing—also known, however redundantly, as "literary fiction"—or pulp fiction. The distinctions are increasingly irrelevant. Certainly in this book-averse generation publishers are wont to see popular novels as mere preludes to camera-ready screenplays. Then again, countless classic novels were born as popular serialized fiction in local newspapers.

This vision of Creole's commercial role is curiously in line with the views of Walter Jekyll and an earlier generation of foreign whites for whom Caribbean Creole was an inferior, "womanish" language, the language of "overheard" black and brown people ventriloquized by those who do not speak "like that." By contrast, James' use of Creole to depict a violent, ideologically riven society is more in line with that of Creole-driven critiques of Jamaican society by the Jamaican "dub" poets of the 1970s and 1980s. The dub poets are themselves associated with an oppositional, masculinist tradition to the point that in 1990 female dub poet Jean Binta Breeze felt compelled to explain her presence in the field with the essay, "Can A Dub Poet Be a Woman?"[29] Ironically, the dub poets themselves are inheritors of the "feminized" dialect performance tradition of Louise Bennett, even if their delivery is closer in spirit to 1970s African American spoken word poets like Gil Scott-Heron and The Last Poets. (Indeed, Linton Kwesi Johnson, whose famous poem is the political diatribe "Inglan is a Bitch," made a memorable guest appearance on one of Louise Bennett's albums.)[30]

Louise Bennett is now a much-anthologized icon of Creole literature in the Caribbean. Nevertheless, Marlon James and Colin Channer have both described her Creole literature and performances as a form of minstrelsy, a critique made more resonant once we understand that the history of minstrelsy is a Caribbean story, not just an American one.[31] When Louis Chude-Sokei claims that "the struggle to claim vernacular culture in the Caribbean revolves around the definitional tensions of the minstrel figure," he summarizes the attraction/repulsion

[28] Christopher John Farley, "Writer Marlon James Reimagines a Watershed in Jamaica," Wall Street Journal (October 2, 2014), accessed December 15, 2015, http://www.wsj.com/articles/writer-marlon-james-reimagines-a-watershed-in-jamaica-1412266564.

[29] Jean Binta Breeze, "Can A Dub Poet Be A Woman?," Women: A Cultural Review, vol. 1, issue 1 (1990), pp. 47–9.

[30] See Miss Lou, Yes M'Dear Live (Kingston: Sonic Sounds, 1995), featuring Special Guest Linton Kwesi Johnson.

[31] See Marlon James, "Iron Balloons Redux," Geoffrey Philp's Blog Spot (June 28, 2006); and Colin Channer, "I Am Not in Exile," Obsidian III: Literature in the African Diaspora, vol. 2, issue 2 (Fall/ Winter 2000–2001), pp. 50–1.

dynamic that animates so much reaction to Louise Bennett and other practitioners of Creole arts, past and present.[32]

The conflicted attitude towards Creole writing is reflected in the consistent reframing of Creole fiction's messy, multicultural, ideologically suspect origins. Pushing against this tendency to dismiss the white ventriloquist writers, in her watershed anthology *The Penguin Book of Caribbean Verse in English* Paula Burnett asserts that white Creole authors such as Michael McTurk and Alexander Cordle belong to the oral tradition of Caribbean poetry right alongside canonized black authors Claude McKay and Kamau Brathwaite. However, Burnett sidesteps the untidy ideological implications of this inclusion by selecting as representative of this orality two of McTurk's relatively innocuous dialect poems about religion and social pretensions rather than any number of wittier—and more acerbically racist—ones.[33] Perhaps this is an unfair expectation: *The Penguin Book of Caribbean Verse in English* reflects its historical moment, published as it was in the 1980s, the high point of a particularly apolitical brand of multiculturalism.

Accepting the historical legacy of Creole means accepting that the ideological motivations were varied. Creole texts were not particularly in line with the nationalist project, or even respectful of black culture—although sometimes they were. Accepting the legacy of Creole literature and performance also means accepting that ventriloquism is not a dirty word. Yes, Cordle, McTurk, and white creole writers before them thrived on an often racist, culturally exploitative ventriloquizing of black voices, black women's in particular. They also produced some remarkable, and remarkably popular, prose. Without these men—for men they were—there would have been no Claude McKays, no Louise Bennetts, no George Lammings, no Derek Walcotts. Indeed Denise Decaires Narain argues that Louise Bennett herself, as a middle-class black woman, in some sense ventriloquizes working-class black women as a narrator.[34]

The problem with ventriloquism is not simply race; it is the author's relationship to the ventriloquized. When Afro-Jamaican "Funny Murray" (Henry Garland Murray's son) wrote and performed his dialect pieces he was condemned by black nationalist editor Robert Love for ridiculing black people. Marcus Garvey similarly condemned Claude McKay for catering to white racism in McKay's dialect-saturated portraits of blacks. Strangely, even as he condemned McKay Garvey approved of the black dialect comedian E. M. Cupidon, who went even further than McKay, inhabiting the very voices of those Creole-speaking

---

[32] Louis Chude-Sokei, *The Last Darky* (2006), p. 154.

[33] See Michael McTurk, "Query," "Deh 'Pon Um Again," in *The Penguin Book of Caribbean Verse in English*, edited by Paula Burnett (1986), pp. 13–14.

[34] Denise Decaires Narain, *Contemporary Caribbean Women's Poetry* (London: Routledge, 2001), p. 53. DeCaires Narain points out that despite Bennett's use of working-class black female voices, "the social distance between the poet and the people chooses to represent does not appear to have generated similarly troubling questions to those generated by early, white, colonial writers."

characters, performing them for laughs before audiences that were decidedly mixed.[35] Was this, then, about race, or about class: the fact that the middle-class McKay had linguistic range—he wrote in standard grammar as well as in Creole—while E. M. Cupidon, famous only for dialect performances, was associated with working class blackness itself?

It is a question that is not quite answered in our present moment. Caribbean writers of all ethnic backgrounds are now *expected* to write, at least in part, in Creole or risk being dismissed as inauthentic. Yet they may, or may not, be suspected of ulterior motives in so doing. Creole is still a dynamic, dangerous language. It is canonical, or on the verge of being so: yet it still waits outside the gates. Black writers or no, perhaps its acceptance *still* depends on who is doing the writing—or speaking. The question of *how* one speaks, *who* one speaks Creole/dialect/vernacular/patois to, or *for*, or *with*, is still fraught. There is a slipperiness to theorizing the politics of Creole, given the class and color ramifications across the Americas. It is enough to say that nothing is quite so satisfying to a Caribbean audience as the most formal of English speech-acts sliced wide open with a heavy shot of Creole. Maybe Creole's originality lies in its ability to "disturb its neighbors," those respectable syntaxes of standard English, French, Spanish, Dutch. Its power lies in its marginality. But can one call marginal anything so central to narrative? There is no Caribbean literature without Creole. Maybe, if critics stopped trying to "crack the code," as the Trinidadian-American poet Roger Bonair-Agard puts it, maybe writers will "stop (maybe) / inventing new syntaxes for survive...."[36]

---

[35] See Our Dramatic Critic, "The Curtain Rises," and "Review of *Susan Proudleigh*," in *The New Cosmopolitan* (February 8, 1931), pp. 20–1.

[36] Roger Bonaire-Agard, "In Defense of the Code-Switch or Why You Talk Like That or Why You Always Be Cussing," in *The Breakbeat Poets: New American Poetry in the Age of Hip-Hop*, edited by Kevin Coval, Quraysh Ali Lansana, and Nate Marshall (Chicago: Haymarket Books, 2015), p. 37.

Bibliography

Abbott, Lynn, and Doug Seroff. *Out of Sight: The Rise of African-American Music, 1889–1895.* Jackson: University of Mississippi Press, 2002.

Abrahams, Roger D., ed. *Afro-American Folktales: Stories from Black Traditions in the New World.* New York: Pantheon Books, 1985.

Adams, L. Emilie Adams. *Understanding Jamaican Patois: An Introduction to Afro-Jamaican Grammar.* Kingston: Kingston Publishers Ltd, 1991.

Allsopp, Richard. *Dictionary of Caribbean English Usage.* London and New York: Oxford University Press, 1996.

Anderson, Izett, and Frank Cundall. *Jamaica Negro Proverbs and Sayings*, 2nd edition. Kingston: Institute of Jamaica, 1927. First published 1910.

Annual Register: A Review of Public Events at Home and Abroad for the Year 1865. London: Longman & Co., etc., 1866.

Anonymous. *Marly, or The Life of a Planter in Jamaica.* Glasgow: Richard Griffin, 1828.

Anonymous. "The Speech of Moses Bon Sàam." *London Magazine*, 1735.

The Anti-Slavery Reporter 9, no. 1, 1861.

Armstrong, John. "To Omicron *Lick-Devil, Esq." In *Universal Almanac: Miscellanies*, vol. 2, 175–6. London, 1770.

Ashcroft, Bill. *Caliban's Language: The Transformation of English in Post-Colonial Literatures.* London: Routledge, 2009.

Atkins, John. *A Voyage to Guinea, Brasil, and the West Indies.* London: Cesar Ward and Richard Chandler, 1736.

Baker, Philip, and Adrienne Bruyn, eds. *St. Kitts and the Atlantic Creoles: The Text of Samuel Augustus Mathews in Perspective.* London: University of Westminster Press, 1998.

Banham, Martin, Errol Hill, and George Woodyard, eds. *The Cambridge Guide to African & Caribbean Theatre.* Cambridge, UK: Cambridge University Press, 1994.

Barbados Pocket Guide, 2nd Edition. London: Thomas Cook Publishing, 2011.

Barringer, Tim, and Wayne Modest, eds. *Victorian Jamaica.* Durham and London: Duke University Press, 2018.

Baugh, Edward. "West Indian Poetry 1900–1970: A Study in Cultural Decolonisation." 1971. Reprinted in *The Routledge Reader in Caribbean Literature*, edited by Alison Donnell and Sarah Lawson Welsh, 99–104. New York: Routledge, 1996.

Baugh, Edward. "A History of Poetry." In *A History of Literature in the Caribbean* Vol. 2, edited by James Arnold, 227–82. Philadelphia: John Benjamins, 2001.

Beke, X. *West Indian Yarns.* Georgetown, 1884.

Benjamin, Joel. 1987. "The Early Theatre in Guyana." *Kyk-over-Al* 37 (December): 24–44.

Bennett, Louise. *Jamaica Labrish.* Portomore, Jamaica: Sangster's Bookstore, 1966.

Berman, Carolyn Vellenga. *Creole Crossings: Domestic Fiction and the Reform of Colonial Slavery.* Ithaca and London: Cornell University Press, 2006.

Bhabha, Homi K. "Unsatisfied: Notes on Vernacular Cosmopolitanism." In *Text and Nation:Cross-Disciplinary Essays on Cultural and National Identities*, edited by Laura García Moreno and Peter C. Pfeiffer. Columbia, SC: Camden House, 1996.

Bogues, Anthony. "Nationalism and Jamaican Political Thought." In *Jamaica in Slavery and Freedom: History, Heritage and Culture*, edited by Kathleen Monteith and Glen Richards, 363–87. Mona, Jamaica: University of the West Indies Press, 2002.

Borg O'Flaherty, Victoria. "Samuel Augustus Mathews: His Life and Times." In *St. Kitts and the Atlantic Creoles: The Text of Samuel Augustus Mathews in Perspective*, edited by Philip Baker and Adrienne Bruyn, London: University of Westminster Press, 1998.

Braithwaite, Edward Kamau. *History of the Voice: The Development of Nation Language in Anglophone Caribbean Poetry*. London: New Beacon Books, 1984.

Brathwaite, Edward Kamau. *The Arrivants*. London and New York: Oxford University Press, 1973.

Brathwaite, Kamau. *The Development of Creole Society, 1770–1820*. Oxford: Clarendon Press, 1971.

Brathwaite, Kamau. *Contradictory Omens: Cultural Diversity and Integration in the Caribbean*. Kingston: Savacou Publications, 1974.

Brathwaite, Kamau. "The History of the Voice." 1984. Reprinted in *Roots*, 265–6. Ann Arbor: University of Michigan Press, 1993.

Breeze, Jean Binta. 1990. "Can A Dub Poet Be a Woman?" *Women: A Cultural Review* 1 (1): 47–9.

Brent, Linda [Harriet Jacobs]. *Incidents in the Life of a Slave Girl*. Massachusetts, 1861.

Brereton, Bridget. *Race Relations in Colonial Trinidad, 1870–1900*. Cambridge, UK: Cambridge University Press, 1979.

Brereton, Bridget. "The Historical Context of Moreton's (1790) Attack on Slavery and Mathews'(1793) Response." In *St. Kitts and the Atlantic Creoles: The Text of Samuel Augustus Mathews in Perspective*, edited by Philip Baker and Adrienne Bruyn. London: University of Westminster Press, 1998.

Broadhead, Richard H. Introduction to *The Conjure Woman and Other Tales*, by Charles W. Chesnutt. Edited by Richard H. Broadhead. Durham and London: Duke University Press, 1993.

Bronkhurst, H. V. P. *Among the Hindus and Creoles of British Guiana*. London: T. Woolmer, 1888.

Brown, Vincent. *The Reaper's Garden: Death, Power, and New World Slavery*. Cambridge, MA: Harvard University Press, 2008.

Brown, William Wells. *The Rising Son: or, The Antecedents and Advancement of the Colored Race*. Boston: A. G. Brown & Co., 1874.

Bryan, Patrick. *The Jamaican People, 1880–1902: Race, Class and Social Control*. Mona, Jamaica: The University of the West Indies Press, 2000. First published 1991 by Macmillan Caribbean (London).

Burnard, Trevor. 2006. "'Rioting in Goatish Embraces': Marriage and Improvement in Early British Jamaica." *History of the Family* 11: 185–97.

Burnett, Paula, ed. *The Penguin Book of Caribbean Verse in English*. London: Penguin Books, 1986.

Buzelin, Hélène, and Lise Winer. "Literary Representations of Creole Languages." In *The Handbook of Pidgin and Creole Studies*, edited by Silvia Kouwenberg and John Victor Singler, 637–65. West Sussex: Wiley-Blackwell, 2008.

Cambridge, Vibert C. "The Muttoo (Mootoo) Brothers Calypso Orchestra." eCaroh Caribbean Emporium. Updated March 19, 2012. First published August 3, 2003 by Stabroek News (Georgetown, Guyana). http://www.ecaroh.com/profiles/muttoobrothers.htm.

Carlyle, Thomas. "Occasional Discourse on the Nigger Question." In *Critical and Miscellaneous Essays*, vol. III. London: Chapman and Hall, 1888.

John R. Chamberlain, "When Spring Comes to Harlem; Claude McKay's Novel Gives a Glowing Picture of the Negro Quarter," *New York Times* (March 11, 1928).

Chambers, Jonathan. *Messiah of the New Technique: John Howard Lawson, Communism, and American Theatre 1923–1937*. Carbondale: Southern Illinois University Press, 2006.

Channer, Colin. 2000–2001. "I Am Not in Exile." *Obsidian III: Literature in the African Diaspora* 2 (2) (Fall/Winter): 50–1.

Cheer Cameron, Margaret. "West Indian Lady's Arrival in London." Produced 1781 for the Kingston Theater.

Chesnutt, Charles. *The Conjure Woman and Other Tales*. Edited by Richard H. Brodhead. Durham and London: Duke University Press, 1993.

Chesnutt, Helen M. *Charles Waddell Chesnutt: Pioneer of the Color Line*. Chapel Hill: University of North Carolina Press, 1952.

Chude-Sokei, Louis. *The Last Darky: Bert Williams, Black-on-Black Minstrelsy, and the African Diaspora*. Durham and London: Duke University Press, 2006.

Cliff, Michelle. *Abeng*. New York: The Crossing Press, 1984.

Cobham-Sander, Rhonda. 2000. "Fictions of Gender, Fictions of Race: Retelling the Morant Bay Rebellion in Jamaican Literature." *Small Axe* 8: 1–30.

Cobham, Stephen. *Rupert Gray: A Tale in Black and White*. Port of Spain, Trinidad: Mirror Printing, 1907.

Cole, Catherine M. *Ghana's Concert Party Theatre*. Indianapolis: Indiana University Press, 2001.

Collins, Edmund John. 1987. "Jazz Feedback to Africa." *American Music* 5 (2) (Summer): 176–93.

Collins, Jane. 2007. "'Umuntu, Ngumuntu, Ngabantu': The Story of the African Choir." *Studies in Theatre and Performance* 27 (2): 95–114.

Collymore, Frank. *Barbadian Dialect*. Bridgetown, Barbados: Cave Shepherd & Co. Ltd, 2005. First published 1955 by Advocate Company (Bridgetown).

Cooper, Carolyn. *Noises in the Blood: Orality, Gender, and the "Vulgar" Body of Jamaican Popular Culture*. Durham and London: Duke University Press, 1995.

Cooper, Carolyn, Ingrid Riley, and Annie Paul. "Celebrating the Success of Marlon James." By Cliff Hughes and Dennis Brooks. *Nationwide News Network*. October 13, 2015.

Cooper, Wayne F. *Claude McKay: Rebel Sojourner in the Harlem Renaissance, A Life*. Baton Rouge: Louisiana State University Press, 1987.

Corcoran, Chris, and Salikoko Mufwene. "Sam Mathews' Kittitian: What Is It Evidence Of?" In *St. Kitts and the Atlantic Creoles: The Texts of Samuel Augustus Mathews in Perspective*, edited by Philip Bruyn and Adrienne Bruyn, 75–102. London: University of Westminster Press, 1998.

Cordle, Edward Alexander. *Overheard: A Series of Poems Written by the Late Edward A. Cordle*. Barbados: C. F. Cole, Printer and Publisher, 1903.

Coval, Kevin, Quraysh Ali Lansana, and Nate Marshall, eds. *The Breakbeat Poets: New American Poetry in the Age of Hip-Hop*. Chicago: Haymarket Books, 2015.

Cowley, John. *Carnival, Canboulay and Calypso: Traditions in the Making*. Cambridge, UK: Cambridge University Press, 1996.

Cowley, John. "West Indies Blues: An Historical Overview 1920s–1950s—Blues and Music from the English-speaking West Indies." In *Nobody Knows Where the Blues Came From: Lyrics and History*, edited by Robert Springer, 187–263. Jackson: University of Mississippi Press, 2006.

Cox, Edward L. *Free Coloreds in the Slave Societies of St. Kitts and Grenada*. Knoxville: University of Tennessee Press, 1984.

Cruickshank, J. Graham. *"Black Talk," Being Notes on Negro Dialect in British Guiana, with (inevitably) a Chapter on the Vernacular of Barbados*. Georgetown: The Argosy, 1916.

Cundall, Frank. "The West Indies Today, 1908." Manuscripts of the Presbyterian Church of Jamaica, 934, 102. National Library of Jamaica.

Dalby, Jonathan. 2016. "Precursors to Morant Bay: The Patterns of Popular Protest in Post Emancipation Jamaica, 1834–1865." *Journal of Caribbean History* 50 (2): 99–129.

Dawes, Kwame. *Natural Mysticism: Towards a New Reggae Aesthetic in Caribbean Writing*. London: Peepal Tree Press, 1999.

de Leon, Rafael [Roaring Lion]. *Calypso from France to Trinidad, 800 Years of History*. General Printing of San Juan, Trinidad and Tobago, 1978.

de Lisser, H. G. *Twentieth Century Jamaica*. Kingston: The Jamaica Times Ltd., 1913.

de Lisser, H. G. *Jane's Career: A Story of Jamaica*. 1913. Reprint, London: Heinemann, 1971.

Devonish, Hubert. *Language and Liberation: Creole Language Politics in the Caribbean*. Trenton: Red Sea Press, 1986.

Devonish, Hubert. "Nature of African-East Indian Contact in 19th Century Guyana: The Linguistic Evidence." Last modified 1991.

Devonish, Hubert. "Interview: Professor Hubert Devonish, Advocate for Jamaican Patois as a Language." Interview by Xavier Murphy. Jamaicans, Speak JA. https://jamaicans.com/jamaicanpatoislanguage-2/.

Dillon, Elizabeth Maddock. *New World Drama: The Performative Commons in the AtlanticWorld, 1649–1849*. Durham and London: Duke University Press, 2014.

Domingo, W. A. "The Tropics in New York." *The Survey*, March 1, 1925, 648–50.

Donkor, David. *Spiders of the Market: Ghanaian Trickster Performance in a Web of Neoliberalism*. Indianapolis: Indiana University Press, 2016.

Douglass, Frederick. *Narrative of the Life of Frederick Douglass*. Massachusetts, 1845.

Edmondson, Belinda, ed. *Caribbean Romances: The Politics of Regional Representation*. Charlottesville and London: University Press of Virginia, 1999.

Edmondson, Belinda. *Caribbean Middlebrow: Leisure Culture and the Middle Class*. Ithaca and London: Cornell University Press, 2009.

Edmondson, Belinda. "Caribbean All-Stars: Sidney Poitier, Harry Belafonte, and the Rise of the African-American Leading Man." In *Poitier Revisited: Reconsidering a Black Icon in the Obama Age*, edited by Ian Strachan and Mia Mask, 61–72. New York: Bloomsbury, 2014.

Edmondson, Belinda. "'Most Intensely Jamaican': The Rise of Brown Identity in Jamaica." In *Victorian Jamaica*, edited by Tim Barringer and Wayne Modest, 553–76. Durham and London: Duke University Press, 2018.

Edwards, Brent. *The Practice of Diaspora: Literature, Translation, and the Rise of Black Internationalism*. Cambridge, MA: Harvard University Press, 2003.

Espiritu, Allison. "Amy Ashwood Garvey (1897–1969)." The Black Past. Updated February 25, 2007. http://www.blackpast.org/aah/garvey-amy-ashwood-1897-1969.

Eyre, Governor John. "Speech to Jamaica Assembly, 1865." *Annual Register*. London, 1865.

Favor, Martin. *Authentic Blackness: The Folk in the New Negro Renaissance*. Durham and London: Duke University Press, 1999.

Foley, Barbara. *Spectres of 1919: Class and Nation in the Making of the New Negro*. Champaign: University of Illinois Press, 2008.

Froude, James Anthony. *The English in the West Indies, or the Bow of Ulysses*. London: Longman's, Green, & Co., 1888.

Fuentes, Marisa J. 2010. "Power and Historical Figuring: Rachael Pringle Polgreen's Troubled Archive." *Gender and History* 22 (3) (November): 564–84.

Fuentes, Marisa J. *Dispossessed Lives: Enslaved Women, Violence, and the Archive*. Philadelphia: University of Pennsylvania Press, 2018.

Garland, Hamlin. "Vernacular Poets and Novelists." In *Roadside Meetings*. New York: Macmillan, 1930.

Gates, Henry Louis Jr. *Figures in Black: Words, Signs, and the "Racial" Self*. London and New York: Oxford University Press, 1987.

Gates, Henry Louis Jr. "The New Negro and the Black Image, from Booker T. Washington to Alain Locke." National Humanities Center. Freedom's Story: Teaching African American Literature and History. http://nationalhumanitiescenter.org/tserve/freedom/1917beyond/essays/newnegro.htm.

Gilroy, Paul. *The Black Atlantic: Modernity and Double Consciousness*. Cambridge, MA: Harvard University Press, 1993.

Governor Edward Eyre to Newcastle, July 5, 1862. "Despatches from the Governor of Jamaica," in "Correspondence respecting the Emigration of Free negroes from the United States to the West Indies. Confidential." CO 884/2/15, National Archives, Kew, England.

Green, Jeffrey. "The Jamaican Choir in Britain." *Jeffrey Green Historian* (blog). http://www.jeffreygreen.co.uk/the-jamaican-choir-in-britain-1906-1908.

Gutzmore, Cecil. "The Image of Marcus Garvey in Reggae Orature." In *Storms of the Heart: An Anthology of Black Arts & Culture*, edited by Kwesi Owusu. London: Camden Press, 1988.

Hall, Catherine. 1989. "The Economy of Intellectual Prestige: Thomas Carlyle, John Stuart Mill, and the Case of Governor Eyre." *Cultural Critique* 12 (Spring): 167–87.

Hamilton, Beverly. 1987. "Marcus Garvey: Cultural Activist." *Jamaica Journal* 2 (3) (August–October): 21–31.

Handler, Jerome, and John Rickford. 1994. "Textual Evidence on the Nature of Early Barbadian Speech, 1676–1835." *Journal of Pidgin and Creole Languages* 9 (2): 221–55.

Hart, Matthew. *Nations of Nothing but Poetry: Modernism, Transnationalism, and Synthetic Vernacular Writing*. London and New York: Oxford University Press, 2010.

Hatfield, Phillip. "Our 'Young Gentleman' Thomas Russell and the Emerging 'Problem' of the Caribbean Language." *British Library: American Collections* (blog). July 24, 2015. https://blogs.bl.uk/americas/2015/07/our-young-gentleman-thomas-russell-and-the-emerging-problem-of-the-caribbean-language.html.

Hearn, Lafcadio. *Gombo Zhebes: Little Dictionary of Creole Proverbs*. New York: Will H. Coleman, 1885.

Heumann, Gad. *The Killing Time: The Morant Bay Rebellion*. Knoxville: University of Tennessee Press, 1994.

Hewitt, Mary Jane. "A Comparative Study of the Careers of Zora Neale Hurston and Louise Bennett as Cultural Conservators." PhD diss., University of the West Indies, 1986.

Hill, Donald. *Calypso Callaloo: Early Carnival Music in Trinidad*. Gainesville: University Pressof Florida, 1993.

Hill, Errol G. *The Jamaican Stage 1655–1900*. Amherst: University of Massachusetts Press, 1992.

Hill, Errol G. "The Caribbean Connection." In *A History of African-American Theatre*, edited by Errol G. Hill and Henry V. Swatch, 273–306. Cambridge, UK: Cambridge University Press, 2003.

Hill, Errol G., Martin Banham, and George Woodyard. *The Cambridge Guide to Theatre*. Cambridge, UK: Cambridge University Press, 2005.

Hill, Richard. *Lights and Shadows of Jamaica History: Being Three Lectures Delivered in Aid of the Mission Schools of the Colony*. Kingston: Ford and Gall, 1859.

Hughes, Langston. *The Big Sea*. New York: Hill and Wang, 1993. First Published 1940 by Alfred A. Knopf (New York).

Hurston, Zora Neale. "The Characteristics of Negro Expression." In *Negro*, edited by Nancy Cunard. New York: Ungar Press, 1970. First published 1934 (London).

Ishmael, Odeen. *The Guyana Story: From Earliest Times to Independence*. Bloomington: Xlibris, 2013.

Jamaica Disturbances: Papers Laid Before the Royal Commission of Inquiry by Governor Eyre (Reports from Commissioners by Great Britain Parliament, House of Commons). London: George Edward Eyre and William Spottiswoode, June 1866.

James, C. L. R. *Beyond a Boundary*. London: Hutchinson, 1963.

James, Winston. *Holding Aloft the Banner of Ethiopia: Caribbean Radicalism in Early Twentieth Century America*. Brooklyn: Verso, 1999.

James, Winston. *"A Fierce Hatred of Injustice": Claude McKay's Jamaica and His Poetry of Rebellion*. Brooklyn: Verso, 2000.

Jekyll, Walter. *Jamaican Song and Story: Annancy Stories, Digging Songs, Ring Tunes, and Dancing Tunes*. London: David Nutt, 1907. First published 1906 (Jamaica).

Jones, Gavin. *Strange Talk: The Politics of Dialect Literature in Gilded Age America*. Berkeley: University of California Press, 1999.

Judge, Erin. "The Annotated Oscar Wao." http://www.annotated-oscar-wao.com/.

Kraut, Anthea. *Choreographing the Folk: The Dance Stagings of Zora Neale Hurston*. Minneapolis: University of Minnesota Press, 2008.

Krise, Thomas. *Caribbeana: An Anthology of English Literature of the West Indies, 1657–1777*. Chicago: University of Chicago Press, 1999.

Lalla, Barbara. 1981. "Quaco Sam—A Relic of Archaic Jamaican Speech." *Jamaica Journal* 45 (May): 20–9.

Lalla, Barbara, and Jean D'Costa. *Language in Exile: Three Hundred Years of Jamaican Creole*. Tuscaloosa: University of Alabama Press, 1990.

Lalla, Barbara, Jean D'Costa, and Velma Pollard. *Caribbean Literary Discourse: Voice and Cultural Identity in the Anglophone Caribbean*. Tuscaloosa: University of Alabama Press, 2014.

Lane, Jill. 1998. "Blackface Nationalism, Cuba 1840–1868." *Theatre Journal* 50 (1): 21–38.

Lane, Jill. *Blackface Cuba, 1840–1895*. Philadelphia: University of Pennsylvania Press, 2020.

Langston Hughes to Louise Bennett, August 13, 1953. The William Ready Division of Archives and Research Collections, McMaster University.

Lewin, Olive. *Rock It Come Over: The Folk Music of Jamaica*. Mona, Jamaica: University of the West Indies Press, 2000.

Lewis, Matthew. *Journal of a West India Proprietor: Kept During a Residence in the Island of Jamaica*. 1834. Edited by Judith Terry. London and New York: Oxford University Press, 1999.

Livingstone, William. *Black Jamaica: A Study in Evolution*. London: S. Low, Marston & Co., 1900.

Locke, Alain, ed. *The New Negro*. New York: Albert and Charles Boni, 1925.

Lombardi, Bernard. "On Reading Louise Bennett Glocally: Langston Hughes, Diasporic Politics, and Nationalist Poetry." Last modified 2015. Microsoft Word file.

Long, Edward. *The History of Jamaica*, vol. 2. London, 1774.

"Lord! What care I for mam or dad?" Lyrics and sheet music. In *Calliope: or, the Musical Miscellany. A Select Collection of the Most Approved English, Scots and Irish Songs, setto music*. London: C. Elliot and T. Kay, 1788.

Lott, Eric. *Love and Theft: Blackface Minstrelsy and the American Working Class*. London and New York: Oxford University Press, 1993.

Lovelace, Earl. *The Dragon Can't Dance*. London: André Deutsch, 1979.

Lyndon, Dominique, ed. *The Woman of Colour: A Tale*. Peterborough: Broadview, 2008.

Martin, Tony. *Literary Garveyism: Garvey, Black Arts, and the Harlem Renaissance.* Dover, MA: The Majority Press, 1983.

Martin, Tony. "African and Indian Consciousness." In *General History of the Caribbean: The Caribbean in the Twentieth Century,* edited by P. C. Emmer, Bridget Brereton, and B. V. Higman, 224–81. London: UNESCO, 2004.

Martin, Tony. *Amy Ashwood Garvey: Pan-Africanist, Feminist, and Wife No. 1 Or A Tale of Two Amies.* Dover, MA: Majority Press, 2007.

Martinéz-San Miguel, Yolanda. *Coloniality of Diasporas: Rethinking Intra-Colonial Migrations in a Pan-Caribbean Context.* New York: Palgrave Macmillan, 2014.

Mathews, Samuel Augustus. *The Lying Hero, or An Answer to J.B. Moreton's Manners and Customs in the West Indies.* St. Eustatius: E.L. Low & Co., 1793.

Mathews, Samuel Augustus. *The Willshire Squeeze: A Ballad Founded Upon Facts to Which Are Added Specimens of the Negro Familiar Dialect and Proverbial Sayings, With Songs.* Demerara: Printed for the Author at the Guiana Chronicle Office, Georgetown, 1822.

Maxwell, Ken. *How to Speak Jamaican.* Illustrated by Livingston McLaren. Humor Us Publications: 1987.

Maxwell, William. *New Negro, Old Left.* New York: Columbia University Press, 1999.

McFarlane, J. E. Clare. "Claude McKay." 1956. Reprinted in *The Routledge Reader in Caribbean Literature,* edited by Alison Donnell and Sarah Lawson Welsh, 97–8. New York: Routledge, 1996.

McKay, Claude. *Constab Ballads.* London: Watts and Co., 1912.

McKay, Claude. *Songs of Jamaica.* Kingston: Aston W. Gardner & Co., 1912.

McKay, Claude. *The Passion of Claude McKay: Selected Poetry and Prose, 1912–1948.* Edited by Wayne Cooper. New York: Schocken, 1973.

McKay, Claude. *My Green Hills of Jamaica.* Heinemann: 1979.

McKay, Claude. *Home to Harlem.* Lebanon, NH: Northeastern University Press, 1987. First published 1928 by Harper and Brothers (New York).

McWatt, Mark, and Marlon James. "Reading, Writing, Religion." By Annie Paul. *The Caribbean Review of Books* (November 2006). http://caribbeanreviewofbooks.com/crb-archive/10-november-2006/reading-writing-religion/

Melnick, Jeffrey. 2005. "Some Notes on the Erotics of 'Black-Jewish Relations.'" *Shofar: An Interdisciplinary Journal of Jewish Studies* 23 (4) (summer): 9–25.

Miller, Herbie. 2009. "Marcus Garvey and the Radical Black Music Tradition." *76 King Street: Journal of Liberty Hall: The Legacy of Marcus Garvey* 1: 102–25.

Milne-Holme, Mary Pamela. *Mamma's Black Nurse Stories.* London: William Blackwood & Sons, 1890.

"Mitchell's West Indian Bibliography." http://www.books.ai/10th/McD-Mem.htm.

"Mme Garvey's Show a Hit at the Lafayette." *Amsterdam News* XVII, no. 50, November 10, 1926.

Mohammed, Patricia. "A Blueprint for Gender in Creole Trinidad: Exploring Gender Mythology through Calypsos of the 1920s and 1930s." In *The Culture of Gender and Sexuality in the Caribbean,* edited by Linden Lewis, 129–69. Gainesville: University of Florida Press, 2003.

Moore, Brian L. *Race, Power and Social Segmentation in Colonial Society: Guyana after Slavery 1838–1891.* Philadelphia: Gordon and Breach Science Publishers Inc., 1987.

Moore, Brian L. *Cultural Power, Resistance and Pluralism: Colonial Guyana 1838–1900.* Montreal: McGill-Queen's University Press, 1995.

Moore, Brian L., and Michele A. Johnson. "Celebrating Christmas in Jamaica, 1865–1920: from Creole Carnival to 'Civilized' Convention." In *Jamaica in Slavery and Freedom:*

History, Heritage, and Culture, edited by Kathleen Monteith and Glen Richards, 144–78. Mona, Jamaica: University of the West Indies Press, 2002.

Moore, Brian L., and Michele A. Johnson. *Neither Led Nor Driven: Contesting British Cultural Imperialism in Jamaica, 1865–1920.* Mona, Jamaica: University of the West Indies Press, 2004.

Moore, Brian L., and Michele A. Johnson. *They Do as They Please: The Jamaican Struggle for Freedom After Morant Bay.* Mona, Jamaica: University of the West Indies Press, 2011.

Moreton, J. B. *Manners and Customs in the West India Islands.* London: Richardson, Gardnerand Walter, 1790. Reprinted 1793 as *West Indian Customs and Manners.*

Morris, Mervyn. "On Reading Louise Bennett, Seriously." *Jamaica Journal* 1 (December 1967): 69–74. First published in 1963.

Murray, Henry Garland. *Tom Kittle's Wake: The Second in a Series of Readings.* Kingston: De Cordova, 1869.

Murray, Henry Garland. *Brown Sammy in Search of a Wife.* Kingston: R. Jordon, 1874.

Murray, Henry Garland. *Brown Sammy Gets Married and Finds Trouble, or Married Hab Teet'.* Kingston: R. Jordan, 1876.

Murray, Henry Garland. 1896. "The Origins of Woman." Edited by William C. Bates. *Journal of American Folklore* 9–10 (32–33) (April-June): 124–5.

Murray, W. C. *A Day with Joe Lennan, the Rosewell Duppy Doctor, and Tommy Silvera or Sucko' Peas Sil.* Kingston: Vendryes and Co., 1891.

Naipaul, V. S. *The Middle Passage.* New York: Vintage, 1981. First published 1962 by André Deutsch (London).

Narain, Denise Decaires. *Contemporary Caribbean Women's Poetry.* London: Routledge, 2001.

"'Natural and Inalienable Right to Freedom': Slaves' Petition for Freedom to the Massachusetts Legislature, 1777." In *Collections of the Massachusetts Historical Society,* 5th Series, III, 436–7. Boston, 1877.

Ngũgĩ wa Thiongo. *Decolonising the Mind: The Politics of Language in African Literature.* Heinemann, 1986.

North, Michael. *The Dialect of Modernism: Race, Language, and Twentieth-Century Literature.* London and New York: Oxford University Press, 1994.

Novak, David. "Noise." In *Key Words for Sound Studies,* edited by David Novak and Matt Sakakeeny, 125–38. Durham and London: Duke University Press, 2015.

Nugent, Lady Maria. *Lady Nugent's Journal of her residence in Jamaica from 1801 to 1805.* Kingston: Institute of Jamaica, 1966. First issued 1839 for private circulation.

Nurhussein, Nadia. *Rhetorics of Literacy: The Cultivation of American Dialect Poetry.* Columbus: Ohio State University Press, 2013.

Office Administering the Government, C. Clementi to Rt. Hon. Viscount Milner, PC, etc. September 2, 1919. CO 111/624, Public Record Office, London.

Ogilvie, W. G. "Many Faces, Different Streams." Unpublished manuscript.

Orderson, J. W. *Creoleana.* London: Macmillan Caribbean, 2002. First published 1842 by Saunders and Otley (London).

Parascandola, Louis J. *"Look for Me All Around You": Anglophone Caribbean Immigrants in the Harlem Renaissance.* Detroit: Wayne State University Press, 2005.

Patterson, Orlando. *The Sociology of Slavery: An Analysis of the Origins, Development, and Structure of Negro Slave Society in Jamaica.* Madison, NJ: Fairleigh Dickinson University Press, 1967.

Paul, Annie. "Plotting a Brief History of Seven Killings: An Exclusive Interview with Marlon James." *Active Voice* (blog). October 6, 2014. http://anniepaul.net/2014/10/06/plotting-a-brief-history-of-seven-killings-an-exclusive-interview-with-marlon-james/.

Paul, Annie. "Bloodcloth! Marlon James and the #ManBooker2015." *Active Voice* (blog). October 28, 2015. http://anniepaul.net/2015/10/28/bloodcloth-marlon-james-and-the-manbooker2015/.

"People and Events: Amy Ashwood 1897–1969." PBS online. http://www.shoppbs.pbs.org/wgbh/amex/garvey/peopleevents/p_ashwood.html.

Peterson, Bernard L. Jr. *The African-American Theater Directory, 1816–1960*. Westport, CT: Greenwood Press, 1997.

Philip, M. NourbeSe. *A Geneaology of Resistance and Other Essays*. Toronto: The Mercury Press, 1997.

Philip, Michel Maxwell. *Emmanuel Appadocca*. London: Charles J. Skeet, 1854.

Phillippo, J. M. *Jamaica: Its Past and Present State*. London, 1843.

Pollard, Velma. *Dread Talk: The Language of Rastafari*. Kingston: Canoe Press, 1994.

Pollard, Velma. "'Slash Me Off a Penny's Worth': The Scots in Jamaica." In *Caribbean-Scottish Relations: Colonial and Contemporary Inscriptions in History, Language and Literature*, by Giovanna Covi, Carla Sassi, Velma Pollard, and Joan Anim-Addo. London: Mango Publishing, 2007.

Prince, Mary. *The History of Mary Prince: A West Indian Slave Narrative*. London, 1831.

Puri, Shalini. "Canonized Hybridities, Resistant Hybridities." In *Caribbean Romances: ThePolitics of Regional Representation*, edited by Belinda Edmondson, 12–38. Charlottesville: University of Virginia Press, 1999.

Putnam, Lara. *Radical Moves: Caribbean Migrants and the Politics of Race in the Jazz Age*. Chapel Hill: University of North Carolina Press, 2013.

Quow [Michael McTurk]. *Essays and Fables in Prose and Verse, Written in the Vernacular of the Creoles of British Guiana*. Georgetown: Argosy, 1899. Published in 1877 and1895 (Georgetown and Demerara).

Radcliffe, John. *Lectures on Negro Proverbs*. Kingston: M. De Cordova, McDougall & Co., 1869.

Rampini, Charles. *Letters from Jamaica: "The Land of Streams and Woods."* Edinburgh, 1873.

Ramsay, Reverend James. *An Essay on the Treatment and Conversion of African Slaves in the British Sugar Colonies*. London: James Phillips, 1784.

Redcam, Tom [Thomas MacDermot]. *One Brown Girl And—A Jamaican Story*. Kingston: Jamaica Times Printery, 1909.

Reid, J. H. "The People of Jamaica Described." In *Jamaica's Jubilee: Or What We Are and What We Hope To Be*, by Five of Themselves. London: Partridge and Co., 1888.

Reisman, Karl. "Tom Kittle's Wake: A West Indian Classic." Fedograph's Weblog (blog). http://fadograph.wordpress.com/tom-kittles-wake-a-west-indian-classic-1877/.

Renny, Robert Esq. *An History of Jamaica*. London: J. Cawthorn, 1807.

Report of the Jamaica Royal Commission in 1866. Digital Library of the Caribbean, Riots and Rebellions. National Library of Jamaica.

Retamar, Roberto Fernández. *Caliban and Other Essays*. Minneapolis: University of Minnesota Press, 1989.

Reynolds, Reverend D. J. 1890. "Jamaica Proverbial Philosophy." *Timehri: A Journal of the Royal Agricultural Society* 4 (Demerara): 47–55.

Rhys, Jean. *Wide Sargasso Sea*. New York: Norton, 1982. First published 1966 by André Deutsch (London).

Rickford, John. *Dimensions of a Creole Continuum: History, Texts, and Linguistic Analysis of Guyanese Creole*. Stanford: Stanford University Press, 1987.

Roberts, Peter A. *From Oral to Literate Culture: Colonial Experience in the English West Indies*. Mona, Jamaica: University of the West Indies Press, 1997.

Rohlehr, Gordon. *My Strangled City and Other Essays*. Port of Spain: Longman, 1993.

Rosenberg, Leah. *Nationalism and the Formation of Caribbean Literature*. New York: Palgrave Macmillan, 2007.

Russell, Thomas. *Etymology of Jamaica Grammar by a Young Gentleman*. Kingston: DeCordova, MacDougall & Co., 1868.

Scarano, Francisco A.1996. "The Jibáro Masquerade and the Subaltern Politics of Creole Identity Formation in Puerto Rico, 1745–1823." *American Historical Review* 101 (5) (December): 1398–1431.

Scott, Michael. *Tom Cringle's Log* (Edinburgh: Blackwood, 1834)." In *St. Kitts and the Atlantic Creoles: The Text of Samuel Augustus Mathews in Perspective*, edited by Philip Baker and Adrienne Bruyn, London: University of Westminster Press, 1998.

Serafin, Steven R., and Alfred Bendixen, eds. *The Continuum Encyclopedia of American Literature*. New York: Continuum, 1999.

Shakespeare, William. *The Tempest*. Edited by Peter Hulme and William H. Sherman. Second Norton Critical Edition. New York: W. W. Norton, 2019.

Sheller, Mimi. *Consuming the Caribbean: From Arawaks to* Zombies. London: Routledge, 2003.

Sheller, Mimi. *Citizenship from Below: Erotic Agency and Caribbean Freedom*. Durham and London: Duke University Press, 2012.

Sheller, Mimi. "Complicating Jamaica's Morant Bay Rebellion: Jewish Radicalism, Asian Indenture, and Multi-Ethnic Histories of 1865." *Cultural Dynamics* 31 (3) (2019): 200–23.

Shipley, Jesse. *Trickster Theatre: The Poetics of Freedom in Urban Africa*. Indianapolis: Indiana University Press, 2015.

Smith, Faith. *Creole Recitations: John Jacob Thomas and Colonial Formation in the Late Nineteenth-Century Caribbean*. Charlottesville: University of Virginia Press, 2002.

Smith, Faith. "'A Mysterious Murder': Considering Jamaican Victorianism." In *Victorian Jamaica*, edited by Tim Barringer and Wayne Modest, 658–74. Durham and London: Duke University Press, 2018.

Some Gentlemen of St. Christopher. *An Answer to the Reverend James Ramsay's Essay on the Treatment and Conversion of Slaves*. Basseterre, St. Christopher: Edward Low, 1774.

Stephens, Michelle Ann. *Black Empire: The Masculine Global Imaginary of Caribbean Intellectuals in the United States, 1914–1962*. Durham and London: Duke University Press, 2005.

Stowe, Harriet Beecher. *Uncle Tom's Cabin: Or, Life Among the Lowly*. Boston: John P. Jewettand Company, 1852.

Swaby, Nydia. "Amy Ashwood-Garvey: A Revolutionary Pan-Africanist Feminist." Re/ Visionist. Updated April 1, 2010. http://revisionistslc.com/2010/04/01/amy-ashwood-garvey-a-revolutionary-pan-african-feminist/.

Taylor, Christopher. *Empire of Neglect: The West Indies in the Wake of British Liberalism*. Durham and London: Duke University Press, 2018.

Theworldvideos1. "Jamaica's Patois Bible: The Word of God in Creole." Online video clip. *YouTube*, December 24, 2011. https://www.youtube.com/watch?v=rRI3srdcia0.

Thomas, Deborah A. *Modern Blackness: Nationalism, Globalization, and the Politics of Culture in Jamaica*. Durham and London: Duke University Press, 2004.

Thomas, Deborah A. *Exceptional Violence: Embodied Citizenship in Transnational Jamaica*. Durham and London: Duke University Press, 2011.

Thomas, John Jacob. *Theory and Practice of Creole Grammar*. Port of Spain, Trinidad: Chronicle Publishing, 1869.

Thomas, John Jacob Thomas. *Froudacity: West Indian Fables by James Anthony Froude*. London: T. Fisher Unwin, 1889.

Thomasson, Frank. *A History of Theatre in Guyana, 1800–2000*. London: Hansib, 2009.

Thompson, Krista. *An Eye for the Tropics: Tourism, Photography, and Framing the Caribbean Picturesque.* Durham and London: Duke University Press, 2006.

Tiffin, Helen. "The Institution of Literature." In *A History of Literature in the Caribbean* Vol. 2, edited by James Arnold, 41–66. Philadelphia: John Benjamins, 2001.

Tryon, Thomas. "A Discourse in the way of Dialogue between an *Ethiopian* or *Negro-Slave*, and a *Christian* that was his Master in *America*." In *Friendly Advice to the GentlemanPlanters of the East and West Indies*, 146–222. London: 1684.

"*Uncle Tom's Cabin* Takes the Nation by Storm." The American Experience, PBS Television. First Aired April 23, 2001. http://www.pbs.org/wgbh/amex/foster/peopleevents/e_cabin.html. Retrieved 3/21/14.

van Sertima, J. *The Creole Tongue.* New Amsterdam, 1905.

Vásquez, Sam. *Humor in the Caribbean Literary Canon.* New York: Palgrave Macmillan, 2012.

Viswanathan, Gauri. "English Literary Study in British India." In *The Postcolonial Studies Reader*, edited by Bill Ashcroft, Helen Tiffin, and Gareth Griffiths, 431–7. Oxford: Routledge, 1995.

Viswanathan, Gauri. *Masks of Conquest: Literary Study and British Rule in India.* New York: Columbia University Press, 2014.

Ward, Candace. *Crossing the Line: Early Creole Novels and Anglophone Caribbean Culture in the Age of Emancipation.* Charlottesville: University of Virginia Press, 2017.

Washington, Booker T., N. B. Wood, and Fannie Barrier Williams. *A New Negro for a New Century: An Up-to-date Record of the Upward Struggles of the Negro Race.* Chicago: American Publishing House, 1900.

Watson, Tim. *Caribbean Culture and British Fiction in the Atlantic World, 1780–1870.* Cambridge: Cambridge University Press, 2008.

Weiss, John McNish. "The Corp of Colonial Marines: Black Freedom Fighters of the War of 1812." http://www.mcnishandweiss.co.uk/history/colonialmarines.html.

Westerman, George W. 1961. "Historical Notes on West Indians on the Isthmus of Panama." *Phylon* 22 (4) (4th Quarter): 340.

Westmaas, Nigel. 2005. "Revolutionary Centennial: Guyana's 1905 Rebellion." *Against the Current: A Socialist Journal* 114 (January/February). https://www.marxists.org/history/etol/newspape/atc/1139.html.

Westmaas, Nigel. "A Mirror of Social and Political Ferment: The Newspaper Press of Guyana, 1839–1899." PhD diss., State University of New York at Binghamton, 2007. ProQuest(AAT 3241792).

Williams, Cynric R. *A Tour Through the Island of Jamaica: From the Western to the Eastern End in the Year 1823.* London: Thomas Hurst, Edward Chance & Co., 1827.

Williams, Cynric R. *Hamel, the Obeah Man.* Edited by Candace Ward and Tim Watson. Peterborough: Broadview, 2010. First published 1827 by Hunt and Clarke (London).

Winer, Lise. 1986. "Socio-cultural Change and the Language of Calypso." *New West Indian Guide* 60 (3/4): 113–48.

Winer, Lise. *Trinidad and Tobago.* Philadelphia: John Benjamins, 1993.

Winer, Lise. "Six Vernacular Texts from Trinidad, 1838–1851." In *Englishes Around the World: Studies in Honour of Manfred Gorlach*, edited by Edgar W. Schneider and Manfred Gorlach, 69–84. Philadelphia: John Benjamins, 1997.

Winokur, Scott. "The Unsparing Vision of V.S. Naipaul." In *Conversations with V.S. Naipaul*, edited by Feroza Jussawalla, 114–29. Jackson: University Press of Mississippi, 1997.

Wright, Richard. *Revels in Jamaica.* Kingston: Bolivar Press, 1986. First published 1937 by Dodd, Mead & Co. Inc. (New York).

Discography

Beckford, Stanley. "Dip Dem Jah Jah." Track 5 on *Stanley Beckford Plays Mento*. Barclay 02466447588, 2002, compact disc.

Bennett, Louise [Miss Lou]. *Yes M'Dear: Miss Lou Live!* Sonic Sounds JA6819CP55, 1982.

Bim and Bam. *Laugh with Bim, Bam and Clover*. Jet Star Records, 2003, compact disc. Originally released 1969 by Pama Records SECO 22, Vinyl.

Bob Marley & the Wailers. "Bad Card." Track A3 on *Uprising*. Island Records ILPS 9596, 1980, vinyl.

Growling Tiger. "Money is King." Decca 17254, 1935.

King Radio. "Man Smart (Woman Smarter)." Decca 17287, 1936.

The Mighty Sparrow. "No Money No Love." Ra NRC 802, n.d.

The Mighty Sparrow. "Jack Palance." Kay CRS.017, 1956.

Public Enemy. "Fight the Power." Track 1 on *Do the Right Thing (Original Motion Picture Soundtrack)*, directed by Spike Lee. Motown MOTD 6272, 1989, compact disc.

Index

For the benefit of digital users, indexed terms that span two pages (e.g., 52–53) may, on occasion, appear on only one of those pages.